Australian Social Attitudes IV

PUBLIC AND SOCIAL POLICY SERIES

Marian Baird and Gaby Ramia, Series Editors

The Public and Social Policy series publishes books that pose challenging questions about policy from national, comparative and international perspectives. The series explores policy design, implementation and evaluation; the politics of policy making; and analyses of particular areas of public and social policy.

Australian social attitudes IV: the age of insecurity
Ed. Shaun Wilson and Markus Hadler

Globalisation, the state and regional Australia
Amanda Walsh

Markets, rights and power in Australian social policy
Ed. Gabrielle Meagher and Susan Goodwin

Risking together: how finance is dominating everyday life in Australia
Dick Bryan and Mike Rafferty

Wind turbine syndrome: a communicated disease
Simon Chapman and Fiona Crichton

Australian Social Attitudes IV

The Age of Insecurity

Edited by Shaun Wilson and Markus Hadler

SYDNEY UNIVERSITY PRESS

First published in 2018 by Sydney University Press
© Individual contributors 2018
© Sydney University Press 2018

Reproduction and communication for other purposes
Except as permitted under the Act, no part of this edition may be reproduced, stored in a retrieval system, or communicated in any form or by any means without prior written permission. All requests for reproduction or communication should be made to Sydney University Press at the address below:

Sydney University Press
Fisher Library F03
The University of Sydney NSW 2006
AUSTRALIA
sup.info@sydney.edu.au
sydney.edu.au/sup

A catalogue record for this book is available from the National Library of Australia.

NATIONAL
LIBRARY
OF AUSTRALIA

ISBN 9781743325742 paperback
ISBN 9781743325759 epub

Cover image: MrVELL/Shutterstock.com
Cover design by Miguel Yamin

Contents

List of figures

List of tables

This book is dedicated to the memory of Professor Bill Martin, 1956–2016.

Introduction: Australia in an age of insecurity

Shaun Wilson and Markus Hadler

Australian Social Attitudes IV is the latest in a series begun in 2005 tracking public opinion. The series aims to communicate with an academic and a broader public about changes in Australian society through a systematic analysis of public opinion surveys. It also aims to address some of the interests and apprehensions of Australians from all walks of life, and to present analysis in ways that make sense of the society around us.

This volume focuses on Australian insecurities. These include, for example, the frustrations and hardships that arise out of insecure work and an unequal economy. And they include the hostilities, confusions and doubts that mark our inability to forge consensus on pressing social challenges – adequate responses to climate change, recognition of social diversity, and the development of inclusive and trusted national institutions.

When the series began, Australia was in the middle of an unprecedented resources boom presided over by a Coalition prime minister who was close to celebrating a decade in office. Within a few years, John Howard was swept aside by a mood for change and an emphatic rejection of WorkChoices industrial relations reforms that voters judged as unfair.

While many Australians would remember the Howard years as a period of temperance, stability and prosperity, others would see it as a time of contentious immigration politics, clashes with unions, and involvement in damaging global conflicts. The Howard government's economic legacy was considered among the strongest of recent governments. Nevertheless, critics argued later that it had cut taxes too far to sustain balanced budgets into the future. In any case, the Howard years were ones of marked political stability at the top, like the Hawke and Keating years that had preceded them. Between 1983 and 2007 – just under a quarter of a century – Australia had just three prime ministers.

The years since the departure of John Howard from the national political scene have involved much more political uncertainty on some key 'indicators'. In 2017, for example, only one state premier had been in office more than three years. And, in the four years between the middle of 2013 and the middle of 2017, Australia had four different prime ministers, with governments on both sides replacing national leaders during their first term in office. Both of these governments survived the subsequent national elections with extremely small margins, with Gillard Labor governing in a minority parliament and the Turnbull Coalition winning the barest of majorities (76 seats from 150).

On the policy level, there has been intense and even bitter partisanship on industrial relations and climate policies. At the same time, a new bipartisanship has emerged in favour of offshore detention and 'border protection', replacing the major divisions over the Howard government's Pacific Solution and the Rudd Labor government's dismantling of that policy. Not surprisingly, as politics and policy have failed to overcome real social and economic divisions, new political actors have flourished. With around 8 to 10 per cent of the national vote, the Greens are now a permanent force on the environmental and socially liberal left. One Nation has returned as the main vehicle for right-wing populism, currently polling at similar levels to the Greens. The two major parties gained just 77 per cent of the federal vote in the House of Representatives in 2016, down from 85 per cent in 2007. Still, this vote share remains high in comparative terms, and Labor and the Coalition continue to win the overwhelming share of seats in the federal parliament.

The 'new instability' facing Australia has two discernible and interlocking features, one relating to the national economy and the other to global insecurities. The first is economic insecurity and slower economic growth. The Rudd Labor government's fiscal stimulus helped Australia through the Global Financial Crisis in 2009, but the slow decline of the terms of trade and the end of the resources boom have meant painful adjustments in Western Australia and Queensland in particular, as well as in many regional centres. Unemployment has risen only slightly since 2007 on official figures, but the labour market continues to fragment into insecure and part-time employment that undermines financial security for many (Stanford 2016; ME Bank 2017). These insecurities are compounded by the extraordinarily high housing costs in Sydney, Melbourne, Brisbane and Perth. Australians now borrow vast sums to remain in cities where there are jobs and opportunity. Given these circumstances, it is not surprising that measures of income distribution indicate that Australia is more unequal than it has been in many decades. The same analysis suggests that many of the equality gains of the post–World War Two era have been eroded (Knight and Biddle 2015).

The second insecurity relates to the global geopolitical context. Although the Obama years promised greater peace, upheavals in the Middle East and the constant threat of extremist violence in Europe and the United States continued to dominate politics. In turn, these insecurities have fuelled right-wing populism and calls for ever-greater efforts to defend national borders and detect sources of potential terrorist aggression. The victory of Donald J. Trump in November 2016 was a turning point for the success for such populism. The president campaigned hard on the theme of emboldening America to 'get tough' on a range of problems that apparently plagued it, from the sociocultural and security threats of risky immigration policies to the decline of American manufacturing. Disaffected Americans responded. At the same time, right-wing populism has swept through Europe, forcefully in some countries like Hungary and Poland. Similar forces threaten to remake the political framework of many other European Union member states, even if right-wing populists continue to fall short of national electoral triumphs.

These contexts are in some ways not new. They reflect severe and persistent tensions in geopolitics and in the global economic order. In Australia, themes of global insecurity have resonated in policies on 'border protection', in immigration and asylum seeker policy (the Operation Sovereign Borders policy of the Coalition), and in amplified political discourse about threats facing Australia. Such discourses are now active across a wide political space, but are most potent when parties like One Nation, who seek restrictions on immigration and a ban on so-called Muslim immigration, take them up.

Insecurities, trust and risks in Australia – contributions to this volume

In developing the chapters for this volume, authors were given a wide brief to interpret these developments in their areas of expertise, exploring insecurities as they relate to sociocultural identities, the economy and employment, and electoral responses to changing national circumstances. The choice to focus on insecurities was further justified by some interesting results reported for the Australian Election Study (AES) 2016 (Belot 2016; Cameron and McAllister 2016). After a long period of stability, AES 2016 picked up signs of deteriorating political trust in Australia. Study author Ian McAllister noted at the time: 'What we are seeing in Australia are the beginnings of a popular disaffection with the political class that has emerged so dramatically in Britain, United States and Italy' (Belot 2016). Several chapters in this volume draw connections between insecurities and such disaffections as they manifest in falling trust, populist voting patterns, suspicions about climate science, and hostilities to immigration. However, the *Australian Social Attitudes* series has a wider ambition. It also aims to keep track of *broader* changes in Australian society, or at least the expression of those changes as stated by thousands of Australians who respond to social surveys.

The rest of this Introduction describes the main content and findings of the individual chapter contributions, identifying broader thematic continuities where they emerge. The logical place to start is Clive Bean's analysis in **Chapter 1** of recent trends in political trust in Australia. Bean acknowledges the most recent decline in political trust is an interesting and unsettling development. Nevertheless, he is cautious about drawing conclusions about the future based on the most recent data. Bean is able to demonstrate that political trust is somewhat dependent on the *political cycle* – old governments reduce it, new governments restore it. Time will tell if these declines turn out to be more secular and long-term, and bring with them some of the syndromes of 'low-trust politics'. Bean also addresses the complex relationship between political trust and different dimensions of insecurity – cultural, socioeconomic, and military/geopolitical. It turns out that insecurities tend to undermine trust in the predicted fashion. Worried and stressed citizens are less trusting of governments and politicians. Nevertheless, *sociocultural* insecurities (related to perceptions of immigration) turn out to have the largest impact on the erosion of political trust in Australia. Not surprisingly, immigration politics is central to the insecurities described in this book.

Chapter 2 by Shaun Ratcliff offers a synoptic account of federal election results from 2016, using a large post-election study conducted by VoxPop Labs. This huge dataset provides Ratcliff with a sufficiently large sample to explore political-sociological trends in voting behaviour right across the political spectrum. He explores the data in detail, to look for explanations for the rising vote for minor parties (many of which are protest parties). He finds that a 'representation gap' – where voter preferences are not adequately reflected in the platforms of either major party – drives support for the Greens, the 'micro left', the Christian right, and populist right parties. The diversity and complexity of the interests and value commitments of voters appear to be driving the fragmentation of voter blocs for the established parties. For example, Ratcliff shows that voters for the populist right are to the *right* of the Coalition on social issues, but slightly to the *left* on economics. Such a policy space is not well represented by either major party. Whether the fragmentation of major voter blocs will continue is a matter for speculation. The UK election of 2017, where voters faced a genuine left–right choice, saw a strong return to two-party voting.

In **Chapter 3**, Shaun Wilson looks at trends in public opinion in one policy area that has produced enormous division in Australia and elsewhere, that of immigration and policy responses to refugees and asylum seekers. Australia for some time now has maintained a 'balancing act' of high migration and tough 'border protection' policies. Wilson finds that, in fact, anti-immigration sentiment has cooled, and argues that this is limiting opportunities for right-wing populism in Australia. In fact, younger voters, city-dwellers and even Coalition voters have all moved towards greater support for current immigration levels. Just as pro-immigration sentiment seems to have developed a broader constituency, policies towards refugees, boat arrivals and asylum seekers continue to polarise Australians. Here, the tough response developed in the Howard years won over voters in the battle of public opinion and at election time. However, Wilson points out that AES data suggests that there is now a permanent opposition to 'boat turnbacks' – one emblematic policy of hard-line border protection. He also suggests that hostility towards Muslims in Australia has not reached levels that suggest majority support for banning so-called 'Muslim' immigration – the policy position of One Nation.

Themes of declining trust are no more revelatory than in the area of the science of climate change. The Labor government of Kevin Rudd failed to secure parliamentary agreement for its carbon-trading scheme in 2009, and went on to abandon the proposal, much to the confusion and disappointment of many in the electorate. Later, when prime minister Julia Gillard introduced a 'carbon tax', her apparent about-face on a pre-election commitment *not* to do so steered her government into a political storm. Opposition Leader Tony Abbott, a climate change sceptic, campaigned persistently on Gillard's broken commitment. He then repealed the tax after winning office, even though the tax was judged as highly effective on the evidence.

Australians like to think of themselves as ultimately pragmatic and realistic people. They compare themselves favourably to the 'crazy Americans' who 'believe in aliens' and who, no doubt, also deny the realities of climate change. However, Bruce Tranter in **Chapter 4** maintains that 'Australians are among the most climate sceptical of people living in advanced industrialised countries'. He builds on his previous work in examining the drivers of what turns out to be a very high level of climate scepticism in Australia, when public opinion is measured comparatively. Partisan divides on this issue suggest that Coalition voters may have followed the lead of climate-sceptical leaders like John Howard and Tony Abbott in doubting climate science. But Tranter also notes strong patterns that relate media habits to climate scepticism: conservative media outlets in Australia play a role in Australia's high incidence of scepticism. Tranter's chapter ends, however, with advice about building consensus. He suggests that advocates of climate policies need to design policies that also appeal to conservatives, i.e. to highlight the growth and jobs potential of a robust renewable energy market.

Tranter notes that men are more likely to be climate sceptics than women. In **Chapter 5**, Katrine Beauregard makes further sociological sense of the 2016 election by pinpointing factors behind a clear 'gender gap' in voting. Although modern gender-based voting, where women vote on the centre-left and men on the centre-right, has been observed in (for example) the United States for some time, such a gap has not been particularly apparent in Australia. That changed decisively in 2016, with more women voting Labor (in two-party terms) and more men voting for the Coalition. Beauregard looks for explanations. Clearly, women have better education and work opportunities than in the past (although the gender pay gap remains disturbingly high) and these two trends are accelerating women's identification with centre-left politics. At the same time, women have more 'progressive' issue preferences on social welfare policies that more closely align with current Labor policy positions than Coalition ones.

Running parallel to the gender-voting gap are divisions in the pattern of women's parliamentary representation, with the Coalition further lagging behind Labor. The clear implication is that Labor's quota system is working to bring about gender equity, and that women are more supportive than men of various forms of affirmative action. Beauregard's findings hint at an important implication for the Coalition: a greater commitment to the policies of gender equality as well as efforts to increase women's representation in politics might help rebuild their support among women.

Chapter 6 continues the focus on the changing political sociology of the national electorate. Ian McAllister and Toni Makkai settle some important debates about what kind of Australians have voted Labor and Coalition over the past few decades. After detailed consideration of possible definitions for both groups, the authors settle on a definition of 'battlers' as low-income voters reporting poor household finances. By contrast, 'aspirationals' are defined by their *orientations* towards an economic model of low taxes that also contains the activities of unions. McAllister and Makkai find something startling about the battlers who turned to John Howard in 1996: 'the stereotypical Howard battler invented by Andrew Robb in 1996 just as rapidly defected from the Liberals in 1998 and did not return for another five elections'. By contrast, aspirationals stayed loyal to the Coalition, though importantly the authors note that, on their definition, these voters are now a smaller share of the electorate as attitudes to lowering taxes and curbing unions have moderated. Taking these findings together, these results suggest that on a very contemporary definition of 'class politics' – voting by income level and attitudes to taxes, spending and unions – class continues to shape electoral outcomes. McAllister and Makkai's analysis also suggests that Labor's attempts to appeal to aspirationals (as they were urged to do in the 2000s) did not succeed and, more to the point, efforts to do so are now less important given the declining attitudinal basis for aspirational voting.

Given the heated partisan debates about clause 18C of the federal *Racial Discrimination Act 1975*, as well as a defence of civil disobedience by the secretary of the Australian Council of Trade Unions, Sally McManus, now is the time to consider how Australians compare on a range of questions about civil freedoms. In their comparative study of attitudes to freedom of assembly, Markus Hadler and Anja Eder use data from 34 countries in **Chapter 7** to situate Australia. So: when it comes to tolerating the views of outsiders, even extremists, are Australians 'liberal' in comparative terms or do we want to keep extreme positions from flourishing or even being heard?

While the emphasis of this book is on the Australian context, data from the Australian Survey of Social Attitudes also feeds into the International Social Survey Programme (http://www.issp.org), which compiles similar data from almost 50 countries around the globe. The latest release of data from this program addressed attitudes towards citizenship, political attitudes, efficacy, and actions (see Scholz et al. 2017). Using International Social Survey Programme data for 2014 on these questions, Hadler and Eder find that Australians sit somewhere in the middle. The United States is the model 'liberal' country in allowing freedom of expression. Countries like Austria and the Netherlands, with a history of fascist politics and occupation (and in the Dutch case a high level of ethnic conflict) are much less tolerant. Australia is rated as more tolerant than most European countries, with the authors attributing this to Australia's participatory democratic life and, despite its multiculturalism, low levels of ethnic fragmentation. When it comes to accounting for social divides in Australia about allowing freedom of assembly, they find that city-dwellers, Greens, Aboriginal and Torres Strait Islanders, and better-educated citizens emerge as more tolerant – and, interestingly, *men* emerged as more tolerant than women on these measures.

In **Chapter 8**, Murray Goot continues to build on his explorations of Australian opinion and election polling. His close overview of polling activities in recent elections, particularly the 2016 federal election, detects something peculiar and worrying: Australian commercial polling (when compared to polling activities in the United Kingdom) is almost singularly focused on *voting* intentions. It has disengaged, according to Goot, from the regular and detailed survey of voter policy preferences. He concludes: 'the very limited attempt by the polling organisations to determine respondents' views on different issue positions signifies the collapse of the Gallup model'.

Goot considers this shortcoming a loss of faith (on the part of poll-commissioning media organisations) in the valuable role that polls can play in the process through which politicians and voters alike come to understand their own and their electorate's policy interests. We note in passing that there is a promising focus on policy preferences of voters in newer commercial polls like the Essential Poll and in the ABC's Vote Compass survey conducted at election time. It is also pleasing that there is a greater range of academic surveys on offer that include issue polling – for example, ANUPoll, the Australian Survey of Social Attitudes, the Australian Election Study, and the Scanlon Foundation's polling on immigration and multiculturalism.

The final two chapters break with a considerable focus in this book on the 2016 election. These analyses focus on shifting social attitudes on two important institutions – the monarchy and marriage. In one sense, these topics share a common theme. Efforts both to replace the monarchy (with a republic) and to legislate for gay marriage have either been checked by public opinion or partisan division. The public ultimately sided with monarchists in rejecting change in the 1999 referendum on the republic, and gay marriage reform was hindered by divisions in federal politics, particularly within the ruling Coalition until its legalisation in December 2017.

In **Chapter 9**, Luke Mansillo tracks the remarkable decline in pro-republic sentiment among voters and the revival in support for Australia remaining a constitutional monarchy with the Queen as head of state. In recalling earlier predictions of a 'rising tide' of voters in favour of the republic as younger republicans replaced older monarchists, Mansillo endeavours to explain why such a trend has *not* been sustained. In a fascinating discovery, he identifies the 'Whitlam generation' (voters who first voted in the years of the Whitlam government and who were politically socialised at the time of the dismissal in 1975) as the most pro-republican generation. Their 'progressiveness' on the question of replacing the monarchy is all the more remarkable because the Whitlam generation does not hold more socially progressive attitudes on other issues. In accounting for the loss of republican enthusiasm, Mansillo identifies the revival of the monarchy as an institution in the United Kingdom and the failure of the republican movement to absorb younger and less-engaged voters in pressing its cause. No doubt, an insecure and uncertain Australia is also not one likely to find much success in changing its constitutional institutions without stronger national leadership on this question.

Finally, Ann Evans and Edith Gray focus their efforts in **Chapter 10** on changing social attitudes to marriage and family. In noting a continuing overall downward trend in the marriage rate, Evans and Gray's analysis finds that that marriage is still a 'high prestige' institution – even if Australians are less inclined to believe that marriage brings happiness or that marriage is preferable when couples have children. There is an emerging socioeconomic dimension to marriage, with the marriage rates of lower-income and less well-educated Australians dropping faster as job security and home ownership become harder to achieve. In building on research findings in the area, Evans and Gray do *not* suggest that marriage will disappear or appear 'outdated'. Rather, they suggest that attitudes to marriage are becoming less 'institutionalised' and now tolerate greater flexibility about the place of marriage.

The use of surveys and data in this volume

This book draws on data from a wide range of national and international social and political surveys as well as some commercial opinion polling from Australia and overseas. Some of the most widely used surveys include the Australian Survey of Social Attitudes (AuSSA), the Australian Election Study (AES), the (Survey of) Household, Income and Labour Dynamics in Australia (HILDA), results from the International Social Survey Program (ISSP), the National Social Science Survey (NSSS), and the large post-election survey for the 2016 federal election conducted by VoxPop Labs. Several contributors (for example, Wilson in Chapter 3 and Goot in Chapter 8) also rely on a range of quality commercial polling from Australia and overseas to develop their analyses. The mode of data collection involved in these surveys varies considerably, but increasingly, academic surveys are using online methods to obtain samples. In all instances, teams of experienced social scientists develop the survey questionnaires and the fieldwork depends on ethics processes at the host universities.

Survey data has its limitations – questions are open to interpretation, issues are so complex that they can require multiple questions to measure with adequate validity, and respondents have reasons to give socially desirable answers to surveys or to ignore the requests of desperate field workers to complete their questionnaires. Moreover, even *when* this data is collected using stratified random sampling with large samples, it is subject not only to sample error but also to sample biases consistent with differing response rates across diverse and sometimes disengaged communities. The researchers who have contributed to this volume are aware of these limitations; and they have used the data with these limits in mind. In more recent years, researchers have had to deal with declining response rates. Accordingly, sample weights are more frequently applied, especially when reporting 'headline' data. The use of statistics and professional judgement helps compensate for some of these problems, but matters of interpretation and emphasis are always involved and rightly the subject of debate and discussion in the community of scholars and in the public sphere. As we have discovered over the years of producing these volumes, much of the interesting analysis emerges when responses are compared over *time* and compared with results from *other nations*. Through these comparisons, we get a greater sense of how Australia is situated globally, where we have come from, and a few hints about what the future may bring.

Acknowledgements of our colleagues

This book is the result of the timely and professional work of our chapter contributors located at the Australian National University, Macquarie University, Queensland University of Technology, the University of Graz, the University of Sydney and the University of Tasmania. We could not have asked for a more cooperative set of authors. We also gratefully acknowledge the support of the staff at Sydney University Press, particularly Susan Murray, Agata Mrva-Montoya, and Denise O'Dea. We express our gratitude for the support of the Public and Social Policy Series editors, Professor Marian Baird and Associate Professor Gaby Ramia, both of the University of Sydney. We would like to thank our copyeditor, Beth Battrick, for her editorial advice and Edith Lanser, administrative assistant to the research group on international comparative research in the Department of Sociology, University of Graz, for her assistance in preparing this manuscript. We are grateful to the Faculty of Arts of Macquarie University for the support, time and resources that allowed us to continue this book series into a fourth volume.

The Introduction is also the place to acknowledge two retirements among our long-time collaborators in the public opinion research community in Australia. We acknowledge the distinguished contributions of Professor Murray Goot of Macquarie University and Professor David Denemark of the University of Western Australia. Known for his remarkable curiosity about Australian history, and his determination to present facts frankly, Murray has shaped writings on Australian politics for decades. Modest and thoughtful of others at all times, David has been an outstanding collaborator in major comparative political science projects that continue to the present. We hope, and fully expect, that retirement from teaching will not mean an end to their fantastic contributions to social and political research.

Finally, it is with much sadness that we put together this volume without the contribution of Professor Bill Martin of the University of Queensland and formerly long-time Flinders University sociologist. Involved in *Australian Social Attitudes* from the beginning, Bill was invited to contribute to this book just before he became ill and, unfortunately, was not able to add anything further from his ongoing program of research into the Australian workplace. This volume is weaker without his input. Bill's loss is mourned by all of us. We will remember him as a decent and warm human being as well as an insightful, critical and professional sociologist.

We dedicate this book to Bill's memory.

References

Belot, Henry (2016). Confidence in democracy hits record low as Australians 'disaffected with political class'. http://www.abc.net.au/news/2016-12-20/2016-australian-election-disaffected-study/8134508.

Cameron, Sarah M. and Ian McAllister (2016). *Trends in Australian Political Opinion: Results from the Australian Election Study, 1987–2016*. Canberra: Australian National University, School of Politics and International Relations. http://www.australianelectionstudy.org/publications.html.

Knight, Genevieve and Nicholas Biddle (2015). FactCheck Q&A: is Australia the most unequal it has been in 75 years? *The Conversation*. 28 September. http://theconversation.com/factcheck-qanda-is-australia-the-most-unequal-it-has-been-in-75-years-47931.

ME Bank (2017). *Household financial comfort report*, 11th Survey (February). https://www.mebank.com.au/media/2511295/Household-Financial-Comfort-Report-Feb-2017.pdf.

Scholz, Evi, Regina Jutz, Jon H. Pammett and Markus Hadler (2017). ISSP and the ISSP 2014 Citizenship II module: an introduction. *International Journal of Sociology* 47(1), 1–9.

Stanford, Jim (2016). A portrait of employment insecurity in Australia: infographic, Australia Institute: Centre for Future Work. Available from http://www.futurework.org.au/ a_portrait_of_employment_insecurity_in_australia_infographic.

Part 1
Australian insecurities

1

Trust and insecurity: is economic and political insecurity eroding trust?

Clive Bean

Around the democratic world, social and political trust have been in decline since the latter part of the 20th century. Previous empirical investigations in Australia, however, while demonstrating that those expressing trust are in the minority, have provided little evidence of an ongoing decline in trust (Martin 2010). For example, political trust, not unreasonably, seems to fluctuate according to the political context in which it is measured (Bean 2001; 2005; Goot 2002). This chapter explores recent data to check whether levels of trust have changed in the early period of the 21st century and considers what might have driven such changes. What factors serve to enhance or diminish trust? Does a sense of insecurity, for instance, impact negatively on trust in Australia, as has been found elsewhere (Wroe 2014; 2016)? And, to the extent that this may be the case, does it mean that insecurity is eroding trust?

With respect to the political sphere, trust has become a common theme at Australian elections in the early part of the 21st century. Political trust is often mentioned when elections are announced, when party campaigns are officially launched, and when winners and losers review the outcome in the aftermath of an election. After the most recent federal election in July 2016, for example, the narrowly re-elected prime minister, Malcolm Turnbull, continued the theme when he said: 'There is no doubt that there is a level of disillusionment with politics, with government, and with the major parties' (Kenny 2016). The same newspaper report referred to the 'high levels of insecurity and even anxiety among voters about the economic pressures of life' and the link these had to the election outcome.

This connection neatly encapsulates the concerns of this chapter. It investigates developments over recent years in political trust and then considers the extent to which trust is associated with various indicators of economic and political insecurity. The relationship between political trust and economic insecurity is a complex one. Many scholars have demonstrated or made the case that trust has declined over several decades since the mid-to-late 20th century, both overseas (Nye, Zelikow and King 1997; Dalton 1999; Putnam 2000; Hetherington 2007) and in Australia (Burchell and Leigh 2002; Leigh 2010; Martin 2010). Ironically, however, the erosion of trust seemed to gather momentum around the same time as various economic indicators across the advanced industrial democracies were improving (McAllister 1999; Dalton 2004). But what has surfaced more recently is growing evidence of individual insecurity about economic and other matters, including uncertainty about present and future employment and financial status in the wake of processes associated with globalisation (Wroe 2016).

The analysis in this chapter begins with an attempt to bring us up to date with developments in political trust in Australia. Earlier work has suggested that trust in government is not experiencing secular decline in Australia. Rather, it is subject to fluctuations that appear to depend on the political cycle (Bean 2001; 2005; Goot 2002). When a new government is elected trust rises, presumably based on the optimistic expectation that it will be more trustworthy than its predecessor. Over time trust then cycles down as the realisation dawns that the current government is no more responsive than previous ones. The peaks and troughs are sometimes higher, sometimes lower, sometimes they cycle down more quickly, sometimes the cycle seems to anticipate a change of government by starting to rise an election or so before a government is ousted. But, broadly speaking, the general pattern persists.

Political trust in early 21st-century Australia

To review how the trends in political trust have played out more recently, in the early part of the 21st century, we review time series data from the Australian Election Study (AES), which is a national post-election sample survey conducted at each federal election since 1987 (McAllister and Cameron 2014). The AES has two key questions on political trust, one of which has been asked consistently since 1993 and the other of which has been asked since 1998. The first question asks: 'In general, do you feel that the people in government are too often interested in looking after themselves, or do you feel that they can be trusted to do the right thing nearly all the time?' The response categories are: 'usually look after themselves', 'sometimes look after themselves', 'sometimes can be trusted to do the right thing', and 'usually can be trusted to do the right thing'. In the analysis this question is referred to as 'trust in government'. The second question asks: 'Would you say that the government is run by a few big interests looking out for themselves, or that it is run for the benefit of all the people?' The response categories are: 'entirely run for the big interests', 'mostly run for the big interests', 'about half and half', 'mostly run for the benefit of all', and 'entirely run for the benefit of all'. In the analysis this question is referred to as 'government by big interests'.

Table 1.1 sets out the responses to these two questions for each year in which they were asked. There are eight time points for the trust in government question and six for the government by big interests question. In this table and throughout the tabular analysis the two trusting and two untrusting response categories are collapsed for ease of presentation. Focusing initially on the trust in government question, the first point to note from the table is that political trust is a minority phenomenon. At no point does a trusting response exceed 50 per cent of the sample and in only one instance does the trusting proportion approach 50 per cent. This came in 1996 when the long-running Hawke–Keating Labor government was finally removed from office after 13 years. In that year, those who said that the government can sometimes or usually be trusted to do the right thing numbered 48 per cent. The next highest point was 43 per cent in 2007, the year in which the Howard Liberal–National government was replaced after 11 years in office. Either side of each of these points, trusting responses ebbed.

Table 1.1: Political trust in Australia, 1993–2016, %.

	The people in government . . .		The government is . . .		
	Look after themselves	Can be trusted to do the right thing	Run for the big interests	About half and half	Run for the benefit of all
1993	66	34	-	-	-
1996	52	48	-	-	-
1998	67	33	52	36	12
2001	68	32	48	36	17
2004	60	40	42	38	20
2007	57	43	38	42	20
2010	63	37	44	43	12
2013	66	34	47	37	16
2016	74	26	56	33	12

Source: Australian Election Study (AES), 1993–2016.

Figure 1.1 Trust in government in Australia, 1993–2013, %.

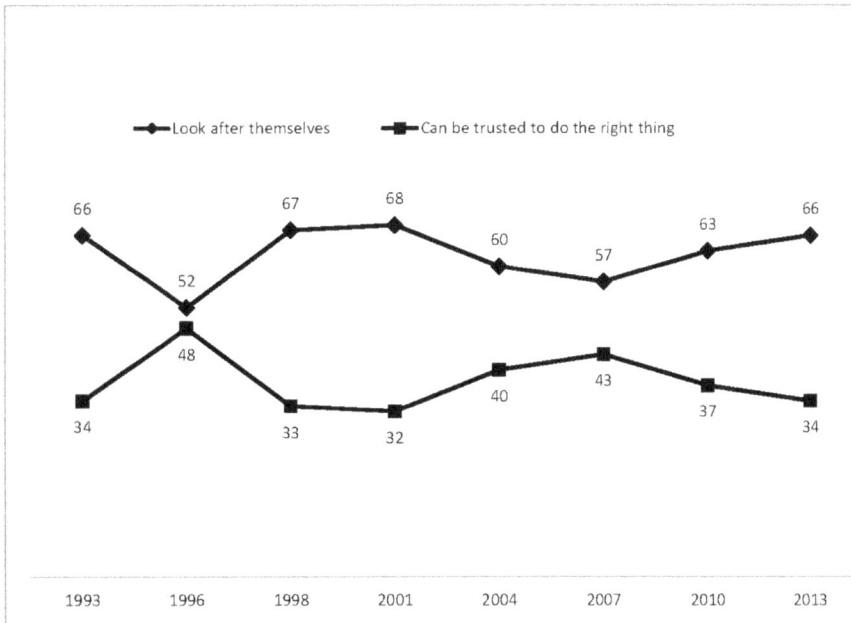

Source: AES 1993–2013.

The earlier observed cyclical fluctuations, with trust trending higher when new governments are elected and lower in between, are thus reinforced over this period. The 2013 federal election, when the Labor government was replaced by the Coalition led by Tony Abbott, proved an exception, with only 34 per cent recording a trusting response in this instance. Coming towards the end of the time series makes it difficult to interpret the significance of this deviation, but one possible interpretation is that it reflects the unusual circumstances of the first minority government at the federal level for 70 years and the highly vexatious parliamentary term that accompanied it (Johnson and Wanna with Lee 2015). The recent 2016 election recorded a further, more exaggerated, extension of this direction, with political trust falling to levels not seen since the late 1970s, in the aftermath of the 1975 constitutional crisis (Bean 2001). Even though the pattern is for trust to trend down when the government in office is re-elected, the 26 per cent of trusting responses in 2016 presents as a critically low level that raises concerns about the current health of Australian democracy. More generally, however, the data in Table 1.1 suggest that the usual baseline level of trust in government appears to be about a third of the electorate giving a trusting response. Figure 1.1 demonstrates how political trust cycles up then down, then back up, then back down again.

Turning to the second question (on who benefits from government), we see that the proportion of trusting responses is lower again. A substantial reason for this is the different question format, which allows for a midpoint response between the trusting and untrusting responses. On every occasion, a third or more of the sample go for the option of saying 'about half and half' on the question of whether the government is run by a few big interests looking out for themselves, or for the benefit of all the people. The pattern of higher trust with a new government and lower trust in between elections is also less distinct, because it is diffused by movement in and out of the central response category. Nonetheless, the pattern is visible in some form at the 2007 election, and there are also some intimations of it in 2013, although untrusting as well as trusting responses rose, as the middle category declined. On this evidence, the election of the Abbott government thus seemed to polarise voters, perhaps more than some electoral contests. Overall, however, the responses to both questions in Table 1.1 reinforce the characterisation of political trust as conforming to a cyclical pattern in Australia, with little to suggest a trend either up or down.

What determines trust?

Studies in the past have shown political trust to be linked to various background characteristics, such as age, gender and socioeconomic status (Dalton 2004; Bean 2005; Bean and Denemark 2007). Here we update such links in the Australian context by examining the association between social structure and political trust in the most recent dataset of our time series, the AES from 2013. Table 1.2 utilises the first question from Table 1.1, trust in government, for this exercise (although employing the 'government by big interests' question would have yielded similar results). Six key social location factors are examined – sex, age, education, occupation, region of residence and birthplace – plus a key indicator of partisan leanings, party identification.

The first notable point from Table 1.2 is the *lack* of association between gender and trust in government in Australia. Neither men nor women are more trusting. In the past

Table 1.2: Political trust within socio-demographic groups, 2013, %.

	Political trust	
	People in government look after themselves	People in government can be trusted to do the right thing
Sex		
Male (n=1,848)	66	34
Female (n=1,972)	66	34
Age		
18–24 (n=402)	67	33
25–44 (n=1,280)	70	30
45–64 (n=1,316)	65	35
65 and over (n=789)	60	40
Education		
No university degree (n=2,550)	67	33
University degree (n=1,206)	65	35
Occupation		
Manual (n=1,030)	70	30
Non-manual (n=2,293)	64	36
Region of residence		
Urban (n=2,713)	66	34
Rural (n=1,067)	67	33
Birthplace		
Australia (n=2,833)	66	34
English-speaking (n=313)	71	29
Non–English speaking (n=587)	62	38
Party identification		
Liberal–National (n=1,473)	61	39
Labor (n=1,354)	66	34
Greens (n=234)	69	31
Other party (n=150)	73	27
No party (n=659)	73	27

Source: AES 2013.

there has been, at most, a small gender gap in trust, but now there appears to be none. Age is different. While the very youngest members of the electorate are not necessarily the least trusting, the highest levels of trust are certainly a characteristic of the more mature age cohorts, to the extent that there is a 10 per cent difference in the proportions expressing a trusting response between those in the 25 to 44 age group and those aged 65 and over. Maturing through the life cycle, it would seem, leads to a more trusting disposition.

Increasing education has often been regarded as a prescription for reducing the deficit in political trust, but here the difference in levels of trust between those with and without university degrees is minimal, while there is a somewhat larger gap between those in 'working-class' (manual) and 'middle-class' (non-manual) occupations. Middle-class, or white-collar workers are some 6 per cent more likely to give a trusting response than working-class, or blue collar, workers.

The next panel in Table 1.2 shows that residing in either urban or rural settings makes little difference to levels of trust in government, but birthplace has an intriguing influence. Compared to the Australian-born, those born outside of Australia in English-speaking countries tend to be less trusting of government, while those born in non-English speaking countries tend to be more trusting. It is interesting to speculate that Australian governments may seem comparatively benign to those who might have come from less stable political regimes. One general message of Table 1.2, however, is that in contemporary Australia political trust does not appear to be strongly shaped by social background.

The strongest differences in political trust are among the partisan groups displayed at the bottom of the table. Previous research has shown that supporters of the party in government at the time exhibit higher levels of trust than supporters of rival parties (Bean 2001). In 2013 this continued to be true, with supporters of the Liberal–National coalition parties showing distinctly higher trust than the rest. Labor Party supporters are next, while those who support the Greens or other minor parties, or who have no party affiliation at all, register much lower levels of trust in government.

Trust and the role of economic and political insecurity

If political trust is not strongly shaped by social structure, has it become linked to insecurities that prevail in relation to personal economic circumstances and other matters? The prominence of such insecurities has increased in the early 21st century and evidence has started to appear recently concerning the impact of economic insecurity, in particular, on political trust in other parts of the world (Wroe 2014; 2016). Economic insecurity has been shown to have a variety of political consequences, having, for example, been linked to electoral support for minor parties (Mughan, Bean and McAllister 2003) and attitudes to the welfare state (Hacker, Rehm and Schlesinger 2013).

In Australia there are certainly indications that many citizens feel insecure about a variety of economic and political concerns. Table 1.3 shows the extent to which the feelings of insecurity abound, based again on the most recent data from 2013. For the purposes of this analysis, three different types of insecurity have been identified: economic, military and cultural. Economic insecurity focuses on personal economic circumstances, particularly in relation to employment. Military insecurity addresses concerns about Australia's defence. Cultural insecurity looks at perceptions of the advantages and disadvantages that accompany immigrants coming to Australia.

Looking first at the economic sphere, the top section of Table 1.3 shows that while the majority of respondents (59 per cent) view it as very or somewhat unlikely that their household income could be severely reduced in the next 12 months, there is a significant proportion (over four in ten) who say the reverse. Furthermore, when asked if they lost their job, or if their spouse or partner lost their job, how easy it would be to find another job in the next 12 months, almost two thirds say it would be very or somewhat difficult in both cases. In combination, these responses are indicative of a substantial degree of personal economic insecurity amongst the Australian public.

Table 1.3: Perceptions of insecurity, 2013, %.

Economic			
Income severely reduced in next 12 months (n=3,873)	Likely 41	—	Unlikely 59
Ease of finding another job in next 12 months (n=3,408)	Easy 35	—	Difficult 65
Ease of partner finding another job in next 12 months (n=2,573)	Easy 37	—	Difficult 63
Military			
Trust US to come to Australia's defence if security threatened (n=3,865)	Trust 82	—	Not trust 18
Australia able to defend itself if attacked (n=3,827)	Agree 28	Neither agree nor disagree 29	Disagree 43
Cultural			
Immigrants increase the crime rate (n=3,837)	Agree 40	Neither agree nor disagree 29	Disagree 31
Immigrants are good for the economy (n=3,834)	Agree 56	Neither agree nor disagree 29	Disagree 15
Immigrants take jobs from people born in Australia (n=3,834)	Agree 35	Neither agree nor disagree 28	Disagree 38
Immigrants make Australia more open to new ideas and cultures (n=3,836)	Agree 73	Neither agree nor disagree 17	Disagree 10

Source: AES 2013.
Notes: Questions: *On economic insecurity*: How likely or unlikely do you think it is that your household's income could be severely reduced in the next 12 months? (Very likely; somewhat likely; somewhat unlikely; very unlikely.) If you lost your job, how easy or difficult would it be to find another job in the next 12 months? (Very easy; somewhat easy; somewhat difficult; very difficult.) If your spouse/partner lost their job, how easy or difficult would it be for them to find another job in the next 12 months? (Very easy; somewhat easy; somewhat difficult; very difficult.) *On military insecurity*: If Australia's security were threatened by some other country, how much trust do you feel Australia can have in the United States to come to Australia's defence? (A great deal; a fair amount; not very much; none at all.) Australia would be able to defend itself successfully if it were ever attacked. (Strongly agree; agree; neither agree nor disagree; disagree; strongly disagree.) *On cultural insecurity*: Immigrants increase the crime rate; Immigrants are generally good for Australia's economy; Immigrants take jobs away from people who are born in Australia; Immigrants make Australia more open to new ideas and cultures. (Strongly agree; agree; neither agree nor disagree; disagree; strongly disagree.)

The next panel in Table 1.3 suggests that insecurity is not limited to the economic realm. Issues of defence and military security have become more salient since the threat of terrorism has increased in recent times (Gibson and McAllister 2007). Although 82 per cent feel that Australia can have a great deal or a fair amount of trust in the United States to come to Australia's defence if Australia's security were threatened by some other country, only 28 per cent agree that Australia would be able to defend itself successfully if it were ever attacked. A similar number neither agree nor disagree with this proposition, leaving 43 per cent who take the view that Australia would not be able to defend itself.

In an era in which debates over refugees, asylum seekers and immigration more broadly abound, both internationally and within Australia (Betts 1999; Goot and Watson 2005; Nair and Bloom 2016), questions on the impact of immigration may also provoke feelings of insecurity. In the bottom panel in Table 1.3 we see that significant minorities express the view that immigrants increase the crime rate and take jobs away from people who are born in Australia (40 and 35 per cent respectively). In the former instance, this group outnumbers those who disagree that immigrants increase the crime rate. The view appears more positive, however, when the proposition is that immigrants are generally good for the economy and that they make Australia more open to new ideas and cultures. Only 15 per cent and 10 per cent, respectively, express 'insecure' views on these questions, while fully 56 per cent and 73 per cent take an open stance on these aspects of the effect of immigration.

The trust–insecurity nexus

Overall, Table 1.3 suggests that insecurity is not rife within the Australian electorate but that it is present in significant amounts, in all three spheres examined – economic, military and cultural. The question of interest is whether this insecurity influences political trust. Table 1.4 takes the first step towards addressing this question by showing how trust in government varies according to whether citizens feel secure or insecure economically. Based on recent research in Europe and the United States (Wroe 2014; 2016), there is certainly an expectation that personal economic insecurity will tend to drag trust down.

Table 1.4 indeed reveals a clear relationship between insecurity and trust when the question focuses on the likelihood of a severe reduction in household income. Those who view this as an unlikely development are 10 per cent *more* inclined to say that people in government can be trusted to do the right thing than those who think it is likely that their income could be severely reduced in the next 12 months. Put another way, 38 per cent of the economically secure trust the government compared to only 28 per cent of the economically insecure. When attention turns to the ease of finding another job if the current one were lost, although the level of insecurity is higher, as we saw in Table 1.3, the gap in trust is smaller – only 3 or 4 per cent. On these questions, the insecure are only slightly less politically trusting.

Table 1.5 covers the same ground for military insecurity. Given that the question about the United States coming to Australia's aid specifically uses the term 'trust', we might expect to see a clear link between this item and trust in government. Such a link is there, but it is not as strong as might have been expected. Some 35 per cent of those who trust the United States to come to Australia's defence in a time of need also trust the people in government, compared to 29 per cent of those who do not have faith in the United States coming to Australia's defence. On the question of Australia's ability to defend itself, the gap in trust

Table 1.4: Political trust by economic insecurity, 2013, %.

	Political trust	
	People in government look after themselves	People in government can be trusted to do the right thing
Income severely reduced in next 12 months		
Likely	72	28
Unlikely	62	38
Ease of finding another job in next 12 months		
Easy	65	35
Difficult	69	31
Ease of partner finding another job in next 12 months		
Easy	65	35
Difficult	68	32

N=3,955. Source: AES 2013.

Table 1.5: Political trust by military insecurity, 2013, %.

	Political trust	
	People in government look after themselves	People in government can be trusted to do the right thing
Trust US to come to Australia's defence if security threatened		
Trust	65	35
Not trust	71	29
Australia able to defend itself if attacked		
Agree	64	36
Neither agree nor disagree	66	34
Disagree	67	33

N=3,955. Source: AES 2013.

is narrower again, with only a 3 per cent gap in political trust between those who think Australia could defend itself and those who think it could not.

The final set of data is perhaps the most intriguing. On the evidence in Table 1.6, cultural insecurity has a stronger relationship to political trust than economic or military insecurity. Each of the four questions on the impact of immigrants shows a noticeable spread of political trust. Thus, while 38 per cent of those who disagree that immigrants increase the crime rate say that people in government can be trusted to do the right thing, only 29 per cent of those who think that immigrants do increase the crime rate express a trusting view. The gap is larger again when the question is whether immigrants are generally good for Australia's economy. Some 37 per cent who agree that immigrants are good for the economy trust the people in government, but of those who disagree only

Table 1.6: Political trust by cultural insecurity, 2013, %.

	Political trust	
	People in government look after themselves	People in government can be trusted to do the right thing
Immigrants increase the crime rate		
Agree	71	29
Neither agree nor disagree	64	36
Disagree	62	38
Immigrants good for the economy		
Agree	63	37
Neither agree nor disagree	67	33
Disagree	76	24
Immigrants take jobs away from people born in Australia		
Agree	72	28
Neither agree nor disagree	64	36
Disagree	63	37
Immigrants make Australia more open to new ideas and cultures		
Agree	63	37
Neither agree nor disagree	72	28
Disagree	78	22

N=3,955. Source: AES 2013.

24 per cent express trust. Similarly, trust in government is distinctly higher among those who do not feel that immigrants take jobs away from the Australian-born (37 per cent) than it is for those who believe that they do (28 per cent). On the final question of whether immigrants make Australia more open to new ideas and cultures, 37 per cent of those who affirm this view also indicate that they trust the people in government to do the right thing, while a low 22 per cent of those who disagree with the proposition display political trust.

This 15 per cent difference in the level of trust on the question of immigration bringing new ideas and cultures is the largest for any variable examined in this analysis. It is conceivable that the association between openness to immigration and trust may reflect a more general trusting outlook which incorporates government, migrants and other spheres. Another key message from Table 1.6 is that, while the proportions expressing an insecure response about the effects of immigration on the economy and new experiences are small, those who do feel insecure are more distrusting than any other group under consideration. Certain items in Table 1.6 – whether immigrants are good for the economy and whether immigrants take jobs away from people born in Australia – also see cultural and economic insecurity coming together, and this combination of factors generating a

Table 1.7: Effects on political trust (multiple regression).

	b	*β*
Sex (male)	-.01	-.02
Age	.002	.09**
Education (university degree)	-.02	-.02
Occupation (non-manual)	.03	.04
Region of residence (rural)	-.01	-.01
English-speaking birthplace	-.05	-.04*
Non-English speaking birthplace	.02	.02
Party identification Labor	-.06	-.09**
Party identification Green	-.11	-.08**
Party identification other/none	-.11	-.13**
Income not likely to be reduced	.22	.11**
Easy to find new job – self	.05	.02
Easy to find new job – partner	.03	.02
Trust US to defend Australia	.15	.06**
Australia able to defend itself	.10	.06**
Immigrants increase crime rate	-.08	-.05
Immigrants good for economy	.10	.06*
Immigrants take jobs	-.04	-.02
Immigrants make Aust. more open	.13	.06*
R-squared		.08

N=3,955. * p < .05; ** p < .01. Source: AES 2013.

sense of insecurity among some members of the Australian public may be more influential in shaping political trust than any single factor on its own.

The final part of the analysis brings together all of the factors examined in the chapter to show which ones have an impact on political trust net of other influences. The analytic technique employed is ordinary least squares regression analysis and Table 1.7 displays both the unstandardised (b) and standardised (beta) regression coefficients. Apart from age (in years) all variables are scored on their original metric, rescaled to run from a low of 0 to a high of 1. Those that have statistically significant effects on trust in government are asterisked. Thus Table 1.7 shows that, of the socio-demographic variables, sex, education, occupation, and region of residence have no significant impact on political trust. Age and birthplace do have an effect: older people are more trusting and those born in English-speaking countries outside of Australia are less trusting. With respect to party identification, Table 1.7 confirms the bivariate data in Table 1.2 by showing that Labor, Green and those with minor party or no party identification are all significantly less trusting of the government than coalition party supporters.

Turning to the various indicators of insecurity, the measure of likely household income reduction has a clear and significant effect, although the questions on ease of finding another job do not. The two measures of military insecurity show significant and distinct effects net of other factors, despite having only modest associations in the bivariate table shown above. And finally, the two cultural insecurity variables that displayed the strongest bivariate associations (about migrants being good for the economy and making Australia more open to new ideas and cultures) retain a statistically significant effect in the multivariate analysis, while the other two do not.

Conclusion

As Wroe (2016) has commented, it has become commonplace for political leaders in established democracies to lament the low and declining levels of political trust. Even louder on the same subject tend to be the voices of political commentators, and such commentary has tended to grow over the years. Australia has been no exception to this practice. Yet in Australia, at least, political trust does not appear to have declined in any systematic fashion. Trust in government is not high – it is, has been and remains a minority phenomenon – but the evidence belies those who argue or imply that it is on an inexorable downward path (Burchell and Leigh 2002; Leigh 2010).

In general, the evidence in this chapter is consistent with the findings of previous work in showing that political trust is trending neither down nor up. Instead, the evidence provides a solid foundation for extending the conclusion that political trust ebbs and flows according to the political cycle (Bean 2001; 2005; Goot 2002). In the main, political trust rises when a new government is elected, particularly if the previous government has had a lengthy term in office. Trust then declines during the term of the new government until that government in turn is replaced, at which point trust registers another high point. In between these times, the norm seems to be that about a third of the electorate expresses trust in government, while the remaining two thirds do not. Whether the low point in trust observed at the 2016 election does or does not represent an aberration will only be seen in time. It could just as well reflect a period of particular public disquiet with Australian politics and politicians as herald a new era of low trust. The cyclical pattern over time points to it being more likely to be the former than the latter.

This chapter set out to consider whether economic and political insecurity is eroding political trust. It found a connection between insecurity and trust, but not a terribly strong one. Based on the findings of the analysis, insecurity might reasonably be said to undermine trust, to a degree at least, but it is too big a stretch to say that it is eroding trust. Furthermore, for the most part, the links between insecurity and political trust are rather modest. An association is present in some form in every instance, but it is mainly in the realm of cultural insecurity that it shows through clearly and consistently. Perhaps surprisingly, economic insecurity on its own does not feature very strongly and the consequences for political trust of military insecurity are minor. There is much more work to be done, but on the evidence here, one of the places where insecurity matters most for trust is at the intersection of cultural and economic insecurity.

Yet, as a phenomenon that has largely come to prominence in the wake of globalisation (Wroe 2016), if insecurity grows it may pose a greater threat to trust than currently. It is difficult to say how likely that is at present, but it does point to the need to monitor the connection between the two. As Hetherington (2007; see also Martin 2010) has argued, political trust matters, in a variety of ways, and economic and political insecurity matter for trust, at least to some extent. It is thus not beyond the bounds of possibility that an increase in insecurity could put further downward pressure on political trust.

References

Australian Election Study (2016). The AES studies: 1993–2016. http://www.australianelectionstudy.org/voter_studies.html.

Bean, Clive (2001). Party politics, political leaders and trust in government in Australia. *Political Science* 53(1), 17–27.

Bean, Clive (2005). Is there a crisis of trust in Australia? In *Australian social attitudes: the first report*. Shaun Wilson, Gabrielle Meagher, Rachel Gibson, David Denemark and Mark Western, eds. 122–40. Sydney: UNSW Press.

Bean, Clive and David Denemark (2007). Citizenship, participation, efficacy and trust in Australia. In *Australian social attitudes 2: citizenship, work and aspirations*. David Denemark, Gabrielle Meagher, Shaun Wilson, Mark Western and Timothy Phillips, eds. 58–80. Sydney: UNSW Press.

Betts, Katharine (1999). *The great divide: immigration politics in Australia*. Sydney: Duffy & Snellgrove.

Burchell, David and Andrew Leigh, eds (2002). *The prince's new clothes: why do Australians dislike their politicians?* Sydney: UNSW Press.

Dalton, Russell J. (1999). Political support in advanced industrial democracies. In *Critical citizens: global support for democratic governance*. Pippa Norris, ed. 57–77. Oxford: Oxford University Press.

Dalton, Russell J. (2004). *Democratic challenges, democratic choices: the erosion of political support in advanced industrial democracies*. Oxford: Oxford University Press.

Gibson, Rachel K. and Ian McAllister (2007). Defence, security and the Iraq war. In *Australian social attitudes 2: citizenship, work and aspirations*. David Denemark, Gabrielle Meagher, Shaun Wilson, Mark Western and Timothy Phillips, eds. 37–57. Sydney: UNSW Press.

Goot, Murray (2002). Distrustful, disenchanted and disengaged? Public opinion on politics, politicians and the parties: an historical perspective. In *The prince's new clothes: why do Australians dislike their politicians?* David Burchell and Andrew Leigh, eds. 9–46. Sydney: UNSW Press.

Goot, Murray and Ian Watson (2005). Immigration, multiculturalism and national identity. In *Australian social attitudes: the first report*. Shaun Wilson, Gabrielle Meagher, Rachel Gibson, David Denemark and Mark Western, eds. 182–203. Sydney: UNSW Press.

Hacker, Jacob S., Philipp Rehm and Mark Schlesinger (2013). The insecure American: economic experiences, financial worries, and policy attitudes. *Perspectives on Politics* 11(1), 23–49.

Hetherington, Marc J. (2007). *Why trust matters: declining political trust and the demise of American liberalism*. Princeton, NJ: Princeton University Press.

Johnson, Carol and John Wanna (with Hsu-Ann Lee), eds (2015). *Abbott's gambit: the 2013 Australian federal election*. Canberra: ANU Press.

Kenny, Mark (2016). Australian federal election 2016: Turnbull takes responsibility for poor campaign as count continues. *Sydney Morning Herald*, 5 July.

Leigh, Andrew (2010). *Disconnected*. Sydney: UNSW Press.

Martin, Aaron (2010). Does political trust matter? Examining some of the implications of low levels of political trust in Australia. *Australian Journal of Political Science* 45(4), 705–12.

McAllister, Ian (1999). The economic performance of governments. In *Critical citizens: global support for democratic governance*. Pippa Norris, ed. 188–203. Oxford: Oxford University Press.

McAllister, Ian and Sarah M. Cameron (2014). *Trends in Australian political opinion: results from the Australian Election Study, 1987–2013*. Canberra: Australian National University.

Mughan, Anthony, Clive Bean and Ian McAllister (2003). Economic globalization, job insecurity and the populist reaction. *Electoral Studies* 22(3), 617–33.

Nair, Parvati and Tendayi Bloom, eds (2016). *Migration across boundaries: linking research to practice and experience*. London and New York: Routledge.

Nye, Joseph S. Jr, Philip D. Zelikow and David C. King, eds (1997). *Why people don't trust government.* Cambridge, Mass.: Harvard University Press.

Putnam, Robert D. (2000). *Bowling alone: the collapse and revival of American community.* New York: Simon & Schuster.

Wroe, Andrew (2014). Political trust and job insecurity in 18 European polities. *Journal of Trust Research* 4(2), 90–112.

Wroe, Andrew (2016). Economic insecurity and political trust in the United States. *American Politics Research* 44(1), 131–63.

2

Minor and populist parties in Australia: does economic insecurity or a 'representation gap' drive support?

Shaun Ratcliff

At the beginning of the 21st century, a larger proportion of the world's population lived in democracies than at any other time in recorded history. Less than two decades later, in many of these democracies trust in leaders, parties and in the institution of democracy itself are at the lowest point they have been in decades (see for instance Cameron and McAllister 2016, 74–5, on trust in Australian political institutions; Heatherington and Rudolf 2015 on the United States; and Armingeon and Ceka 2014 on trust in the European Union). In some cases, nations' democratic systems are themselves under threat of breaking down (Diamond 2011). This environment creates a breeding ground for insurgent candidates and parties running against the establishment and traditional politics. This chapter examines the role that economic insecurity and poor issue representation play in voters' support for these kinds of parties.

The growing vote for minor parties and populist candidates in recent years throughout much of the democratic west has been particularly pronounced since the economic shock of the Global Financial Crisis (GFC). In the United States, Donald Trump first captured the Republican nomination and then the presidency in 2016 with 'anti-system' and anti-immigrant rhetoric; and from the left, Bernie Sanders came close to winning the Democratic nomination with a platform aimed primarily at reducing the influence of corporate elites and economic inequality. Neither candidate had been a long-term member of their party. Across Europe, the average share of the populist vote in national and European parliamentary elections has increased from approximately 5 per cent in the 1960s to more than 10 per cent in recent years (Inglehart and Norris 2016). This success includes the formation of government in Greece by the populist-left Syriza, which gained office in 2015 in opposition to the austerity measures imposed on the country by its creditors, the European Union and the International Monetary fund. Similarly, in recent years, the perennial (almost) breakthrough party in France, the National Front, has seen a resurgence in support, with its leader Marine Le Pen campaigning on a mix of protectionist economics and opposition to mass immigration; at the same time, an entirely new party captured the presidency and the National Assembly. In the United Kingdom, Nigel Farage led the populist right United Kingdom Independence Party (UKIP) to win its first seats in the British Parliament with an anti-Europe and anti-immigration manifesto; and, with elements of the centre-right Conservative Party, UKIP helped achieve victory for the anti-EU vote in the 2016 'Brexit' referendum. In many cases, these have been political successes that would have been difficult for most scholars and commentators to imagine a few short years ago.

Australia is not immune from the appeals of populism, or new parties challenging the status quo. As Figure 2.1 shows, the share of the vote gained in the Senate by non-major parties and candidates has gradually increased over several decades, burgeoning in 2010 following the GFC and consequent low wages growth (Australian Bureau of Statistics, 2017, Table 1). This high level of minor party support was maintained at the 2013 and 2016 elections.[1] This growth, if it continues, may change the electoral balance in favour of a more fragmented party system, making governance more complicated and potentially affecting policy outcomes.

In this chapter, I explore the large vote received by these parties in the Australian Senate at the 2016 election. I examine how this record-high minor party vote may have resulted from a combination of economic insecurity and poor issue representation. Voters who feel the major parties are not providing them with acceptable economic outcomes and policy settings consistent with their preferences are behaving 'rationally' by supporting other parties. Although not all the parties and candidates included here are populist in nature, many are. Those that are not populist frequently represent a protest against the established centre-left Labor Party and centre-right Liberal–National Coalition parties, which between them have (in various forms and incarnations) formed the national governments of Australia since 1901.

I use the term minor parties generally to refer to parties not aligned with the established political parties that form government in Australia. Although a substantial literature has grown addressing these types of political actors, there is no single authoritative account with which to classify them. Many of the studies concerning anti-establishment and protest politics focus on populism. However, this term also lacks a widely accepted definition. Mudde (2007) argued that populism was an ideological phenomena, with the 'nation' forming the core of the ideology, around which there are three broader features: nativism, authoritarianism, and the championing of the (perceived) general will of 'the people' over the preferences of the 'elite'. Conversely, Moffitt and Tormey (2014) described populisim as a political *style* – rather than any particular sets of ideologies or policies – which can be used by actors from the far left to the far right, and includes appeals to the people (versus elites), focuses on crises, breakdowns and threats, and involves a rejection of traditional political norms and language.

In this chapter, I examine all non-major candidates and party groups that contested the 2016 Australian Senate election. These parties have been included on several criteria. These include a rejection of either the style or substance of the major parties' positions (or both). They also focus on issues or policy positions that they see as 'underrepresented' by the major parties. These foci include the advocacy of environmentally and socially progressive policies (the Greens) and opposition to free trade, regional economic

---

1   The upper house of the Australian federal parliament. Each of Australia's six states is represented by 12 senators, and the two territories are represented by two each. Like members of the United States Congress, Australian Senators serve staggered terms, with voters electing half their states' cohort to the upper house at federal elections (with each territory position open every election). This system increases the chance of success for minor parties, with voters able to rank candidates (or parties) from most to least preferred, allowing an individual to support a more desirable candidate or party who has little chance of election, followed by a more electable candidate, without feeling as though they may have 'wasted' their vote.

Figure 2.1 Vote share of minor parties and independents in the Australian Senate, 1949–2016.

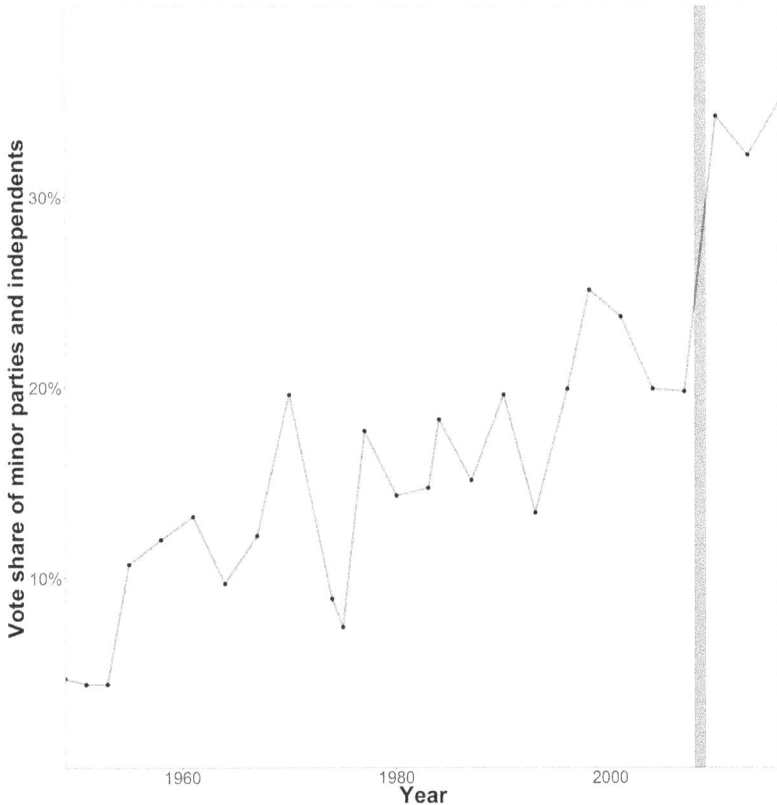

Source: Australian Electoral Commission.
Notes: Each point represents the results of a Senate election. The dark vertical bar represents the approximate period of the global financial crisis.

stagnation, and the decline of manufacturing (the Nick Xenophon Team). They also include opposition to high immigration and the ongoing arrival of asylum seekers (One Nation) and the loss of traditional morality and the diminished role of Christianity in society (Christian parties including Family First and the Christian Democrats). Minor parties also take opposing positions on the welfare state, which is seen as being either too generous (the Liberal Democrats), or not generous enough (the Greens again).

Several explanations help to provide an understanding of the increased support of these parties and candidates in Australia, and other representative democracies, in recent years (or in some cases, decades). One of these is that these parties and candidates represent a temporary 'glitch' in the system. In this view, the successes of Donald Trump in the United States, UKIP in the United Kingdom, and One Nation in Australia are an aberration – the result of short-term factors that will dissipate shortly after emerging. However, the relative longevity of the National Front in France, green parties in Germany and Australia, and similar parties in other democracies, suggests this may not be the case. An alternative view suggests new parties, occupying different niches in the political ecosystem, reflect deeper, longer-term social and economic trends.

Economic insecurity as an explanation

One of the most commonly cited reasons for the growth of populist and authoritarian parties, and others challenging the status quo, is the rise in economic insecurity in Western democracies. This phenomenon is often seen as the result of slowing growth and increasing inequality, which places strains on democratic legitimacy and systems of government. The difference between consistent economic growth (three years or more in a row) and malaise (two years of contraction) has been found to increase the probability that a state will revert from a democratic to non-democratic system from less than 1 to nearly 8 per cent (see Przeworski, Alvarez, Cheibub and Limongi 2000, 9). This is not to suggest that the parties I am examining here are anti-democratic, or that *established democracies* are necessarily at risk, but to highlight the stresses that economic stagnation can place on the established norms and traditions that are required to maintain democratic systems. Beyond slower economic growth, several mature liberal democracies have seen a decline in manufacturing employment, an erosion of trade union membership, and the withdrawal of progressive welfare safety nets (Hacker 2006). These economic changes impact upon voters' perceptions of whether the existing economic and political system is working in their interest.

In a context of shrinking employment opportunities for blue-collar workers and those with fewer formal qualifications, voters with lower levels of economic security (driven by their education and work history, as well as location) may perceive their livelihoods as precarious or declining. This insecurity may, in turn, reduce trust in the established parties to provide outcomes that meet these voters' expectations. As this form of economic insecurity grows, new parties that are separate from the existing establishment (and therefore able to escape responsibility for any of its shortcomings) can appeal to voters – particularly the less advantaged – by shifting the blame for the financial and consequent social distress of these groups onto others. For example, populism may encourage perceptions that voters exist in a state of 'zero-sum competition' with immigrant groups for resources (a frequent target of the populist right), and that free trade reduces their employment opportunities (a claim made by both the populist left and right). Protectionist trade policies, reduced immigration, and the return of manufacturing jobs are offered as panaceas. With centre-left parties generally unwilling or unable to promise the same (relatively) simple-sounding solutions, this account argues, some economically insecure voters have directed their support towards populist parties (see, for instance, Albertazzi and McDonnell 2008; Betz 1994; Ramiro and Gomez 2016). These longer-term trends are likely exacerbated by severe financial crises, which further erode confidence in established political and economic systems, and increase the support of the far right in particular (Funke, Schularick and Trebesch, 2016).

In the Australian context, there have been claims that economic insecurity was one of the significant causes of the rise of the populist One Nation Party between 1996 and 1998 (Turnbull and Wilson 2001). The rapid increase in minor party support in the Australian Senate in 1990 – immediately prior to the beginning of Australia's worst recession since the Great Depression – and again since 2010 following the GFC, shown in Figure 2.1, supports this assertion. However, this has also been disputed (Goot and Watson, 2001a), and there are other plausible explanations.

Sociocultural explanations

Support for populist protest parties can also be seen as a response to cultural and social change (Inglehart and Norris 2016). According to this account, growth in postmaterialist politics concerning the environment and gender equality, changes in the nature and level of immigration, and increasing social liberalism, incite negative responses from those who disagree with, or feel excluded by, these shifts in social norms. These constituencies include older voters, men, those with lower levels of education, and traditionally dominant groups. These groups sense either that their privileges are being supplanted, or that traditional norms are being undermined (see for instance Inglehart 1990; 1997; Norris 2005).

Frequently, this conflict manifests around concerns about immigration. Goot and Watson (2001b), for instance, see support for One Nation in Australia as primarily a product of racial tensions and a backlash against large-scale Asian immigration. This concern about high levels of immigration and multiculturalism may be the result of perceived competition for tangible resources – employment opportunities, public services and goods – that new arrivals may pose (Campbell 1965; Sherif 1967; Sherif and Sherif 1953). Those most likely to view immigration as a source of competition for scarce resources – and therefore oppose it – include voters without barriers to competition in the employment market. This group includes workers in occupations that do not require specific qualifications (manual occupations, for instance), and who have generally lower incomes.

Concerns about immigration may also derive from social or cultural rather than economic drivers. These are based on the belief that high levels of immigration (and the existence of out-groups more generally) are a threat to the dominant culture (covered by symbolic threat theory, see Blalock 1967; Key 1984 [1949]), as well as the status of the 'in-group' in the social hierarchy. These threat perceptions largely relate to the idea that immigrants change the societies they join (described by social dominance theory, see Sidanius and Pratto 1999). It may be that they challenge the dominance of established groups, or that through their mere presence they fundamentally alter the composition of the host society (Sides and Citrin 2007, 491). This effect is particularly strong when the perceived cultural distance between the country of origin and the host society is large (Vala, Pereira and Ramos 2006, 136), which may be mediated by more or less contact with different groups, and the resulting propensity to stereotype and perceive threat from difference (Allport 1954).

In this view, concern about immigration, multiculturalism, and ethnic difference can be the result of socialisation and a lack of positive interaction with out-groups. In support of this theoretical framework, several studies in Australia and elsewhere have found that older voters – who were socialised with different norms concerning immigration – are more likely to oppose immigration (Goot 1993; McAllister 1993). Additionally, there are indications the association between education and support for immigration is as much a product of the socialisation involved in attaining higher levels of education as of the labour market advantages these voters possess (Hainmueller and Hiscox 2007, 437; Sides and Citrin 2007; Wilkes, Guppy and Farris 2008).

Issue representation and support for minor parties

In a context where the established political parties fail to provide policy offerings that are seen to reduce the economic insecurity felt in some parts of society, and which address the concerns of those voters opposed to social change and high levels of immigration, parts of the electorate may feel poorly represented by the political system. This problem creates conditions in which minor parties thrive. Associated with this hypothesis, there has been a growing critique that established parties are no longer willing or able to properly represent the policy interests of different groups in society (Mair 2013; Marsh and Miller 2012). Research from the US and Australia has indicated that, rather than responding to the policy preferences of all parts of the electorate equally, the policy positions adopted by political elites, and public policy outcomes themselves, are more likely to favour the preferences of affluent voters (Bartels 2010; Giger, Rosset and Bernauer 2012; Gilens 2012).

A possible outcome of the outsized influence that economic and cultural elites have on party policy has been the general acceptance of markets as the primary resource allocation mechanism in society. In recent years, a number of scholars, including political scientist Peter Mair (2013, 72) and philosopher Michael Sandel (2012), have raised concerns about this embrace of market economics, and Bob Birell and others have critiqued Australia's immigration program, which they characterise as primarily serving the interests of business and higher-income professionals (Birrell 2006; Birrell and Healy 2003). These scholars and commentators argue that by failing to provide alternative solutions to problems of economic management, established parties have reduced the functionality (and legitimacy) of liberal representative democracy itself.

With the economic policies of the established parties constrained to market solutions in a range of areas, and social change occurring at a relatively fast pace across several domains in recent decades, there exists the potential for some members of the electorate to feel economically insecure and socially excluded. Even if this group is relatively small, it provides a pool from which some minor and populist parties may recruit voters. Similarly, others may not believe change has occurred fast enough, providing parties supportive of social change (such as the Greens) a base. According to the 'responsible party' model, political parties must take stable and clearly differentiated policy positions to provide effective representation (Adams 2001; Esaiasson and Holmberg 1996; Schmitt and Thomassen 1999). If they do not, it becomes difficult for voters to place these parties within a coherent issue space, and therefore decide which party best represents their preferences (Converse 1975; Schmitt and Thomassen 1999; van der Brug 1999). Elements of the literature have found that voters tend to be more satisfied when parties better represent their policy interests (Brandenburg and Johns 2014) and actually provide substantive alternatives (Laver 2011).

A lack of issue representation by the established government-forming parties may result in a dissatisfied electorate,[2] one that is willing to show its displeasure through the

---

2   Calvert (1985), Roemer (2001) and Wittman (1973; 1977; 1983) all produced theoretical models explaining this process by showing that party systems cannot retain equilibrium over the long term in a state where the main parties are providing similar policy offerings. As Mair, Sandel and others argue, this is currently the case with market economics. In these models, when the established, government-forming parties are unwilling or unable to offer meaningful policy differences in salient areas where differences are demanded by some segment of the population, another party will attract the support of those disaffected with the status quo (which might include former activists, donors and candidates of the established parties). Even Anthony Downs (1957, 131), who predicted the parties would moderate their policy offerings in order to maximise their electoral success, outlined how excessive policy convergence between established parties could result in new parties forming on the ideological fringe, acting either to pull a major party away from the centre, or (less likely) to attract away enough of its supporters to replace it on the left or right. The growth in populist party support may be this process in action.

ballot box. One outlet for expressing dissatisfaction is anti-establishment, populist and insurgent parties. In Australia, New Zealand and Canada, supporters of minor parties on both the left and right expressed higher levels of dissatisfaction with democracy in their country than other voters (Bowler, Denemark, Donovan and McDonnell 2017).

Data sources and measures for economic insecurity

Given the literature documented above, we expect a strong positive relationship between voters' perceived economic insecurity and the probability they would support a populist, protest or other minor party. More economically insecure voters – those stating that their own economic situation and the state of the wider economy are worse – should be more likely to support these parties, with variation across different types of minor parties. Assuming voters are 'utility maximisers' with bounded rationality (see, for instance, Popkin 1991), they should be expected to support the party most likely to govern closest to their preferences – therefore, voters who have issue preferences farther from the policy positions of the established parties are defined as less well represented. When they are poorly represented across a few policy areas – measured here as the average distance between their preferences and the positions of both the Coalition and Labor Party across several issues – they should be more willing to support populist or minor parties taking policy positions closer to their preferences.

These ideas are tested using a novel dataset, collected through an online study of approximately 50,000 voters run by Vox Pop Labs, conducted during and immediately after the 2016 Australian federal election (with respondents recruited through the Vote Compass voter engagement tool during the campaign; see Vox Pop Labs 2016). These data are unique for Australia, in both their sample size and content. They include responses on the positions of both voters and the established parties (Coalition and Labor) on a set of 30 issues, which allows for the measurement of the distance between voter issue preferences and the positions taken by the parties across a range of policy areas. Five questions were also included on economic security, allowing for different dimensions of economic 'stress' to be measured. These are then used to model voter behaviour as an outcome of these (and other) factors. Additionally, the large sample provides the opportunity to examine patterns in the support for Australia's smaller political parties, which might otherwise be difficult to examine in a standard sample with 2,000 observations or less. These are then organised into seven parties or party groups: the Greens (n=19,234); other Minor parties on the left (n=2,635); the Nick Xenophon Team (n=6,429); other parties and independents in the political centre (n=2,384); Libertarians (n=501); the Christian right (n=696); and, the 'Populist and protest right' (n=1,839).[3] The specific coding of parties into groups can be found in Appendix 2.1.

---

3   The large number of party categories is also something that makes Australia an interesting case study to examine the increasing support for populist and protest parties in mature liberal democracies. As this list of parties suggests, there has been a rapid increase in the number of (and support for) these parties. Possibly more than most countries, Australia has a fractured set of minor parties on both the left and the right of the political spectrum. This is potentially caused (or exacerbated) by the proportional and preferential system used to elect senators (discussed above).

Table 2.1: Voter economic insecurity (sociotropic and personal).

Variable	Dimension 1 (sociotropic)	Dimension 2 (personal)
Economy, next 12 months	.73	.21
Economy, next 5 years	.80	.20
Family, next year	.42	.47
Family, past year	.20	.95
Good time to buy	.40	.32

Source: Vox Pop Labs post-election survey data.
Notes: Loading of economic security items onto latent traits in an exploratory factor analysis with varimax rotation. Each row in this table represents a survey item. The columns show how strongly these load onto the two economic security dimensions estimated by this analysis. The first column represents sociotropic security and the second personal economic security. A high positive loading of an item on a dimension indicates an issue strongly separates respondents with preferences with high and low security. A value close to zero indicates an item that does a poor job of doing so.

To better understand the effect of economic insecurity on the Australian electorate at the 2016 federal election, five questions were included in the Vox Pop Labs online post-election study. They were: (i) Do you think that during the next 12 months Australia will have good times financially or bad times? (measured on a 2-point scale); (ii) Would you say that you and your family are better or worse off than you were a year ago? (3-point scale); (iii) Do you think now is a good or a bad time to buy major household items? (2-point scale); (iv) Looking ahead, which of the following two scenarios would you say is more likely – Australia will have continuous good times during the next 5 years or so, or Australia will have periods of widespread depression or unemployment? (2-point scale); and (v) Do you think that a year from now, your family will be better off financially, worse off or about the same as now? (3-point scale).

Latent perceptions of economic insecurity are estimated using a two-dimensional factor analysis, with the factor scores produced along each dimension scaled to have a mean of 0 and a standard deviation of 1. The two dimensions are shaped by *sociotropic* economic insecurity (dimension 1), including the *general* financial situation of Australia as well as perceptions of the economic situation in the next five years; and perceptions of personal economic security (dimension 2), which were driven by respondents' retrospective views of their *own* financial situation. (Responses to questions about whether it was a good time to buy a major household appliance and about expectations of their financial situation loaded about equally onto both dimensions.)

These two measures of economic insecurity can be understood as products of voters' opportunities and lived experiences. To better understand this, the average insecurity scores (derived from this factor analysis) for different demographics are displayed in Figure 2.2, with the horizontal lines around the midpoint representing 95 per cent confidence intervals. The dashed vertical line is the overall population average. To improve accuracy, these data were weighted using age, sex, industry, geography (federal electoral division), education, religious affiliation, and both previous and current vote choice.

Figure 2.2 Economic security by demographic group.

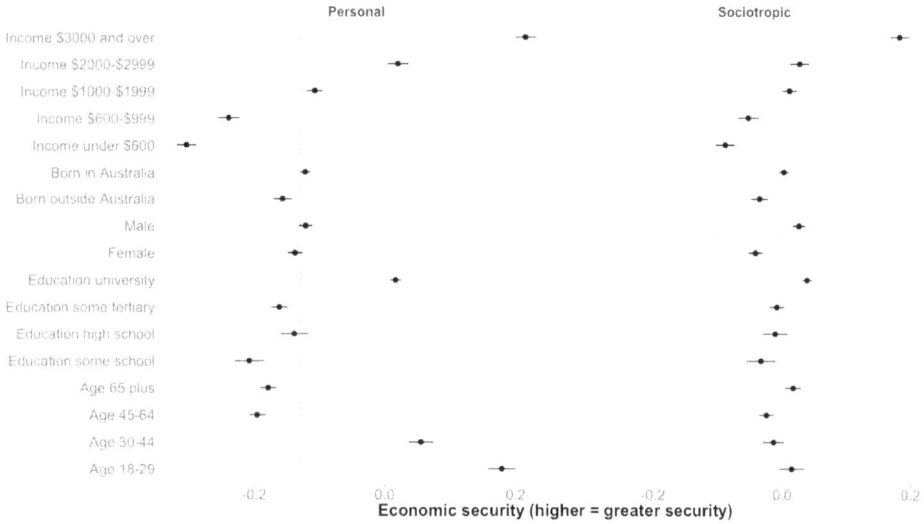

Source: Author's analysis of Vox Pop Labs post-election survey data.
Notes: Exploratory data analysis of economic insecurity by socioeconomic variables. Each closed circle represents the weighted mean level of security for each group. Horizontal error bars are 95 per cent confidence intervals. The dashed vertical line is the overall weighted mean economic security across the entire population.

Figure 2.3 Economic insecurity by urban geography and state.

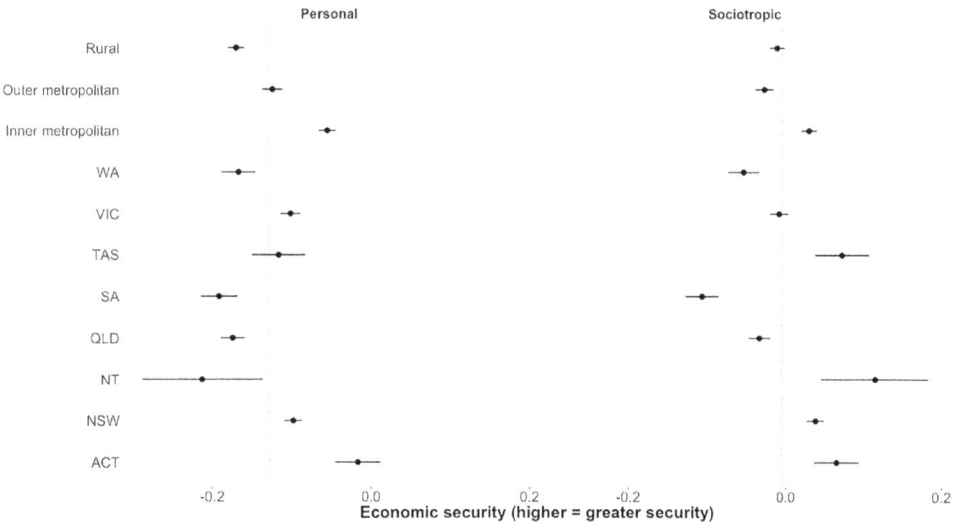

Source: Author's analysis of Vox Pop Lab's post-election survey data.
Notes: Exploratory data analysis of economic insecurity by geographic groups (the first three categories compare voters in rural, outer and inner metropolitan areas, the second states). See Figure 2.2 for methods.

Figure 2.4 Economic security by Senate vote.

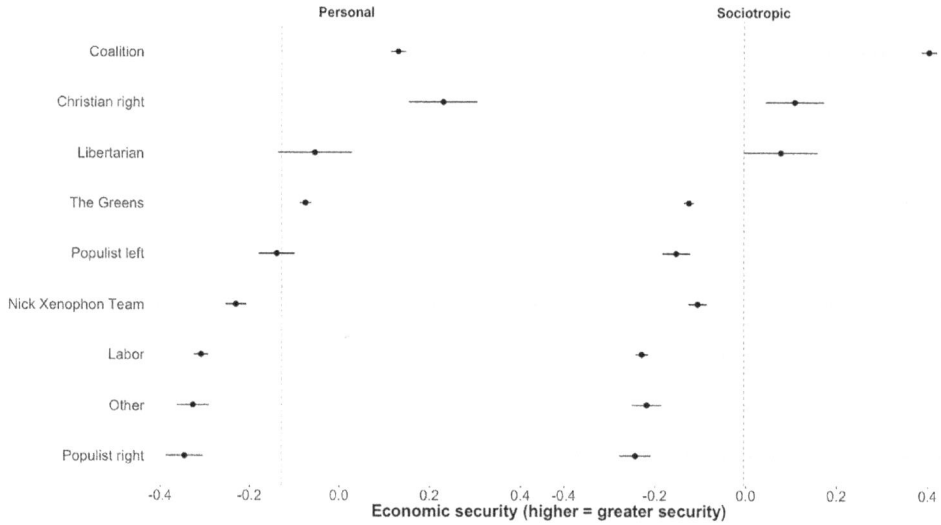

Source: Author's analysis of Vox Pop Lab's post-election survey data.
Note: Economic insecurity by Senate vote. See Figure 2.2 for methods.

Do income and education matter to reported insecurity? Education levels are weaker predictors of sociotropic security, with the university-educated reporting more positive views of the overall economy, but only by a small degree. But there were large differences for perceptions of *personal* economic security. Those with university qualifications reported perceptions of individual economic wellbeing more than a fifth of a standard deviation higher than those who had not finished high school. Household income was the strongest predictor for perceptions of economic security, with this pattern being largely linear and particularly strong for personal security. Respondents with weekly incomes above $3,000 (over $156,750 per annum) reported levels of personal economic security half a standard deviation higher than those with incomes of less than $600 per week ($31,350 per year).

Age played a mixed role in assessments of economic security. Voters aged 65 years and over perceive the overall economy as doing well, but their personal economic security was worse than younger voters. Those aged 18–29 years had similar levels of sociotropic economic security, but saw their own situation as relatively good. Voters aged 45–64 years had relatively negative perceptions of *both* their own personal and sociotropic economic security, suggesting their overall levels of economic security were particularly low.

It is hardly surprising that there is a stronger relationship between voters' *personal* demographic and economic backgrounds and their evaluation of their *personal* economic security. However, sociotropic economic evaluations also vary significantly by gender and birthplace: the Australian-born sample had higher rates of personal and sociotropic security than those born elsewhere, while men had slightly higher levels of sociotropic security than women, but showed little difference on personal economic security. There were also important regional variations, likely the result of diversity in the employment opportunities and life chances available in different parts of the country. The result of this, displayed in Figure 2.3, is that sociotropic security varies as much between respondents in different states as personal economic security. However, the difference between voters living in inner-metropolitan and rural areas – with the former reporting higher levels of both – was largely found along the personal security dimension.

These data also allow us to examine the association between respondents' perceptions of economic security and how they voted at the 2016 Senate election. Figure 2.4 indicates Coalition voters had the highest level of sociotropic security, and a similar level of personal security as Christian right voters. Supporters of the Nick Xenophon Team, the populist left and right parties, and Labor and other parties had lower levels of security on both dimensions. Respondents voting for the Greens in the Senate had higher levels of personal security and lower levels of sociotropic security. This suggests there is a relationship between economic security and partisan choice, which is examined further below.[4]

The representation gap and the vote for minor parties

Voters may support populist and protest parties when they are poorly represented by the major parties. Uniquely for Australia, these data provide the ability for voters' preferences to be measured against the positions taken by the parties prior to and during the campaign, with both voters and the major political parties coded on 30 policy issues, measured on five-point Likert scales (listed in Appendix 2.2). The coding of the positions of political parties was accomplished using publicly available information on the positions they had taken using the kind of information available to voters (interviews, policy documents and party websites). This policy coding was made public, and changed at the request of the parties if it could be shown that better public information was available to place their position.

We can simplify the measurement of preferences for these 30 issues by fitting an exploratory factor analysis to these data, estimating a two-dimensional set of issue preferences for voters. The items included in this factor analysis and how they load onto each dimension can be seen in Figure 2.5. Items associated with the distribution of economic power and resources loaded most strongly onto the first dimension, which was therefore labelled the economic issue dimension. These include attitudes towards taxation and social spending as well as free trade and foreign ownership of assets. Respondents closer to the traditional economic right (i.e. opposed to significant changes to existing economic hierarchies) score higher on this dimension, preferring less state intervention in the economy and workplace, and being less concerned with trade and foreign ownership.

The second dimension was most strongly associated with attitudes to asylum seekers, foreign aid, terrorism, sexuality, gender equality, and the recognition of Australia's Indigenous people in the federal Constitution. Voters who score highest on this dimension can be considered closer to a social conservative position that supports the status quo and opposes measures that alter existing norms and hierarchies. Consistent with the first

---

4   Of course, it is also possible that causality runs from partisanship to perceptions of the economy. This is likely to be more so the case for perceptions of the wider economy (sociotropic security) than it is for personal economic security, as individuals are more likely to be fully aware of their own circumstances than they are of the state of the overall economy, and therefore less likely to see this through partisan lenses. Figure 2.4 supports this to some extent, with larger differences between the Coalition and other parties along the sociotropic dimension.

Figure 2.5 How survey items load onto economic and social issue dimensions.

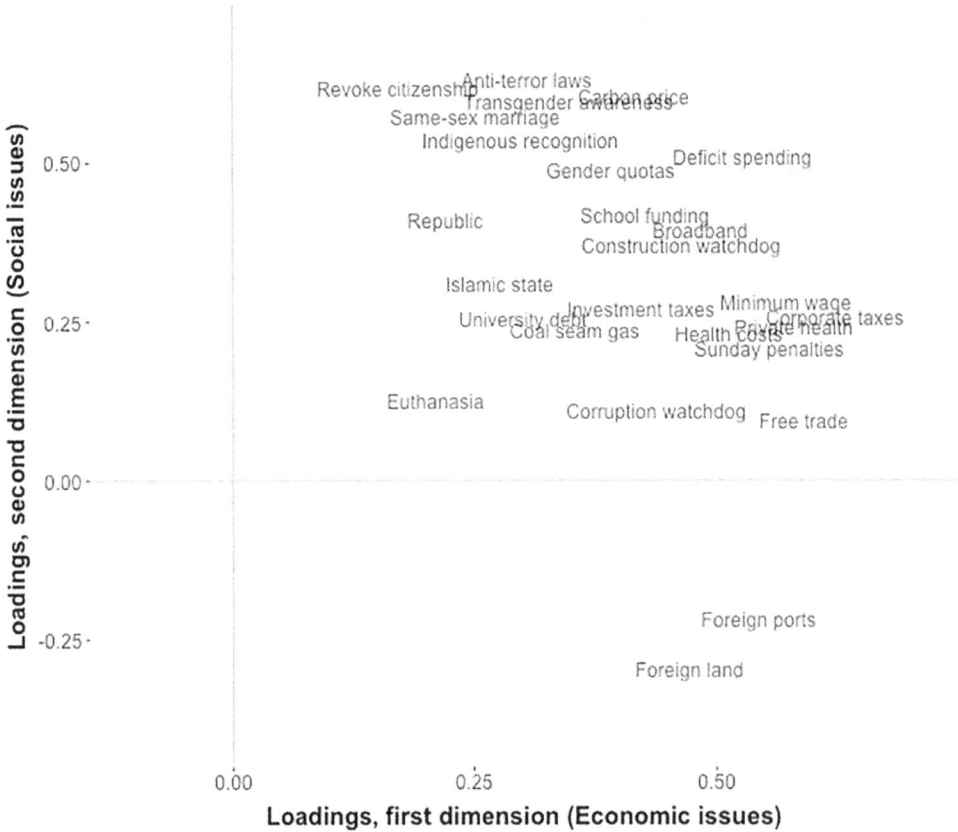

Loadings, first dimension (Economic issues)

Source: Loading of issue items onto two dimensional factor analysis, fit to Vox Pop Labs post-election survey data by the author.

Notes: Mapping campaign issues onto social and economic issue dimensions estimated with an exploratory factor analysis with varimax rotation. Each label represents the loading of items from the Vox Pop Labs survey on both dimensions estimated by the factor analysis. The x-axis represents the first dimension (labelled economic) and the y-axis the second dimension (labelled social). A high positive loading of an item on a dimension indicates an issue strongly separates respondents with preferences on the left and right. A value close to zero indicates an item that does a poor job discriminating between them.

dimension, the preferences related to a positive score on this dimension were more likely associated with the political right in Australia.

These variables, covering a set of economic and social issues, allow us to better understand voters' preferences on these dimensions. The distances of these preferences from the positions taken by the major parties are associated with the probability of supporting minor or populist party groups. The scores estimated by this factor analysis (also standardised to have a mean of 0 and standard deviation of 1) are then used to estimate the positions of the major political parties in the same policy space, using the positions coded during the election campaign. These party policy positions, and the weighted distributions of voters, is shown in Figure 2.6. These graphs compare the preferences of voters with personal (top row) and sociotropic (bottom row) economic insecurity scores in the top and bottom quintiles, represented by the light and dark curves respectively. The positions taken by the Coalition and Labor Party on these issues at the 2016 election are represented by the darker and lighter shaded vertical bars. The x-axis shows preferences on the economic (left-hand plots) and social (right-hand) dimensions, left to right. The y-axis is the (weighted) proportion of respondents at each point.

The distribution of voters' issue preferences, conditional on their economic security, is shown in Figure 2.6. Those with lower levels of economic security on both dimensions (represented by the light grey curve) tended to have issue preferences on the *left* on economic issues, but to the *right* on the social dimension. This indicates that the economically *insecure* prefer more social spending and protectionist trade policies, but less social change, stronger anti-terror laws and more restrictive policies to deal with asylum seekers arriving in Australia by boat. With the Labor Party occupying a position in the middle of both issue dimensions, and the Coalition on the right (particularly on economic policy), these voters are on average poorly represented by the established parties.[5] We may expect this to have political ramifications, with the abandonment of the established parties in favour of options that provide policy outcomes closer to their preferences a highly rational move.

We can then use these estimates of voter and party policy positions to measure issue representation as the average Euclidean distance of a voter's preferences from both parties' positions (see Appendix 2.3 for more on how issue distance is measured). Using this measurement schema, the position of the Coalition parties was 1.89 (nearly 2 standard deviations to the right of the average respondent), and the Labor Party 0.33. The voter with a preference sitting at 0 would have an average distance of 1.11 from the established parties, while one that was -2 to the left would have an average distance of 3.11, and would have been poorly represented by the party system on this dimension. The distances of voters with different economic and demographic characteristics are shown in Figure 2.7, with a higher score indicating that the mean issue preferences of respondents in that group are farther from the positions taken by the established parties.

Consistent with the existing literature (Bartels 2010; Giger et al. 2012; Gilens 2012), Australian voters living in higher-income households are better represented by the established parties on the economic dimension (with the pattern for social issues less clear). Men are slightly better represented than women on economic issues, but not on the social dimension. Overseas-born voters are better represented by the major parties on the social dimension. University-educated and younger voters are better represented on both dimensions, and older voters and those who did not finish high school are on average poorly represented.

Issue representation, insecurity, and support for minor parties

The data examined above suggest that voters with higher personal insecurity have preferences to the left of centre on economic issues, but are also further to the right on social issues. In fact, those with low personal economic security were twice as likely to be 3 standard deviations right of centre than those with high personal security. However, there also are associations between

---

5   These findings may be a product of the questions asked. If there had been questions about industrial relations and trade unions, the relative positions of the parties (particularly Labor) and voters may have been different.

Figure 2.6 Distribution of issue preferences of voters with high and low economic security.

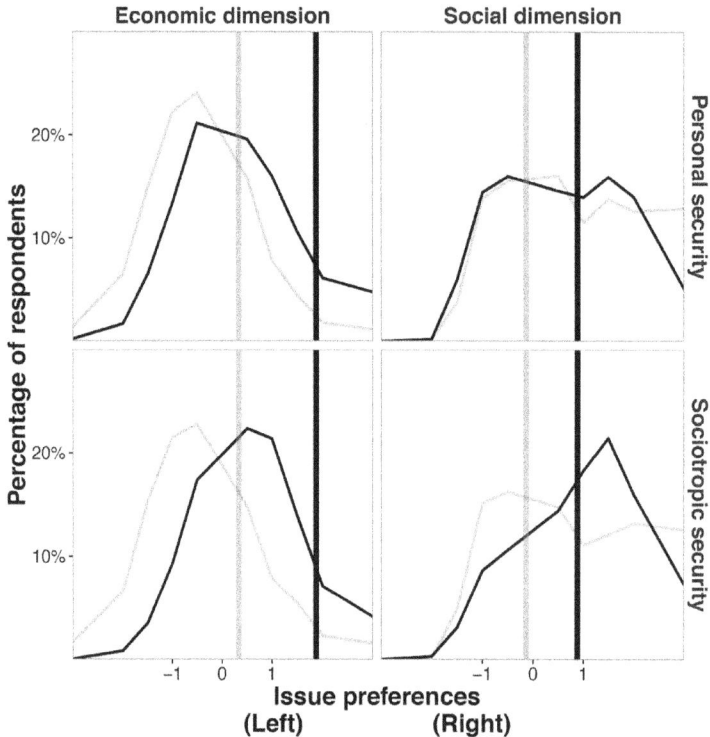

Source: Author's analysis of Vox Pop Labs post-election survey data.
Notes: These plots show the distribution of issue preferences of voters that self-report economic security in the highest and lowest 20 per cent of the sample respectively. Economic security and issue preferences are measured on two dimensions each using the factor analysis fit to post-election survey data, outlined above. Rows on the plots represent the two types of economic security and the columns the issue dimensions. The dark curve represents voters with high economic security and the light curve those with low security. The light vertical line is the estimated position of the Labor Party on each issue dimension, the dark line the Coalition. These data were weighted by age, sex, industry, geography, education, religious affiliation, and both previous and current vote choice.

vote choice, the demographic and economic backgrounds of voters, their issue preferences, and their perceptions of economic security. To take all of these factors into account, voters' distance from the major parties is estimated and then a series of logistic regressions are fit to these data to better understand the patterns observed so far.

These models are fit separately for each party (or party group), and are used to estimate the probability that voters would provide each party or candidate with their first preference vote. This modelled outcome is conditional on voters' perceived sociotropic and personal economic security, and their distance from the major parties on the social and economic issue dimensions (their level of issue representation). Both the variables for economic security and distance from the parties are standardised with a mean of 0 and a standard deviation of 1, so that the coefficients are more easily interpreted. For these models, we measure economic insecurity (higher scores = higher insecurity) to align the

Figure 2.7 Issues representation by demographic group.

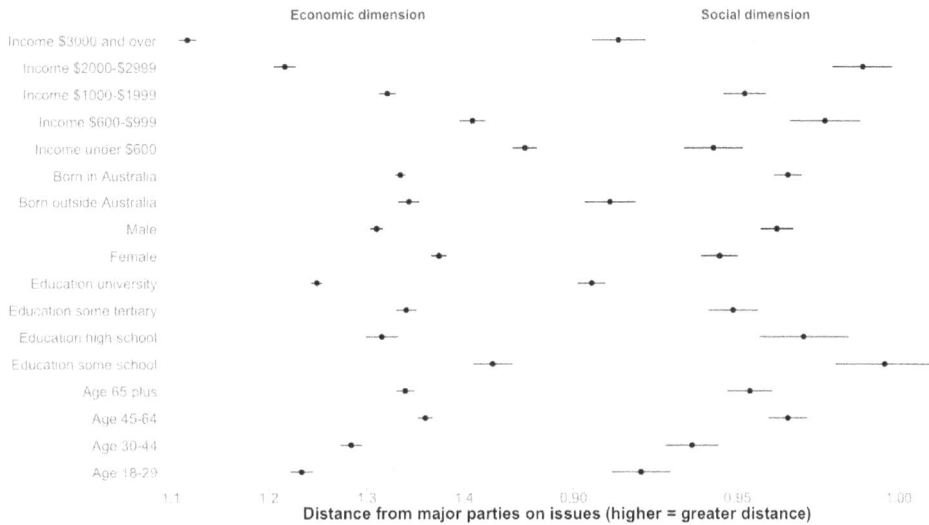

Source: Author's analysis of Vox Pop Labs post-election survey data.
Notes: Voter distance from positions of the major parties on economic and social dimensions. Each point represents the weighted mean level of security for each group.

expected effects of security and policy distance, with support for minor parties expected to increase with both distance from the policies of the established parties and insecurity.

After this initial model specification including economic insecurity and issue representation, interaction terms between security and issue representation were also included. These were found to add generally only a small, but in some instances meaningful, increase in the explanatory power of the models, and were retained. To account for the potentially confounding effects of demographics, as well as over and underrepresentation of particular groups, controls for age, education, religion and division type (inner city, suburban, regional and rural) were also included in these models. Those observations with missing data were excluded, with these models fit to data consisting of 38,826 respondents each. The coefficients for each model fit to these data can be found in Appendix 2.4.

To better understand the patterns in support for minor parties as a product of both economic insecurity and issue representation, the predicted probabilities of support for the parties and candidates of interest were estimated using the logistic regression coefficients obtained from these models, which were then plotted and displayed in Figures 2.8 to 2.11. These graphs show how vote choice shifts as economic security changes (with the darker curves representing voters with security two standard deviations above the mean, and lighter curves those two standard deviations below), and as voters move away from the parties (with a higher value on the x-axis indicating greater distance from the parties).

Figure 2.8 shows the predicted change in support for the Greens and for minor parties on the left in the 2016 Senate election as a function of economic security and issue representation. Examining the left-hand side plot first, we can see that voters with higher personal security are more likely to support the Greens when age, education, religion and location were taken into account. However, even after these other factors were held

Figure 2.8 Support for the Greens (and minor left parties) by issue representation and economic security.

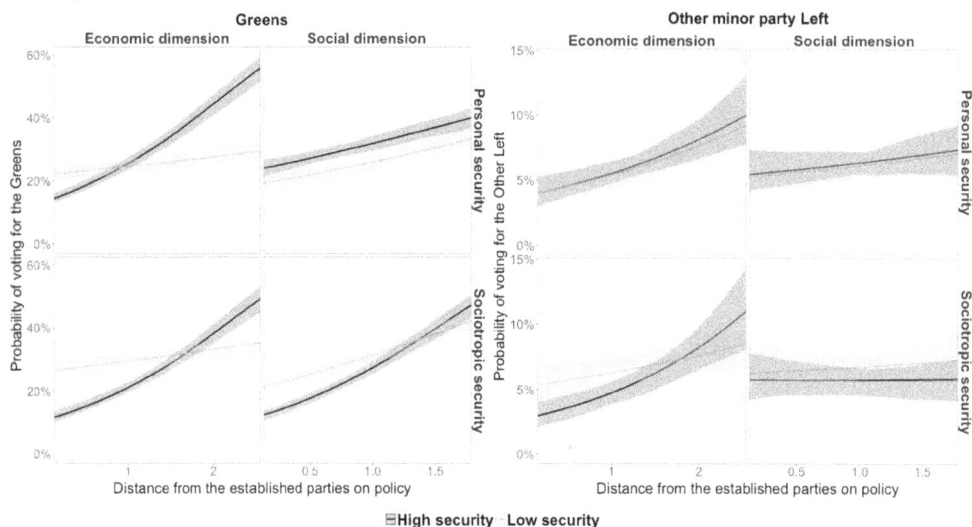

Source: Predicted probabilities from regression models fit to Vox Pop Labs post-election survey data by the author.

Notes: Predicted change in support for the Greens and other parties on the left in the Senate among high and low economic security voters as distance from the major parties increases. The y-axis is the probability of support for the populist right, and the x-axis the distance from the parties, with a higher figure indicating a greater distance. The light curve represents voters with economic security in the lowest fifth of the population, and the dark curve those with economic security in the highest fifth. The shaded areas are 95 per cent confidence intervals. Issue preferences and distance from the parties are all standardised to have a mean of zero and a standard deviation of one.

constant, lower levels of sociotropic security also predicted a Greens vote, particularly when voters' issue preferences were closer to the positions of the major parties. This indicates Greens voters generally felt positive about their own personal situation, but were less optimistic about the national economy – not necessarily surprising given that the government was formed by centre-right parties at the time. Additionally, we observe that voters with preferences farther from the policy positions of the major parties (mostly to the left) were more likely to support the Greens. This was particularly the case on the economic dimension for voters with high levels of both types of security, and on the social dimension for those with high levels of sociotropic security. Other minor parties and candidates of the left did particularly well among voters who were poorly represented by the established parties on *economic* issues, with those enjoying high sociotropic economic security particularly likely to support these parties as the distance of their preferences from the positions taken by the major parties on this dimension increased. These parties did best with similar voters to Greens: younger voters, the university-educated, the non-religious, and those living in the inner city (although compared to the Greens, education mattered less, and age and location more).

Different patterns were observed for the Nick Xenophon Team (NXT) and other non-establishment centrist parties and candidates (see Figure 2.9). In both instances, these parties

Figure 2.9 Support for the Nick Xenophon Team (and 'Other' parties and candidates) by issue representation and economic security.

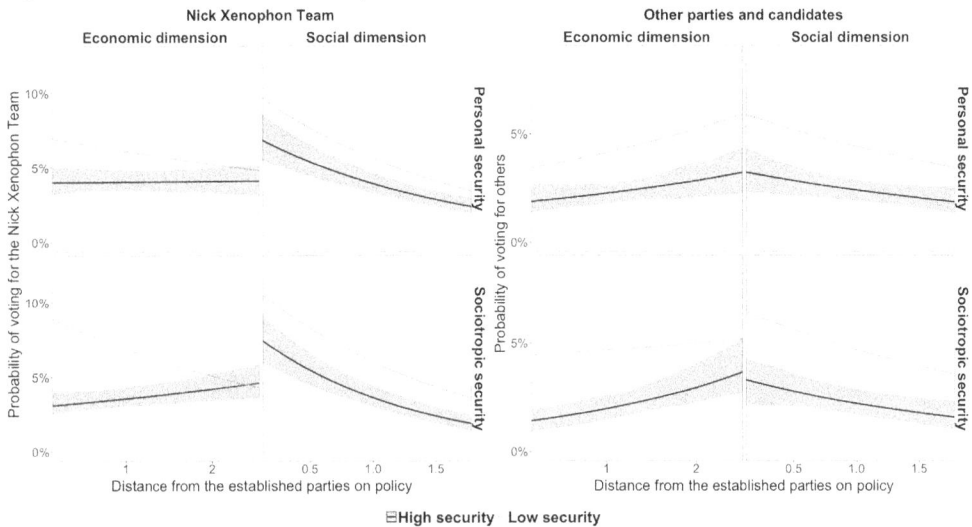

Source: Predicted probabilities from regression models fit to Vox Pop Labs post-election survey data by the author.

Notes: Predicted change in support for the Nick Xenophon Team, or other parties and candidates, in the Senate amongst high- and low-economic security voters as distance from the major parties increases. The shaded areas are 95 per cent confidence intervals.

were more likely to obtain votes from respondents with *low* levels of economic security (on both dimensions). Unlike those supporting the non-Labor left, a lack of representation does not appear to be a major driver for supporting these parties. Instead, support for NXT was estimated to be *lower* among voters with preferences farther from the established parties, especially on social issues (except for high-security voters, on economic issues). These results indicate that parties like NXT were tapping into economic insecurity, with voters concerned about the state of their personal financial situation or the wider economy.

As can be seen in the regression coefficients shown in Appendix 2.4, when all other factors in the model were held constant, NXT still performed better with voters whose socioeconomic situation would generally tend them towards greater economic insecurity. This model predicted they would do much better with older voters, somewhat better amongst those who did not have a university degree, worse with those identifying as Catholics, and slightly better in rural electorates. Like NXT, other centrist minor parties did best with voters who did not complete a university degree, and in particular, those who did not finish high school. They also did particularly poorly among inner-city voters and best with those living in rural electorates.

Estimated support for the libertarian and Christian right is shown in Figure 2.10. The libertarian Senate vote was weakly predicted by personal economic security, with highly secure voters slightly more likely to support these parties. However, issue representation does *not* appear to have been particularly important. Voters were also more likely to support Christian right parties if they have higher levels of personal economic security,

Figure 2.10 Support for libertarian and Christian right parties by issue representation and economic security.

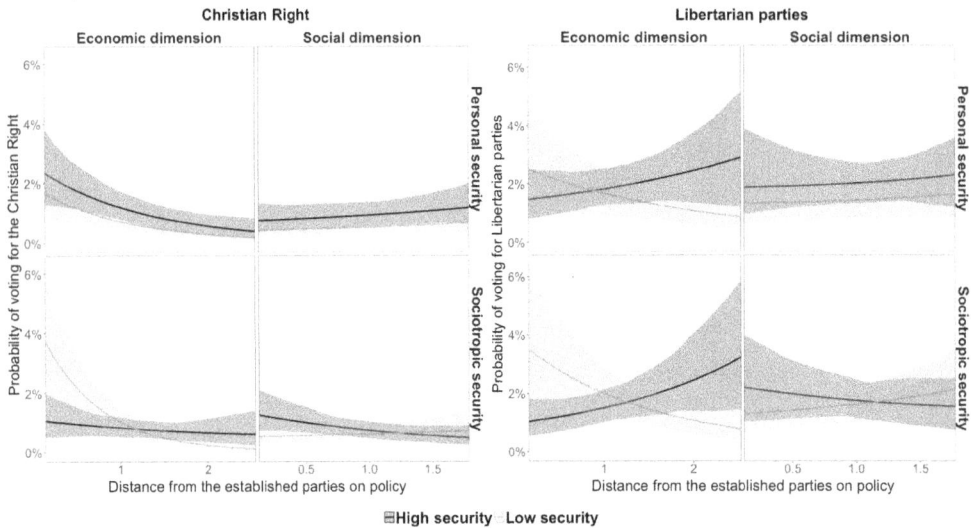

Source: Predicted probabilities from regression models fit to Vox Pop Labs post-election survey data by the author.

Notes: Predicted change in support for libertarian and Christian right parties in the Senate among high and low economic security voters as distance from the major parties increases.

and if they had issue preferences closer to the positions of the major parties, particularly on economic issues. We can conclude that support for these parties appears to be primarily driven by voters' identities (as can be seen in Appendix 2.4). Libertarian voters were more defined by age (with younger voters more likely to support libertarian parties) and to a lesser extent by their location (with greater support in rural areas). The Christian right was better predicted by religion, location and age, with older, non-urban, Protestant voters also more likely to support them.

In contrast, a Senate vote for the populist and protest right (i.e. One Nation) was strongly driven by a combination of poor issue representation on social issues and economic insecurity. These parties filled a 'niche' in Australian politics in 2016, attracting voters who felt the economy was performing poorly in particular, and to a lesser extent that their own economic position was insecure. Most importantly, these voters had preferences on social issues that varied considerably from the major parties' positions, supporting stronger measures against asylum seekers arriving by boat, terrorism, and changes to traditional societal norms. Unlike some of the other parties on the right, it was not older voters who were necessarily the key support base for these parties. Rather, our model predicted it was those voters aged between 30 and 44 years, and 45 to 64 years, who were their core support base. They also did best among those voters who had not finished high school, and particularly poorly with the university-educated. They did worst with atheists and best with Protestants. They did particularly poorly in the inner city, and best in provincial cities and rural electorates.

Explaining minor and populist party voting in 2016

Economic insecurity and a lack of issue representation *both* provide important explanations for the support enjoyed by minor and populist parties at the 2016 federal election. Above, I outlined a theoretical framework characterising voters as 'utility maximisers' (Popkin 1991), and from this it was hypothesised that they would want to support parties that best represent their perceived interests, which includes providing economic security and enacting policies that closely match their issue preferences. If this is a valid assumption, then in situations where voters feel economically insecure, and their preferences across a range of issues are not represented by the established government-forming parties, they may believe the political system itself is failing to represent their interests, and be more likely to support anti-system parties.

Consistent with the existing literature, voters with lower household incomes and lower levels of education were poorly represented by the major parties on both economic and social issues at the 2016 election (Bartels 2010; Giger et al. 2012; Gilens 2012). They were on average to the *left* of the major parties on economic issues, preferring higher corporate taxes, more spending on health and education and more protectionist trade policy. However, they were also to the *right* of the established parties on social issues, wanting harsher deterrents for asylum seekers arriving by boat and expressing less support for rapid change in social norms in areas of gender and sexuality. These voters also tended to have lower levels of economic security. Assuming they are motivated by a desire to obtain the best possible outcomes from the political system, these individuals have considerable reasons to support non-establishment parties in greater numbers than more secure voters. This is precisely what was observed, although with different patterns for different non-establishment parties. In the US in 2016, voters with these kinds of issue preferences were more inclined to take the anti-establishment option, and supported the presidential bid of Donald Trump (Carmines, Ensley and Wagner 2016).

The Greens and the minor parties on the left attracted voters who were mostly personally economically *secure*, and who were driven by disagreement with the established parties on both issue dimensions. Those who voted for the Nick Xenophon Team, and other minor parties and independent candidates of the centre, were driven by both their own poor financial situation *and* general perceptions of the economy. However, they appear to have been largely well represented by the established parties on the two issue dimensions measured in this chapter. The minor parties of the right appear largely to be a product of identity politics, supported by a mix of groups concerned about their traditional status in the social hierarchy and about social change. Christian and populist right voters in particular appear to have been largely middle-aged and older Protestants with lower levels of education living outside the cities. This, combined with lower levels of economic security and poor social issue representation, appears to have largely fuelled the support for the populist right.

These findings provide some insight into the political implications of the rising support for these parties and candidates, and the challenges faced by the major parties. The government-forming parties in Australia may need to address the economic insecurity experienced by some voters, and provide policy options closer to the preferences of citizens who are poorly represented by their current positions. Of course, this is a two-edged sword. If the Coalition moved to the right on social issues to better represent voters who believe society is changing too fast, or Labor moved to the left on economic issues

Figure 2.11 Support for the populist right by issue representation and economic security.

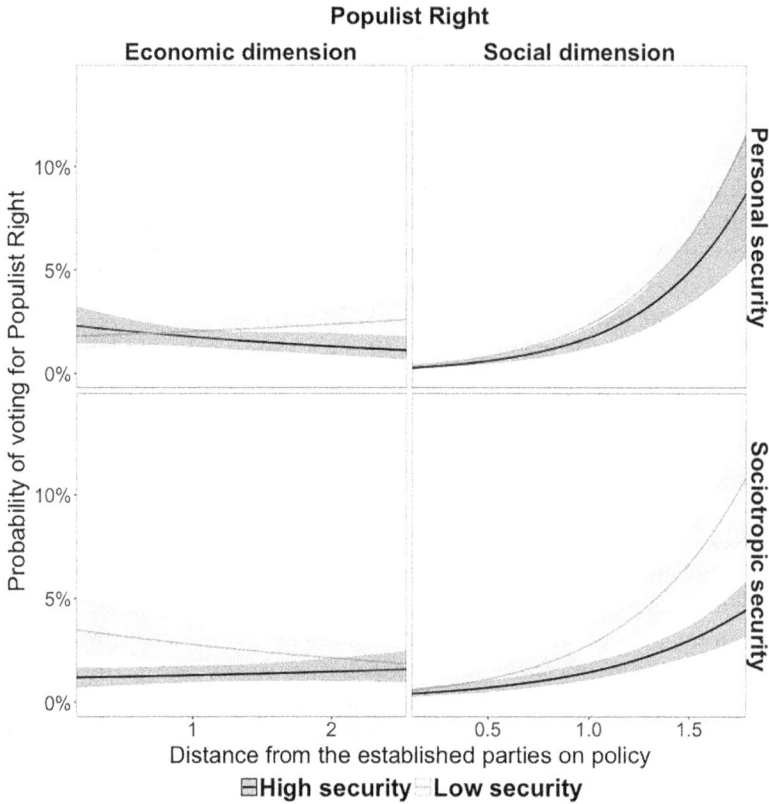

Source: Predicted probabilities from regression models fit to Vox Pop Labs post-election survey data by the author.

Notes: Predicted change in support for the populist right in the Senate among high and low economic security voters as distance from the major parties increases. The predictions are calculated from a logistic model fit to vote choice given voters' distances from the established parties on economic and social issues, and their level of personal and sociotropic economic insecurity. The y-axis is the probability of support the populist right, and the x-axis distance from the parties, with a higher figure indicating a greater distance. Issue preferences and distance from the parties are all standardised to have a mean of zero and a standard deviation of one.

to address the concerns of the economically insecure, it could result in greater political polarisation. Failure to respond, however, may result in a growing share of the vote shifting to parties other than the Coalition or Labor. This would alter the electoral balance in favour of a more fragmented party system in the Senate at least, making governance more complicated and potentially affecting policy outcomes.

The economic crises since the GFC have created turmoil. This has had a political effect, including the rise of populist right parties in Europe, Brexit in the UK, and the election of Donald Trump in the US. Although Australia avoided the worst of the global recession, real disposable income growth has stalled for several years. The political impact here has been to create instability and dissatisfaction with public policy and governing parties. Although we cannot be certain whether the recent increase in support for these minor parties will continue – these data are a snapshot of 2016 and not a time series, and history is rarely linear – Australian politics could be transformed, with the established parties forced into governing coalitions with these other parties. Labor may become more reliant on an alliance with the Greens, just as the Liberal Party has done with the National Party since the 1920s (in various forms). The Coalition may need to come to an accommodation with Christian and libertarian parties, or of One Nation, if they remain electorally successful. However, a reason to believe this may not happen is the fragmented nature of these parties, particularly on the right, with a large array of parties emerging to fill the gaps left open by the major parties on policy or economic security.

Different combinations of poor issue representation and economic insecurity have provided the ingredients for support for non-establishment parties and candidates. Australia's major parties appear not to be representing elements of the economic left, nor the social right, adequately (based on the data examined here, at least). Voters with lower household incomes and lower levels of education appear not to be well represented by these parties' political platforms. This has resulted in a collection of minor, protest and populist parties forming to fill different niches in the political ecosystem. The populist and Christian right between them have built electoral coalitions similar to those that supported Donald Trump (see, for instance, Carmines et al. 2016). However, unlike in the US, none of these groups has been able to unite the economically insecure and poorly represented into a single voting bloc. Similarly, the NXT has secured a large base of support amongst the economically insecure, limiting the ability of the populist left and right to expand their base of support in this area. This may suggest that, short of a vast realignment of Australian politics, the rise of a non-establishment political force of the magnitude of a Donald Trump is unlikely in the near term in Australia.

References

Adams, James (2001). *Party competition and responsible party government*. Ann Arbor: Michigan University Press.

Albertazzi, Daniele and Duncan McDonnell, eds (2008). *Twenty-first century populism: the spectre of Western European democracy*. New York: Palgrave Macmillan.

Allport, Gordon (1954). *The nature of prejudice*. Cambridge: Addison-Wesley Publishing Company.

Armingeon, Klaus and Besir Ceka (2014). The loss of trust in the European Union during the great recession since 2007: the role of heuristics from the national political system. *European Union Politics* 15(1), 82–107.

Australian Bureau of Statistics (2017). 6345.0 – Wage Price Index, Australia, December 2016.

Bartels, Larry (2010). *Unequal democracy: the political economy of the new gilded age*. Princeton, NJ: Princeton University Press.

Betz, Hans-Georg (1994). *Radical rightwing populism in Western Europe*. New York: St Martin's Press.

Birrell, Bob (2006). Productivity commission on the economics of immigration. *People and Place* 14(1), 1–7.

Birrell, Bob and Ernest Healy (2003). Migration and the housing affordability crisis. *People and Place* 11(3), 43–56.

Blalock, Hubert M. (1967). *Towards a theory of minority-group relations*. New York: Wiley.

Bowler, Shaun, David Denemark, Todd Donovan and Duncan McDonnell (2017). Right-wing populist party supporters: dissatisfied but not direct democrats. *European Journal of Political Research* 56, 70–91.

Brandenburg, Heinz and Rupert Johns (2014). The declining representativeness of the British party system, and why it matters. *Political Studies* 62, 704–25.

Calvert, Randall (1985). Robustness of the multidimensional voting model: candidates' motivations, uncertainty, and convergence. *American Journal of Political Science* 29, 69–95.

Cameron, Sarah M. and Ian McAllister (2016). *Trends in Australian political opinion: results from the Australian election study 1987–2016*. Retrieved from Canberra.

Campbell, Donald T. (1965). *Ethnocentric and other altruistic motives*. Lincoln: University of Nebraska Press.

Carmines, Edward, Michael J. Ensley and Michael W. Wagner (2016). Ideological heterogeneity and the rise of Donald Trump. *The Forum* 14(4), 385–97.

Converse, Philip E. (1975). Public opinion and voting behavior. In *Handbook of Political Science*. Fred I. Greenstein and Nelson W. Polsby, eds, 75–169. Reading, Massachusetts: Addison-Wesley.

Diamond, Larry (2011). Why democracies survive. *Journal of Democracy* 22(1), 17–30.

Downs, Anthony (1957). *An economic theory of democracy*. New York: Harper.

Esaiasson, Peter and Sören Holmberg (1996). *Representation from above: members of parliament and representative democracy in Sweden*. Aldershot, UK: Dartmouth.

Funke, Manuel, Moritz Schularick and Christoph Trebesch (2016). Going to extremes: politics after financial crises, 1870–2014. *European Economic Review* 88, 227–60.

Giger, Nathalie, Jan Rosset and Julian Bernauer (2012). The poor political representation of the poor in a comparative perceptive. *Representation* 48(1), 47–61.

Gilens, Martin (2012). *Affluence and influence: economic inequality and political power in America*. Princeton, NJ: Princeton University Press.

Goot, Murray (1993). Multiculturalists, monoculturalists and the many in between: attitudes to cultural diversity and their correlates. *Journal of Sociology* 29, 226–53.

Goot, Murray and Ian Watson (2001a). One Nation's electoral support: economic insecurity versus attitudes to immigration. *Australian Journal of Politics and History* 47(4), 512–15.

Goot, Murray and Ian Watson (2001b). One Nation's electoral support: where does it come from? What makes it different and how does it fit? *Australian Journal of Politics and History* 47(2), 159–191.

Hacker, J. (2006). *The great shift: the new economic insecurity and the decline of the American dream*. New York: Oxford University Press.

Hainmueller, Jens and Michael J. Hiscox (2007). Educated preferences: explaining attitudes toward immigration in Europe. *International Organization* 61(2), 399–442.

Hetherington, Marc J. and Thomas J. Rudolph (2015). *Why Washington won't work: polarization, political trust, and the governing crisis*. Chicago: University of Chicago Press.

Inglehart, Ronald (1990). *Culture shift in advanced industrial society*. Princeton, NJ: Princeton University Press.

Inglehart, Ronald (1997). *Modernization and postmodernization*. Princeton, NJ: Princeton University Press.

Inglehart, Ronald and Pippa Norris (2016). *Trump, Brexit, and the rise of populism: economic have-nots and cultural backlash*. Faculty Research Working Paper Series.

Key, Vladimer Orlando (1984 [1949]). *Southern politics in state and nation*. New York: Knopf.

Laver, Michael (2011). Why vote-seeking parties may make voters miserable. *Irish Political Studies* 26(4), 489–500.

Mair, Peter (2013). *Ruling the void: the hollowing of Western democracy*. London: Verso.

Marsh, Ian and Raymond Miller (2012). *Democratic decline and democratic renewal: political change in Britain, Australia and New Zealand*. Cambridge: Cambridge University Press.

McAllister, Ian (1993). Immigration, bipartisanship and public opinion. In *The politics of Australian immigration*. James Jupp and M. Kabala, eds. South Carlton, Vic.: The Bureau of Immigration Research.

Moffitt, Benjamin and Simon Tormey (2014). Rethinking populism: politics, mediatisation and political style. *Political Studies* 62, 381–97.

Mudde, Cas (2007). *Populist radical right parties in Europe*. New York: Cambridge University Press.

Norris, Pippa (2005). *Radical right: voters and parties in the electoral market*. Cambridge: Cambridge University Press.

Popkin, Samuel L. (1991). *The reasoning voter: communication and persuasion in presidential campaigns*. Chicago and London: The University of Chicago Press.

Przeworski, Adam, Michael E. Alvarez, José A. Cheibub and Fernando Limongi (2000). *Democracy and development: political institutions and well-being in the world, 1950–1990*. New York: Cambridge University Press.

Ramiro, Luis and Raul Gomez (2016). Radical-left populism during the Great Recession: Podemos and its competition with the established radical left. *Political Studies* 65(1) (suppl.), 108–26.

Roemer, John E. (2001). *Political competition: theory and applications*. Cambridge, MA: Harvard University Press.

Sandel, Michael J. (2012). *What money can't buy: the moral limits of markets*. London: Farrar, Straus and Giroux.

Schmitt, Hermann and Jacques Thomassen, J. (1999). *Political representation and legitimacy in the European Union*. Oxford: Oxford University Press.

Sherif, Muzafer (1967). *Group conflict and cooperation: their social psychology*. London: Routledge & Kegan Paul.

Sherif, Muzafer and Carolyn W. Sherif (1953). *Groups in harmony and tension*. New York: Harper.

Sidanius, Jim and Felicia Pratto (1999). *Social dominance: an intergroup theory of social hierarchy and oppression*. Cambridge: Cambridge University Press.

Sides, John and Jack Citrin, J. (2007). European opinion about immigration: the role of identities, interests and information. *British Journal of Political Science* 37(3), 477–504.

Turnbull, Nick and Shaun Wilson (2001). The two faces of economic insecurity: reply to Goot and Watson on One Nation. *Australian Journal of Politics and History* 47(4), 512–15.

Vala, Jorge, Cicero Pereira and Alice Ramos (2006). Racial prejudice, threat perception and opposition to immigration: a comparative analysis. *Portuguese Journal of Social Science* 5(2), 119–140.

van der Brug, Wouter (1999). Voters' perceptions and party dynamics. *Party Politics* 5(2), 147–69.

Vox Pop Labs (2016). Vote Compass methodology. Available at http://voxpoplabs.com/votecompass/methodology.pdf.

Wilkes, Rima, Neil Guppy and Lily Farris (2008). 'No thanks, we're full': individual characteristics, national context, and changing attitudes toward immigration. *International Migration Review* 42(2), 302–29.

Wittman, Donald (1973). Parties as utility maximizers. *American Political Science Review* 67(2), 490–498.

Wittman, Donald (1977). Candidates with policy preferences: a dynamic model. *Journal of Economic Theory* 14(1), 180–89.

Wittman, Donald (1983). Candidate motivation: a synthesis. *American Political Science Review* 77(1), 142–57.

Appendix 2.1: Party groups

The parties or party groups examined in this chapter are:

The Greens

Other minor left parties

- Animal Justice Party
- Australian Cyclists Party
- Australian Equality Party (Marriage)
- Australian Progressives
- Australian Sex Party
- Bullet Train for Australia
- Marijuana (HEMP) Party
- Secular Party of Australia
- Socialist Alliance
- The Arts Party
- Voluntary Euthanasia Party
- Sustainable Australia
- Pirate Party
- Socialist Equality Party
- Renewable Energy Party
- Science Party

The Nick Xenophon Team

Libertarian parties

- Smokers' Rights Party
- Liberal Democrats

Christian right

- Australian Christians
- Christian Democratic Party (Fred Nile Group)
- Family First

Populist and protest right

- Australia First Party
- Australian Liberty Alliance
- Jacqui Lambie Network
- John Madigan's Manufacturing and Farming Party
- Katter's Australian Party
- Shooters, Fishers and Farmers Party
- Pauline Hanson's One Nation
- Rise Up Australia
- DLP Democratic Labour
- Australian Country Party

Other parties

- Palmer United Party
- VOTEFLUX.ORG Upgrade Democracy
- Mature Australia
- Online Direct Democracy (Empowering the People)
- Independents
- Australian Motoring Enthusiasts Party
- Derryn Hinch's Justice Party
- Other parties or candidates
- Seniors United Party of Australia
- Veterans Party
- Australian Mental Health Party
- Glenn Lazarus Team

Appendix 2.2: Issue items

These were coded so that the position farthest to the left was coded left–right, from -2 to +2, and then included in the factor analysis outlined above.

Five-point agree—disagree scales:

1. The government should further restrict foreign ownership of Australian agricultural land.
2. Boats carrying asylum seekers should be turned back.
3. Asylum seekers should be held in offshore detention centres while their claims are being processed.
4. Transgender awareness should be taught in primary schools.
5. The federal budget deficit should be reduced, even if it means fewer public services.
6. Schools with lower-performing students should receive more government funding than those with higher-performing students.
7. The Australian constitution should recognise Indigenous people as Australia's first inhabitants.
8. Australia should put a price on carbon emissions.
9. There should be fewer restrictions on coal seam gas exploration.
10. The economic benefits of free trade outweigh the costs.
11. Australia should end the monarchy and become a republic.
12. The government should establish a federal corruption watchdog.
13. Anti-terrorism laws in Australia have gone too far.
14. The government should be able to revoke Australian citizenship from suspected terrorists abroad.
15. People who work on a Sunday should get paid more than people who work on a Saturday.
16. The government should reinstate the construction industry watchdog, the ABCC.
17. Foreign companies should be prohibited from leasing Australian ports.
18. The National Broadband Network should deliver faster speeds even if it costs the government more.
19. Gender quotas should be used to increase the number of women in Parliament.
20. Tax breaks for investment properties should be restricted to newly-constructed properties.
21. Marriage should only be between a man and a woman.
22. Terminally ill patients should be able to legally end their own lives with medical assistance.

Five-point less (or fewer/lower)—more (or higher) scale

1. How many refugees should Australia admit?
2. How much income should former students earn before they have to start repaying their university debt?
3. How much should Australia spend on foreign aid?
4. How involved should the Australian military be in the fight against Islamic State?
5. How much tax should companies pay?
6. How much of their health care costs should individuals have to pay directly?
7. How much of a role should the private sector have in health care?
8. How high should the minimum wage be?

Appendix 2.3: Measuring the distance between the issue preferences of voters and the positions of the established parties

In this chapter voters' distance from the major parties is measured as the average Euclidean distance from both parties' positions. This can be written as:

$$\text{avgdist}_i = \frac{\sqrt{(\text{preference}_i - \text{positionCoalition})^2} + \sqrt{(\text{preference}_i - \text{positionLabor})^2}}{2}$$

where *preference* is the answer provided by respondent *i* for their preferred outcome on each of the issue dimensions outlined above, *positionLabor* is the position taken by the Labor Party on an issue dimension at the election, and *positionCoalition* the policy location of the Liberal–National Coalition parties. In this case, if we look at the economic dimension for instance, the position of the Coalition parties was nearly two standard deviations to the right (1.89, or to the right of nearly 95 per cent of the sample), and the Labor Party took a centrist position (0.33). The voter with the mean position (0) would have a distance of 1.11, while a voter with a position two standard deviations to the left (-2) would have an average distance from the parties of 3.11, and might be said to be poorly represented by the party system on this issue.

Appendix 2.4: Regression coefficients

	Greens	Minor left	Xenophon	Other	Christian right	Libertarian	Populist right
Sociotropic economic insecurity	.05 (.01)	.04 (.03)	.13 (.02)	.19 (.03)	-.06 (.07)	-.02 (.06)	.16 (.04)
Personal economic insecurity	-.07 (.01)	-.01 (.03)	.10 (.02)	.16 (.03)	-.15 (.06)	-.10 (.06)	.08 .04
Economic issue distance	.30 (.01)	.23 (.03)	-.04 (.02)	.14 (.03)	-.52 (.07)	-.06 (.06)	-.05 .03
Social issue distance	.36 (.01)	.02 (.03)	-.32 (.02)	-.17 (.03)	-.08 (.05)	.01 (.05)	.70 .03
Age 30–44	-.09 (.05)	-.16 (.08)	.62 (.10)	.15 (.11)	.02 (.19)	-.29 (.18)	.31 .14
Age 45–64	-.36 (.04)	-.66 (.08)	1.04 (.09)	.15 (.10)	-.58 (.18)	-.76 (.17)	.28 .13
Age 65 plus	-.62 (.04)	-1.28 (.09)	1.24 (.09)	.01 (.11)	-1.05 (.20)	-.71 (.18)	.04 .13
Education university	.75 (.04)	.25 (.09)	-.21 (.04)	-.26 (.06)	.27 (.16)	-.03 (.16)	-.53 .07
Education some tertiary	.01 (.04)	-.07 (.09)	-.05 (.04)	-.20 (.06)	.03 (.16)	-.12 (.15)	-.33 .07
Education high school	.26 (.04)	-.05 (.08)	-.05 (.04)	-.05 (.06)	-.27 (.16)	-.08 (.15)	-.28 .07
Religion atheist	.73 (.03)	.75 (.07)	.03 (.03)	-.12 (.05)	-2.71 (.22)	.02 (.11)	-.61 .05
Religion other	.18 (.03)	.05 (.08)	-.01 (.04)	.04 (.06)	-1.38 (.19)	-.23 (.13)	-.35 .07
Religion Catholic	-.10 (.04)	-.29 (.09)	-.18 (.05)	-.01 (.08)	-1.98 (.15)	-.20 (.15)	-.19 .08
Division type outer metropolitan	-.22 (.03)	-.16 (.07)	.08 (.04)	.37 (.07)	.71 (.13)	.22 (.14)	.69 .09

	Greens	Minor left	Xenophon	Other	Christian right	Libertarian	Populist right
Division type provincial	-.14 (.04)	-.22 (.08)	-.10 (.05)	.38 (.08)	.66 (.16)	.10 (.17)	.90 (.09)
Division type rural	-.19 (.03)	-.39 (.07)	.14 (.04)	.50 (.07)	.71 (.14)	.31 (.14)	.90 (.08)
Sociotropic insecurity x economic issue distance	-.10 (.01)	-.05 (.03)	-.08 (.02)	-.05 (.03)	-.18 (.08)	-.17 (.07)	-.06 (.04)
Sociotropic insecurity x social issue distance	-.05 (.01)	.01 (.03)	.02 (.02)	.01 (.03)	.08 (.06)	.06 (.06)	.04 (.03)
Personal insecurity x economic issue distance	-.10 (.01)	-.01 (.02)	-.02 (.02)	.00 (.03)	-.03 (.07)	-.12 (.06)	.07 (.03)
Personal insecurity x social issue distance	-.09 (.01)	.03 (.03)	.02 (.02)	.01 (.03)	.10 (.05)	.01 (.05)	.09 (.03)

Source: Coefficients from regression models fit to Vox Pop Labs post-election survey data.

Notes: Each column represents a model predicting support for a different party group. Figures represent the values of logistic regression coefficients when all other factors in the model are held at their baseline values (and those in parentheses standard errors). Baselines are Age 18–29, Some school education, Protestant religious affiliation, and inner-metropolitan division.

3

Attitudes to immigration and asylum seekers in Australia: contested territory or an opportunity for right-wing populism?

Shaun Wilson

This chapter deals with trends in Australian attitudes to immigration and asylum seekers. It does so by considering an important political development: the return of the populist right to Australian politics, primarily in the form of a revived One Nation. The return of One Nation is not surprising given wider global events – voter support for nationalist and anti-immigration parties in Europe, the influence of anti-immigration sentiment on the United Kingdom's decision to leave Europe, and the disquieting success of Donald J. Trump's campaign in the 2016 presidential elections in the United States. One Nation's fortunes have depended on political opportunities available to it and indeed, its ability to maintain a coherent party organisation. However, its success in the 2016 federal Senate elections (and improved polling since) raises questions about One Nation's prospects.

The goal of this chapter, then, is to make sense of three related developments. These are the return of One Nation to politics, the changing character of opposition to immigration, and the role of sociocultural and economic insecurities in explaining this opposition. One Nation, as the main vehicle of popular-right expression, has been weakened over the years by party disorganisation, the difficulties of maintaining small-party representation given Australia's electoral systems, and competition from the Coalition, particularly on border protection. However, its revival demands a fresh round of analysis.

My task here is to consider the role of public opinion and social attitudes in creating opportunities for parties like One Nation. It makes sense to focus on patterns in attitudes to immigration as an important factor in the shifting fortunes of populist right politics without making the strong assumption that political opportunities can be neatly 'forecast' from trends in public opinion. Even though the international literature finds solid evidence of the association between anti-immigration sentiment and support for the populist-right (Rydgren 2008, 740), it is also clear there are other significant influences on the political opportunities for the populist right (Mudde 2013, 6). These factors are also highlighted in what follows here.

In considering recent polling evidence,[1] I shall argue that trends in support for immigration levels and changing patterns of opposition to asylum seekers probably limit electoral opportunities for right-wing populism for the time being. There is now a significant constituency for high migration in Australia and a genuine partisan divide over Australia's handling of asylum seekers. The latter fact points to difficulties governments face in either liberalising or making tougher conditions for asylum seekers.

Recent commercial polling that suggests a substantial minority of Australians support a ban on so-called 'Muslim immigration' should be interpreted in this light. Attempts to alter the immigration mix along these lines will embolden some. However, these kind of policies also encounter public opinion constraints and resistance from social movements, both of which were still in formation two decades ago.

A resurgent populist right in the land of multiculturalism?

The near-absence of populist right political representation in Australia over the past decade is remarkable given developments in Europe and elsewhere. In searching for explanations, one can start with the pressures faced by minor parties like One Nation in a two-party system that makes sustaining parliamentary representation difficult. Next, one might consider the organisational dysfunction of One Nation as a factor. However, the Coalition's ability to appeal to populist voters through its immigration and national security policies is another consideration. Indeed, the evidence internationally suggests that the *mainstream* right, not the populist right, has been chiefly responsible for tougher immigration policies (Mudde 2013, 12). In any case, I will argue that underlying trends in Australian attitudes to immigration and asylum seekers over the past decade or so have not been particularly favourable to parties seeking to exploit anti-immigration politics.

As Mudde points out, the politics of race and immigration is a complex, multidimensional space. A relevant starting point, especially for a country like Australia with a migration program that is both large and culturally diverse, is to see whether support for multiculturalism has remained high. Governments have remained committed to a broadly multicultural policy framework, though that support has become more qualified in some contexts. Markus' (2016) intensive opinion research on this subject has not detected any decline in support for multiculturalism on a direct measure – 'Multiculturalism has been good for Australia' – with over 80 per cent agreement for successive survey years (2016, 50). However, another measure in the Australian Election Study (AES) 2016 hints at some fraying. The proposition that 'immigrants make Australia more open to ideas and cultures' measures the role of migration in achieving openness and diversity – two features of multiculturalism. On that measure, total support has also been high – in the 75 per cent–81 per cent range between 1996 and 2007. Since 2010, however, it has fallen, now sitting in a range between 69 per cent and 73 per cent (Cameron and McAllister 2016, 101).

---

1   This survey of public opinion cannot hope to replicate the detailed analysis of polling and data available in Markus (2016) or Goot and Watson (2011). Instead, my main goal is to identify changing patterns of support and opposition to immigration as a way of making sense of opportunities for the growth of right-wing populism.

Australia compared internationally

A society broadly committed to multiculturalism can still find reasons to oppose immigration – for example, when joblessness is high. One commonly used barometer of immigration sentiment asks respondents about their feelings towards the *level* of immigration. How do Australians compare on this score?

Data from nine rich countries presented in Table 3.1 suggests that Australians support current immigration levels. A minority (42 per cent) prefer lower immigration – the lowest of these nine countries selected for this comparison. Anti-immigration sentiment is higher elsewhere – a staggering 79 per cent of UK respondents, 62 per cent of Belgian respondents, and 60 per cent of French respondents want lower immigration. Moreover, two of the countries mentioned have significantly lower net migration rates than Australia (see last column of the Table).

However, a closer look at this data adds nuance. There is evidence that a relatively high number of those Australians opposed to immigration have strong views about it. Some 24 per cent want immigration reduced *a lot*. On that measure, Australia's anti-immigration population jumps to a higher place on the list.

Table 3.1 also presents data from a WIN/Gallup (2016) poll conducted in 69 countries about approval of foreign *workers*. Here, Australian support for migration appears more qualified. Net approval for these workers is at a sobering minus 22 per cent. Still, the balance of opinion in Australia was more favourable to foreign workers than in Belgium (minus 49 per cent) and in France (minus 37 per cent), and was similar to the opinions of voters in the Netherlands and in the United Kingdom (minus 21 per cent and 28 per cent respectively). However, Australian opinion was considerably less favourable than that recorded for voters in Sweden (+27 per cent), Germany (+5 per cent), the United States (+5 per cent), and Denmark (minus 11 per cent).

Finally, Table 3.1 gives some basic data on the performance of major right-wing populist parties in these nine countries. With the exception of Denmark, the countries where the populist right is electorally stronger than in Australia *tend* to have stronger preferences for reducing immigration. Nevertheless, the relationship is not particularly strong, and is likely mediated by other considerations such as voting systems and the responsiveness of mainstream parties to anti-immigration agendas. One might consider the impact of Howard-era immigration policies and Donald Trump's repositioning of the Republicans as examples of such responsiveness.

As noted, immigration sentiment offers only some insight in accounting for populist right voter support. To the extent that it *does* have explanatory value, the data suggests that *overall* Australian attitudes to immigration are not particularly hostile, especially when cast in comparative terms. Still, around a quarter of Australians want much-reduced immigration and attitudes to foreign *workers* are fairly 'cool'. These results suggest there is a considerable electorate for populist right politics centred on immigration, even if these issues are not running 'white hot' as they are in some parts of Europe. However, recent moderation in hostility to immigration levels helps explain why populist right-wing politics in Australia have been less successful in the past decade than it was in the anti-immigration 1990s.

Table 3.1: Major populist right party vote (main house of parliament) and attitudes to immigration in selected rich democracies.

	Populist right vote last national election (%) (or poll)	Reduce immigration (total) %	Reduce immigration (*a lot*) %	Net support for foreign workers %	Net migration rate (per 1,000 pop; 2016)
Denmark	21	43	21	-11	2.1
United Kingdom	15	79	57	-21	2.5
France	14	63	48	-37	1.1
Sweden	13	60	29	27	5.4
The Netherlands	13	n/a	n/a	-28	1.9
Germany	11	49	24	5	1.5
Belgium	5	62	48	-49	5.6
Australia	3	42	24	-22	5.6
USA	--	43	19	5	3.9

Sources: **Column 1:** for Australia's populist right classification, see footnote 2. For other classifications, refer to the most recent national election Wikipedia pages for: Belgium (2014; combined vote for VB/Flemish Interest and PP/People's Party); Denmark (2015; DF/Danish People's Party); France (2012; National Assembly elections; FN/ National Front); The Netherlands (2017; PVV/Party for Freedom); Sweden (2014; Sweden Democrats); the United Kingdom (2015; UKIP); and refer to the 'Opinion polling for the next German federal election, 2017' Wikipedia page (poll average of January to March 2017 polls for the AFD (Alliance for Germany). **Columns 2 and 3:** data on preferences for reducing immigration comes from ISSP (2015) (country samples ranging from N=904 to N=2,202) and AES 2016 (N=2,818; weighted). **Column 4:** data from WIN/Gallup (2016). Question: 'Generally speaking do you think the immigration of foreign workers is a good thing or a bad thing for [insert your country]'. Sample sizes approximately N=1,000 in each country. **Column 5:** estimated net migration rates for 2016; CIA (2016).

Immigration and populist right electoral performance in Australia

In Australia, favourable conditions for a strong anti-immigration force in politics – that is, widespread voter resistance to immigration levels – peaked in the post-recessionary 1990s (Markus 2016, 39; Cameron and McAllister 2016, 100). One Nation emerged out of this, achieving its strongest performance in the 1998 elections in its 'heartland' state of Queensland. It gained almost 23 per cent of the primary vote and 11 of 89 seats. Nevertheless, One Nation made only minor headway elsewhere in gaining parliamentary representation.

Since the early 2000s, anti-immigration sentiment weakened considerably for reasons explored in the rest of this chapter. Not surprisingly, the populist right – as a distinct political force – disappeared from Australian politics for a decade. Even at their strongest, populist right parties in Australia have never gained above 10 per cent of the vote for the main chamber of parliament at a national election, something achieved in a number of European countries. Still, One Nation polled well in the 15 House of Representative seats it contested in 2016 (averaging 13 per cent per cent of the primary vote) and populist right parties achieved around 6 per cent of the vote in the Senate (mainly votes for One Nation) (see Green 2016).

Why this partial revival? First, the political cycle mattered. Right-wing disappointment with a first-term Coalition government that replaced its conservative-populist prime minister, Tony Abbott, fomented a protest vote in 2016. Second, political opportunities were enhanced by Prime Minister Turnbull's decision to call a double dissolution election in July 2016, making it easier for One Nation to win its four Senate seats. Third, international politics is favouring both leftist and right-wing populist movements, with the latter amplifying the kind of anti-immigration and now anti-Muslim rhetoric that One Nation promotes.

Just as these factors help explain One Nation's success in elections and in recent polling, they hint at limits to the party's future performance. Its relatively poor result in the Western Australian state election of March 2017 (a primary vote of 4.9 per cent, no seats in the Legislative Assembly, and three in the Legislative Council) is a reminder of the fragility of its appeal, its organisational vulnerability, and the patchy charm of its long-time party leader. In November 2017, despite a resurgent primary vote, One Nation gained only one seat in the Queensland state election, well short of their 1998 performance.

Conditions for longer-term and broader success of a party like One Nation depend on more than favourable short-term opportunities. Robust party organisation, even greater electoral salience of its core issues, and a broader appeal to Labor and Coalition voters would all count. The fact that anti-immigration politics in Australia – as we shall see, *the* bread-and-butter issue for One Nation – has lost force since the 1990s, and also invites greater public contestation when it returns, suggests that conditions for populist mobilisation may not be as easy to obtain.

Does hostility to immigration distinguish voters on the populist right?

Judging from recent elections, One Nation and other populist right parties continue to appeal to a significant minority of Australian voters. What policy differences distinguish their voters? And does anti-immigration sentiment feature as strongly in their support as I have suggested? These questions have been analysed using a large post-election survey conducted by VoxPop Labs. Shaun Ratcliff's research presented in Chapter 2 suggests that a 'representation gap' on social issues – on asylum seekers, for example – played a central role in populist right vote choice in 2016 (see also Marr 2017, who cites McAllister's research). However, Ratcliff also finds that general beliefs about the (poor) state of the economy, and to some extent personal economic insecurity, drove voters to these parties.

Here, we can add to Ratcliff's findings by considering a much smaller (but randomly selected) sample of around 120 voters who voted for one of the populist right parties according to AES 2016.[2] This is a small sample size, so we look for large differences

---

2   In the AES 2016 sample, populist right voters were identified by any vote in either the House or Senate for the following parties that were classified as having populist right-wing positions in one or more of these areas: race and immigration, Muslims/Islam, law and order, and economic and military nationalism. These parties were: One Nation; Citizens Electoral Council of Australia; Shooters, Fishers and Farmers; Katter's Australian Party; Rise Up Australia; Derryn Hinch Justice Party; Jacquie Lambie Network; and the Australian Liberty Alliance. The populism of some of these parties is highly politically eclectic (but generally tends to right-wing themes) and the category of populist right used here is not synonymous with *extreme* right. The corresponding 'populist right' vote data in Table 3.1 has been extracted from the Official Results for the House of Representatives at the 2016 federal election (http://results.aec.gov.au/20499/Website/HouseStateFirstPrefsByParty-20499-NAT.htm).

that are likely to be statistically significant as well as sociologically meaningful. As the data presented in Table 3.2 shows, these voters overwhelmingly disagreed with Malcolm Turnbull replacing Tony Abbott as prime minister in 2015 (85 per cent disapproval). This is direct evidence that the new prime minister was rejected by the Coalition's right flank.

Table 3.2 also shows that not all social issues drive support for these parties with equal force. The results make clear that attitudes to *immigration and race* – asylum seekers, the number of migrants, and Aboriginal rights – strongly differentiate this voter bloc, with perceptions of government control by 'big interests' featuring similarly. It is not too much of a stretch to suggest that issues of immigration and big interests *merge* for many in this group, culminating in a world-view asserting that multiculturalism has been 'forced' on Australia from above (see Marr 2017, 57).

However, populist right voters do *not* appear to oppose other forms of social progress. Most express support for same-sex couples having the same rights as others (58 per cent) and most do *not* believe equal opportunities for women have gone too far – even though they are more conservative on both questions than other voters. Moreover, just as Ratcliff finds with the VoxPop Labs data, the AES 2016 sample of populist right voters also express greater dissatisfaction with the economy and higher levels of personal economic insecurity.

What is clear is that both the VoxPop Labs and AES data point to issues of race and immigration as the strongest points of differentiation between populist right voters and everyone else. Public opinion in this area appears to be central to explaining prospects for right-wing populism in Australia.

Trends in Australian attitudes to immigration

As data presented in the previous section suggests, populist right voters are distinguished by their hostility to immigration and asylum seekers. However, they also express higher levels of dissatisfaction with politics generally, and they have higher levels of economic insecurity than other voters. So do these findings suggest that the revival of One Nation is an indication of rising hostility to immigration in general and to migrants and asylum seekers in particular?

To answer this question, let's go back to 1996, and focus initially on opinions about the level of immigration.[3] At the time of the Keating Labor government's defeat, a very high 63 per cent of Australians wanted to reduce immigration, according to AES 1996. (See Table 3.3.) This hostility had remained even after the Labor government had slowed the rate of immigration following the recession of 1991–92 (see Sherrell and Mares 2016). Moreover, this negative sentiment persisted well into the period of economic recovery.

Strong anti-immigration sentiment in Australia in the 1990s is a reminder of how recessions can undermine immigration, even after economic growth is restored. This is a problem for the UK and Europe, almost a decade after the beginnings of the Global Financial Crisis (GFC). The ability of a weak economy to stir up anti-migrant sentiments tends to be understated in the literature, which emphasises sociocultural backlash (Inglehart and Norris 2016, for example). We cannot explore this problem in detail here, but both types of explanations appear to matter. As Markus' analysis for Australia shows,

---

3   For a detailed overview of polling on immigration levels, see Goot and Watson (2011, 20–28).

Table 3.2: Attitudes and demographics of populist right voters versus all other voters, %.

	Populist right voters (n=120)	All other voters (n=2,698)	Gap##
Attitudes			
Disapprove of Turnbull replacing Abbott	85	50	+35
All boats carrying asylum seekers turn back	78	46	+32
Prefer lower immigration	71	40	+31
Government run by a few big interests	82	54	+28
Aboriginal rights gone too far	51	27	+24
Self-identified working class	59	39	+20
Very dissatisfied with state of economy#	33	15	+18
Big business has too much power	89	73	+15
Household finances worse in last 12 months	48	34	+14
Same-sex couples equal rights	59	71	-12
Equal opportunities for women gone too far	21	9	+12
Very difficult to find another job next 12 months	47	36	+11
Demographics			
Born in Australia	89	77	+12
Aged under 40 years	26	35	-9

Source: Australian Election Study 2016 (weighted).
Notes: # 'Very dissatisfied' coded as 0–2 on a 10-point scale where 0 is very dissatisfied and 10 is very satisfied. ## All the differences between populist right voters and 'All other voters' are significant on bivariate Gamma tests at $p<0.05$ using unweighted data.

preferences for reduced immigration over time track extremely closely to the level of unemployment (2016, 39; Goot and Watson 2005, 184).

Over the course of the 2000s, voter demands for lower immigration started to fall away. In fact, support for reduced immigration fell to around 35 per cent in 2004 before trending up again over the next decade. Explanations for acceptance of immigration levels must centre on Australia's improved economic and employment performance, especially during the resources boom. This is an argument highlighted in Goot and Watson (2005: 184) and in Meagher and Wilson (2006). As Table 3.3 shows, voter assessments of *general* job insecurity improved between 1998 and 2007. Voters believing it would be 'very difficult' to find another job fell sharply from 42 per cent to 14 per cent over that time. Greater support for immigration levels also tracks Australian Bureau of Statistics unemployment/ underemployment measures (Table 3.3) – consistent with Markus' findings.

At the same time, fewer voters believed that 'immigrants take jobs away from people who are born in Australia'. The number of respondents agreeing with this statement declined from 41 per cent in 1996 to 29 per cent in 2007. Perceptions that 'immigrants increase the crime rate' also declined, from 52 per cent to 37 per cent in 2016. This decline tracked the falling incidence of crime throughout the 2000s (Weatherburn 2016). It is likely therefore that employment and crime conditions helped stabilise support for immigration numbers. Moreover, increases in (personal) job insecurity in the 2010s have not yet translated into rising perceptions that immigrants take jobs.

Improved employment and crime rates have probably weakened the immigration backlash. But could changes in immigration levels or the *type* of immigration have also played a role? As Table 3.3 shows, the net migration rate in fact *rose* during the Howard era, and stayed high during the early Rudd years. Claiming, therefore, that greater acceptance of immigration levels was a 'thermostatic' response (Wlezien 1995) to reduced immigration levels is inconsistent with the facts.[4]

Numbers are only one part of the puzzle. The type of immigration may also concern voters. Authors like Goot and Watson (2005: 184) as well as former prime minister Tony Abbott claim Coalition policies restored confidence in immigration (Shanahan and Kelly 2010).[5] The argument goes as follows: once the Howard government encouraged skilled migrants over family resettlement (Phillips 2006), confidence rose.

This hypothesis is hard to explore without data on whether voters endorsed, or even recognised, this policy shift. However, the detail may not have mattered. There are reasons to expect such a shift in voter sentiment – without assuming voters knew such detail. Building on earlier analysis (Goot and Watson 2005, 182), Table 3.3 shows the Coalition leading Labor on the immigration issue in five of the last seven elections for which there is data.[6] Their leads ranged from 12 per cent to 27 per cent. It follows that voters are more accepting of immigration numbers when their preferred 'manager' of this program is in power. By contrast, Labor has not held a decisive lead on immigration at any of these elections.

The Coalition's long-standing lead on immigration policy relates to its ability to frame immigration politics. This applies not only to immigration and 'border protection' policies when in office, but to the pursuit of immigration themes when Labor governs. Opposition Leader Tony Abbott relentlessly pursued Labor over renewed boat arrivals after Labor in government dismantled the Pacific Solution. Labor policy was reframed as a loss of control over Australia's borders at a time of global risk and insecurity.

One further possible factor in greater acceptance of immigration levels relates to *political learning*. The ongoing contest over immigration in the public sphere encouraged by activists has 'educated' the public. The result has been the emergence of a constituency in favour of asylum seekers and high levels of immigration. There is now international evidence to support this hypothesis, in that immigration attitudes are becoming more polarised over time (Bohman and Hjerm 2016). The clear implication here is that partisan politics is becoming central to the shaping of support and opposition to immigration.

The story is slightly more complex than one stressing partisanship. When we look at trends in attitudes to immigration levels, they actually appear to be *losing* some of the

4 Rising opposition to immigration levels during Labor's term in office that followed, especially in 2010, may suggest a *lagged* response to surging migration during the Howard years, but this shift may have been a *general* response to perceptions of immigration levels under Labor rule.
5 It is certainly the case that 'skilled migrant' immigration attracts high voter support (77 per cent) but *not* significantly more supported than 'family reunion' immigration at 75 per cent (see Morgan Poll 2016).
6 Note that there are no figures for 2010.

Table 3.3: Drivers of anti-immigration sentiments, 1996–2016.

	1996	1998	2001	2004	2007	2010	2013	2016	Change
Reduce immigration	63	48	37	35	46	52	41	42	*-21*
Immigrants take jobs	41	37	35	30	29	35	35	30	*-11*
Immigrants increase crime rate	52	47	47	41	43	43	40	37	*-15*
Immigrants make Australia more open	79	80	75	81	78	69	73	70	*-9*
Measure of job insecurity#	--	42	36	24	14	--	33	37	--
ABS unemployment measure*	15.8	15.5	14.3	12.7	11.0	13.0	14.3	14.8	*-1.0*
Net migration rate##	0.58	0.43	0.71	0.50	1.12	0.79	0.94	0.80	*+0.32*
Coalition lead on best on immigration	+26	-3	+27	+18	-2	--	+16	+12	*-14*
Incumbent party at federal election	Labor	Coal.	Coal.	Coal.	Coal.	Labor	Labor	Coal.	

Source: AES 1996–2016 (weighted for 2010–2016).
Notes: Most AES data is taken from Cameron and McAllister (2016, 40). # AES data on job insecurity for AES 1998–2007 is a *general* measure of voter assessment of difficulty in finding a job while AES 2013–2016 data measures *personal* difficulty; see Appendix Table 3.A1 for details.
* Derived combined unemployment and underemployment statistics (seasonally adjusted) for quarterly data closest to the date of respective federal elections, and available from Australian Bureau of Statistics, Labour Force 6202.0 Excel files (Spreadsheet 22).
Phillips et al. (2010) and author calculations from (ABS) 3101.0 Australian Demographic Statistics (Sept. 2016).

partisan character. By contrast, attitudes to asylum seeker arrivals, discussed further in the next section, are becoming more partisan.

Table 3.4 shows that, between 1996 and 2016, there have been particularly large falls in anti-immigration preferences among respondents aged under 40 years and among those living in big cities (30 and 27 percentage-point declines respectively). Some of the fall can be attributed to the shifting social demography of the younger electorate as it acquires even more education: the views of younger Australians overlap considerably with the pro-immigration preferences of the university-educated cohort.

Coalition voters have become significantly *more* accepting of current immigration levels. Again, compositional change may play some role here. For example, some of the Coalition's most strongly anti-immigration voters defected to populist right parties in 2016. This had the effect of shifting average Coalition voter preferences on immigration in a liberal direction.

So, in sum, One Nation's return does not appear to be the product of rising opposition to immigration levels. Its return appears to have had its basis in short-term political opportunities, perhaps without the sustaining 'resource' of widespread anti-immigration feeling.

Trends in Australian attitudes to asylum seekers: the unsettled politics of offshore detention policies

Since 2001, the Coalition has taken a 'hard-line' position towards asylum seekers who arrive by boat, offshore detention, and visas for asylum seekers (Kelly 2017 summarises

Table 3.4: Patterns of opposition to immigration levels (1996 v 2016) and boat arrivals (2001 v 2016), %.

	Opposition to current immigration levels			Opposition to asylum seekers (turn back boats)		
	1996	2016	change	2001	2016	change
Voting						
Overall	63	42	-21	62	48	-14
Labor	53	38	-15	53	38	-15
Coalition	71	46	-25	75	64	-11
Greens	--	11	--	32#	10	-22
Populist right*	--	71	--	85#	78	-7
Demographics						
Women	65	41	-24	61	40	-21
Men	62	43	-19	63	55	-8
University degree	42	25	-17	38	34	-4
No degree	68	51	-17	78	56	-22
Age under 40	65	35	-30	55	32	-23
Born in Australia	67	43	-24	64	47	-17
Large city	60	33	-27	55	42	-13
Middle class	56	33	-23	57	41	-16
Working class	70	51	-19	66	56	-10
Battlers*	76	52	-24	64	54	-10

Sources: AES 1996 (N=1,797), 2001 (N=2,010), 2016 (weighted).
Notes: # sample size<100. * For populist right parties' classification in 2016, see footnote 3; in 2001, populist right voters are One Nation voters in either the House of Reps or Senate. * Battlers defined as McAllister and Makkai do in Chapter 6.

the Coalition's position). The electoral payoff was significant. Prime Minister Howard's response to the *Tampa* incident and policy of offshore detention helped win back One Nation voters at the 2001 elections (McAllister 2003). With Labor coming to adopt policies of offshore detention, creating bipartisan support for Australia's hard-line approach, it might follow that the public remains overwhelmingly committed to this policy consensus. In fact, by 2016, the policy of boat turnbacks no longer attracted majority support, and stood at 48 per cent (see Table 3.4; Figure 3.1). Opposition to the policy has climbed to around one third of the voting population since 2013 (Cameron and McAllister 2016, 96).[7]

What has produced this shift in public opinion, and what groups of voters have shifted most? Women have shifted *against* the turnback policy more than men have, with support

---

7   Goot and Watson (2001, 37) comment on the considerable variation of opinions on asylum seeker policy that appears to depend on the question and framing of the question. No doubt, these variations also reflect the genuinely conflicted positions in the opinions of some voters.

falling a dramatic 22 percentage points between 2001 and 2016. There is now a clear gender divide on this policy question in keeping with other findings in Chapter 5. Not surprisingly, younger voters (under 40 years) have also moved more sharply away from boat turnbacks than older voters. Voters without a university degree have also shifted in the same direction, with the gap between degree-educated voters and those without degrees narrowing sharply from 40 per cent in 2001 to 22 per cent in 2016. This result may be an indication that the politics of opposing hard-line asylum policies has moved beyond the 'university campus', as it were, and now has broader influence on centre-left voters, particularly women. But working-class and 'Battler' voters (see Chapter 6) have shifted less on turnbacks – 10 per cent declines for both groups. Working-class and battler men remain on balance supporters of these tough policies.

Table 3.4 also reveals much sharper *polarisation* by party on asylum seeker policy. Coalition and One Nation/populist right voters maintain agreement with boat turnbacks by large majorities (64 and 84 per cent respectively). Labor voters agree less (38 per cent) and Greens voters are sharply opposed (10 per cent agree). When attitudes to immigration levels and boat turnbacks are compared, we can also see the particular impact of the politics of asylum seeking in operation. Table 3.4 suggests that, by 2016, there are now relatively small partisan divides between Labor and Coalition voters about the level of immigration. By contrast, the political divides on refugees are large and *expanding*.

In 2001, a sizeable share of voters who supported immigration opposed asylum seeker arrivals. They were more inclined to see asylum seekers as a separate problem from immigration – speculatively, what Howard-era policy tried to establish. By 2016, attitudes were in closer alignment. Voters who *support* immigration levels are now more likely to *reject* hard-line asylum policies. And the same goes for the tightening relationship between those who *reject* current immigration levels and *support* tough asylum policies. This 'convergence' is depicted in Figure 3.1. A simple measure (Gamma scores) that tracks consistency of individual voter opinion between the two survey items rose from 0.58 in 2001 to 0.69 in 2016.[8]

Labor, the working class, and asylum seekers

Political polarisation over asylum policy has had its largest impact on the Labor Party. The Coalition have consistently embraced a 'hard-line' policy on asylum seekers and the Greens have opposed this policy consistently and vociferously (Wilson 2016). By contrast, Labor has struggled to define itself consistently on these issues since then Labor leader Kim Beazley yielded to Prime Minister Howard's decision to turn back the *Tampa*, begin offshore detention, and excise Australian territorial islands from the nation's migration zone (Phillips and Spinks 2013). However, the Rudd Labor government did end up dismantling the Pacific Solution. This decision invited attack from the Coalition, who blamed the policy for causing a rapid increase in boat arrivals, numbers of people in detention, and deaths at sea. In 2013, Kevin Rudd decided to reverse Labor's earlier 'liberal' position in his very short second term as

---

8   Gamma (scaled between 0 and 1) measures the level of consistency in responses to the respective items on immigration levels and asylum seekers for individual respondents. A higher Gamma score means more consistency i.e. respondents who want immigration 'reduced a lot' more consistently *also* strongly approve of boat turnbacks.

Figure 3.1 Opinions about lower immigration and turning back asylum boats start to converge, 2001–2016, %.

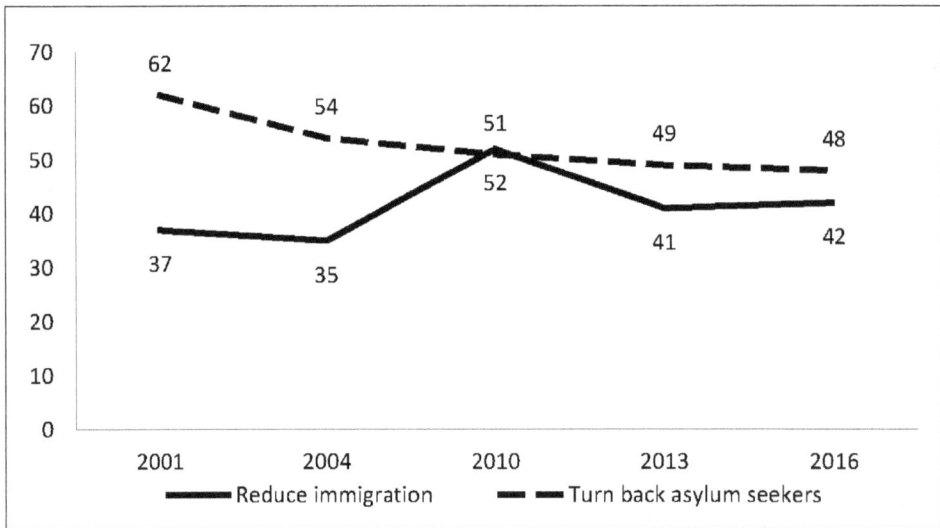

Source: AES 2001–4; 2010–16 (weighted).

prime minister. He effectively endorsed a Coalition approach to this issue via the construction of an offshore detention centre on Manus Island.

Why so much policy instability from Labor? As we shall see, the reasons for this go beyond criticisms of political indecision. Labor's uncertainty over the issue emerges from the policy preferences of its long-time electorate of working-class voters, as Table 3.5 illustrates. Overall, in 2016, Labor won self-identified working-class voters by 9 points – not a particularly large margin in historical terms, but still a handy lead. However, when we consider Labor's two-party vote from a smaller sample of working-class voters who *support* boat turnbacks, Labor's vote drops by a substantial 9.5 points (see column 2). To be expected, Labor does much better among working-class voters who support *redistribution* of income (60 per cent voted ALP). But when we look at working-class voters who support *both* turnbacks and redistribution, we see that Labor's two-party vote stays at just 50 per cent (column 4).

Labor's hesitation, then, emerges out of bitter electoral experience with more liberal asylum policies and the reaction to these policies by an important voter base. The ALP's troubles on this issue have not ended there. Middle-class, left-leaning voters prefer the Greens' unambiguous opposition to asylum policies over Labor's more accommodating and at times unclear position.

In suggesting that asylum seeker politics is polarised into two constituencies, I am not claiming these groups are of equal size, or that public opinion does not sway against the direction of policy in the ways that Wlezien (1995) and Stimson (2004) have suggested. Indeed, it appears to do just that. For example, a substantial minority of voters appear to have rejected the hard-line Pacific Solution in the lead-up to the 2007 defeat of the Howard government. But voters eventually rejected Labor's liberal approach after 2007, forcing the ALP government into humiliating retreats that culminated in its election-eve Manus Island proposals of 2013.

Table 3.5: House of Representatives vote in 2016 among self-identified working-class voters by attitudes to boat turnbacks and redistribution.

	Working-class (WC) voters	WC voters agreeing with boat turnbacks	WC voters agreeing with redistribution	WC voters agreeing with *both*
Coalition	37	46	31	42
Labor	42	36	46	40
Greens	7	2	8	2
Populist right	5	7	6	7
Other	10	10	10	9
Labor (two party)	**54.5**	**45**	**60**	**50**
N	927	555	555	329

Source: AES 2016 (weighted).
Notes: Self-identified measure of working class. For populist right parties in 2016, see footnote 3. Author's estimate of the Labor two-party vote. Sample weighting produced a much high 'Other' vote, but the two-party Labor votes on unweighted and weighted samples varied very little.

As the breakdown of voter attitudes in the two Essential polls presented in Table 3.6 shows, part of the electorate does react *against* the policy direction of the ruling party. The first poll was taken under Labor just before Kevin Rudd resigned as prime minister in 2010. A clear majority of voters believed that the Labor government was 'too soft' on asylum seekers (65 per cent agreed). This was a view shared by practically all Coalition voters (90 per cent) and a majority of ALP voters (56 per cent).

The second poll was taken in November 2016 during Malcolm Turnbull's time as prime minister. It is clear that the public had shifted substantially again, this time in reaction to the Coalition's Operation Sovereign Borders, which Malcolm Turnbull preserved as prime minister. While most Coalition voters believed that their government had got it 'about right', Labor and Greens voters on balance considered the policy 'too hard'. In Labor's case, those results produced a net lead for 'too hard' of 14 per cent in 2016, but this lead was dramatically higher among Greens at 40 per cent.

So clearly, as well as following distinctly partisan patterns, elements of the public react to the asylum policies of the government of the day. In Labor's case, it was vulnerable to widespread perceptions that it was 'too soft' after dismantling the Pacific Solution. In the Coalition's case, reports of inhumane conditions in offshore detention and breaches of international law upset centre-left voters. The result is that a substantial electorate unhappy with tough policies emerges during Coalition rule.

Explaining resistance to immigration levels and asylum seekers: regression analysis

To further explore demographic and attitudinal factors that shape public opinion on immigration levels and boat turnbacks, we can specify regression models that capture likely influences. The two dependent variables are statements on (i) the immigration level

Table 3.6: Agree that the government is too hard (soft) on asylum seekers, %.

	April 2010 poll under Labor (under PM Rudd)			Most recent poll under Coalition (November 2016)		
	Too hard	*Too soft*	*Net too hard*	*Too hard*	*Too soft*	*Net too hard*
Overall	6	65	-59	23	24	-1
Coalition	3	90	-87	9	22	-13
Labor	6	56	-50	37	23	+14
Greens	24	25	-1	54	14	+40

Source: Essential Poll 2010 (6 April; N=1,009); 2016a (8 November; N=1,008).
Notes: Questions: 'Do you think the Federal Labor government is too tough or too soft on asylum seekers or is it taking the right approach?' (6 April) and 'Do you think the Federal Liberal/National Government is too tough or too soft on asylum seekers or is it taking the right approach?' (November 8).

and (ii) agreement with boat turnbacks. Demographics in the models include: gender, age in years, income (measured on a 22-point scale), education (university degree/none), self-identified class status (working class/not), religiosity (frequency of attendance; 6-point scale), and location (lives in big city/does not). To test the impact of voting and job insecurity, two dummy variables are specified: the first captures Coalition voting (versus all others), and the second is a 4-point measure of voter difficulty in finding a new job in the next 12 months. For details, see Appendix Table 3.A1.

Attitude scales are included in the extended-model scenarios for both statements (see Models 2 and 4 in Table 3.7). The first is a 20-point scale constructed out of four items on voters' assessments of *characteristics of immigrants* (increase crime, take jobs, good for the economy, and make Australia open to ideas and cultures). The second captures voter concern about *law and order threats* (stiffer sentences for law-breakers). And the third captures voter concern over *fiscal threats* (prefer lower taxes to more social spending).[9] Again, refer to Appendix Table 3.A1 for details. The hypotheses explored here are that negative views of immigration levels and boat arrivals depend on particular threats from immigrants (i.e. taking jobs) as well as beliefs about associations between migration and threats to law and order and fiscal stability.

A standard way of modelling dependent variables as 5-point Likert scales is to specify ordered logit models. However, these models performed poorly on the test of parallel lines, so they were re-specified as partial proportional odds models (Williams 2005). These models allow the specified relationship between some of the independent variables and the response variable to vary by the level of the independent variable. Analysis was undertaken in Stata/IC14.2 using gologit2 software and an 'autofit' modelling option. The results are presented in Table 3.7.

Supporters of *reduced* immigration (Model 1) are likely to be working-class self-identifiers, experience job insecurity, be less religious, and earn lower incomes. Although coefficients vary, supporters of reduced immigration are also more likely to be Coalition

9   These *threat* hypotheses are derived from the formulations discussed in Hainmueller and Hiscox (2010), who write of various types of threats that voters fear from migration (job competition and a fiscal burden).

voters, not hold degrees, and live outside big cities. Overall, this profile suggests that lower-income, insecure voters who live outside large cities – i.e. the kind of voters who are attracted to One Nation – are most likely to seek reduced immigration.

When attitudinal measures are included, they dominate the results as presented in Model 2, rendering most demographic variables insignificant. Not surprisingly, holding negative views about immigrants is the most powerful predictor of preferring lower immigration. However, preferences for stiffer sentences for law-breakers and preferring lower taxes are also strong predictors. Results can be interpreted as suggesting that voters who prefer reduced immigration see immigrants as contributing to crime, greater social expenditures, and more competition for jobs. Immigration is thus construed as a very broad threat to social and economic security.

Turning to support for refugee boat turnbacks (Model 3 and 4), a similar picture emerges. However, there are differences too. Men, low-income earners, working-class identifiers, Coalition voters, and respondents outside big cities are all significantly more likely to approve of turnbacks, with older voters and non-degree holders tending in a similar direction in most comparison scenarios. Again, attitudinal responses dominate Model 4 when they are included, but importantly, *men* remain significantly more likely to support turnbacks.

To summarise, the demographics of respondents seeking lower immigration and boat turnbacks are similar. Based on these findings, we can surmise that these voters see immigrants and asylum seekers as a *threat* to security across several dimensions. By contrast, support for current immigration levels emerges from a different electorate made up of the city-dwelling educated middle class. Supporters of liberal refugee policies also have these characteristics but that 'coalition' of support weakens significantly among Coalition voters and men.

Considering the contrasting features of these constituencies, it makes sense to interpret the conflict as a sociocultural one, between the 'cosmopolitan' outlooks of younger, educated cosmopolitans and the 'white ethnocentrism' of an older regional Australia. But economic and employment insecurity plays a role in shaping attitudes, especially attitudes towards boat turnbacks (Models 3 and 4).

Varieties of anti-immigration politics: 457s and 'Muslim immigration'

Lastly, we consider public opinion on two important topics in the recent immigration debate: temporary labour migration and, to adopt crude political shorthand, 'Muslim immigration'. As noted earlier, Australians are not particularly resistant to immigration in comparative terms. This may reflect better post-GFC economic conditions in Australia. However, as is apparent from results in Table 3.1, public opinion on 'foreign workers' in Australia was more negative.

Why is the presence of foreign workers a problem for some voters? The use of short-term 457 visas grew over time. In Western Australia, 457s were focused on mining and construction, but across Australia, demand for 457s in 2013 was expanding fastest in industries such as accommodation and food services and retail trade (Larsen 2013). The countries of origin of 457 visa holders in 2013 included India (21 per cent), the United Kingdom (19 per cent), Ireland (10 per cent) and the Philippines (6 per cent) (Larsen 2013). Supporters claim that temporary work programs give business flexibility to meet

Table 3.7: Ordinal regression models on immigration levels and asylum turnbacks.

	Panel 1: Reduce level of immigration	
	Model 1	Model 2
Demographics		
Female	-0.16	-0.11
Older	0.00	0.01
Income	-0.01	-0.00
Degree	-0.67**	-0.08
Working class ID	0.53**	0.14
Religiosity	-0.05*	-0.07**
Live in big city	-0.56**	-0.31**
Coalition voter	0.58**	0.12
Job insecurity	0.18**	0.06
Attitudes		
Law and order scale	--	0.16**
Lower taxes scale	--	0.17**
Immigration scale	--	0.56**

Source: AES 2016. Notes: Dependent variable is 5-point scale from 'Increase a lot' through to 'Decrease a lot'; *p<0.05; **p<0.01; Pseudo R-squares: Model 1: 0.06 (n=1,996); Model 2=0.26 (n=1,958); intercept values not reported.

	Panel 2: Approve of turning back boats carrying asylum seekers	
	Model 3	Model 4
Demographics		
Female	-0.62**	-0.72**
Older	0.01**	0.02**
Income	-0.02*	-0.01
Degree	-0.64**	-0.07
Working class ID	0.52**	0.11
Religiosity	-0.01	-0.03
Live in big city	-0.23**	0.09
Coalition voter	1.28**	0.94**
Job insecurity	0.16**	0.08
Attitudes		
Law and order scale	--	0.43**
Lower taxes scale	--	0.31*
Immigration scale	--	0.38**

Source: AES 2016. Notes: Dependent variable is 5-point scale from 'Strongly approve' through to 'Strongly disapprove'; *p<0.05; **p<0.01; Pseudo R-squares: Model 1: 0.09 (n=1,986); Model 2=0.24 (n=1,950); intercept values not reported.

demand for labour where there are shortages and gives foreign workers opportunities to earn better wages and use their skills. Critics point to exploitative practices by unscrupulous employers who they say use the scheme to undercut wages and working conditions. They also highlight the availability of unemployed locals. Voter apprehension is evident. An Essential Poll from November 2016 indicated that 64 per cent of Australians would support 'Government legislation to reduce the number of overseas workers being brought to Australia under short-term 457 visas' (Essential Poll 2016b). The Turnbull Government's reforms to temporary work visas in 2017 must be read in this light.

Table 3.8 offers insight into the contours of unpopularity of 457s. Asking about migration priorities, Essential Poll data suggests that *Labor* voters are more concerned about the use of 'foreign workers under short term (457) visas each year' (29 per cent). Just 26 per cent of Labor voters nominated 'the arrival of asylum seekers by boat each year'. By contrast, Coalition voters prioritised concerns about asylum seekers over 457 migration by an overwhelming margin, 51 per cent to 19 per cent. Greens voters were least likely to have any concern (32 per cent); among those who did, most chose the 'overall increase in Australia's total population' option (25 per cent).

The figures point to the *varieties* of anti-immigration themes in Australian society. Coalition and populist right voters resist immigration for reasons of both security and ethnocentrism. Labor voters are more resistant to immigration for reasons of employment threat – perhaps both the job competition it implies and the threat to wages and conditions from exploitative elements of migration schemes. Greens voters are most resistant to immigration for reasons of environmental threat, i.e. the impact of population growth in fragile ecosystems. Given the increasing publicity and concern about abuses under the 457 visa system, immigration politics in Australia may well focus in future years on the extent of labour-based migration and the limited protections for workers available under these schemes (Kelly 2017). Indeed, the Turnbull government's decision to modify this scheme in 2017 is the first direct evidence of this impact.

Finally, to the politically charged question about the migration of people who express a Muslim faith or originate from so-called 'Muslim countries'. An Essential Poll from September 2016 found 49 per cent support in response to the question, 'Would you support or oppose a ban on Muslim immigration to Australia?' The finding attracted major attention in politics and the media. A subsequent Essential Poll from February 2017, taken at the time of the Trump administration's proposed ban, found a lower 41 per cent support in response to the question, 'Would you support or oppose the Australian government instituting a similar ban on people from Muslim countries from entering Australia?' These results suggest a substantial minority of Australians are prepared to consider more exclusionary migration policies. Presumably, these results are a response to ongoing violent conflicts and terrorist action internationally, and to the populist politics they have fortified.

Markus (2016) disputed Essential's findings on Muslims in his annual *Mapping Social Cohesion* report, challenging both the methodology (online panels produce socially *undesirable* responses) and the question selected for this poll. Markus agrees that negative opinions about Muslims are relatively high – in his research, around 25 per cent of the population offer such opinions. But his study finds lower hostility towards Muslims than implied by Essential. Moreover, he notes the stability in Australian attitudes towards Muslims over the past few years (2016, 44). Taking due note of Markus' observations about panel surveys, one might add that Markus' question asks about Muslims *in general*, and not

Table 3.8: Voter immigration concerns: boat arrivals versus foreign workers, %.

	Total	Labor	Coalition	Greens
The arrival of asylum seekers by boat	36	26	51	17
The use of foreign workers under short-term (457) visas	21	29	19	18
The overall increase in Australia's total population	20	22	16	25
None of them	17	18	10	32
Don't know	6	5	4	8

Source: Essential Poll (2016b; N=1,012).

Table 3.9: Attitudes to multiculturalism and Muslim immigration, %.

	Total 'positive' response	Total 'negative' response	Net 'positive' response
Multiculturalism has been good for Australia #	83	12	+71
Immigrants make Australia more open to ideas and cultures *	69	10	+59
Overall, has multiculturalism (that is, the acceptance of people from different countries, cultures and religions) made a positive or negative contribution to Australian society? ##	61	23	+38
Is your personal attitude positive, negative or neutral towards Muslims? #	--	25	--
Are you concerned about the number of Muslim people in Australia? (total not concerned=column 1; total concerned=column 2) ##	42	53	-11
Please say whether you support or oppose Muslim immigration (total support=column 1; total do not support=column 2) **	59	32	+27
When a family applies to migrate to Australia, should it be possible for them to be rejected purely on the basis of their religion? (should not be rejected=column 1; should be rejected=column 2) ##	56	24	+32
Would you support or oppose a ban on Muslim immigration to Australia? (oppose=column 1; support=column 2) ##	40	49	-9
[2011] In your view, should the Australian government exclude Muslims from our migrant intake? (no=column 1; yes=column 2) ##	55	25	+30

Sources: # Markus (2016c: 50; N=1,002); ## (in order) Essential Poll (2016c; N=1,000); Essential Poll (2016d; N=1,000); Essential Poll (2011; N=1,082); * AES 2016 weighted; **Morgan Poll 2016 (N=656).

about Muslim *immigration*. Accordingly, the question may not fully capture public desire to limit further immigration from these groups in the current political climate.

Table 3.9 offers insights into the *range* of opinions about multiculturalism, Muslims, and so-called 'Muslim immigration'. The sources are the AES, Essential Polls, and the Morgan Poll, as well as Markus' own research. What is obvious is the extent of variation in responses on similar themes, noting as Markus does the influence of question wording and survey mode. Essential polling, for example, tends to produce the most populist opinion on immigration questions.

The three questions on multiculturalism test opinion about the *benefits* rather than the principles of multiculturalism (refer to the first three rows of the table). Although the results differ depending on polling agency and the question asked, there is a clear tendency in the data. Most Australians affirm these benefits, with agreement ranging from 61 per cent (Essential) to 83 per cent (Markus).

However, for responses on Muslims and Muslim immigration, the results reflect more serious variation and inconsistency in voter sentiments (refer to the final six rows of the table). Essential detected majority concern (53 per cent) in 2016 about the numbers of Muslims in Australia. But these kind of results bear some similarity to poll results from the 1980s that highlighted alarming resistance to so-called 'Asian immigration' (see Markus 2016 who also cites Murray Goot's work on these polls). Once a real force in public opinion, attitudes to immigrants from Asian backgrounds no longer shape either debate or policy rhetoric to the same extent.

What about attitudes to Muslim immigration? Neither survey item presented in the table produced majority support – an important finding in itself. However, it is clear that, as in the US under the Trump administration, such a policy proposition has substantial minority support. Essential's polling altered the wording of its question about banning Muslims between 2011 (see final row) and 2016 (see second last row). This change prevents direct comparisons. Still, at least *some* of the increase in support for such a ban between 2011 and 2016 represents a hardening in attitudes, independent of changes to question wording. It is likely the product of the increased salience of the issue, aided by political events and the emergence of political entrepreneurs on the populist right.

Conclusion

I conclude this chapter by returning to the tasks set out at the beginning. The first is to make an assessment of the relationship between immigration attitudes and opportunities for right-wing populism in Australia, particularly expressed through One Nation. There seems little doubt that strong anti-immigration feeling was a major factor in the emergence of One Nation in the late 1990s. Moreover, attitudes to immigration and race continue to distinguish voters attracted to right-wing populist parties in Australia.

These observations, however, leave us with a puzzle – to explain the revival of One Nation at a time when the available survey evidence suggests a substantial shift away from strongly anti-immigration sentiment in the community and even a slow decline in approval of boat turnbacks. Two possible explanations emerge. The first is that political opportunities, relating to both the leadership of the federal Coalition and ongoing external threats posed by violent extremism, revived voter interest in One Nation, particularly in Queensland. The second is that One Nation's recovery has been only partial, perhaps because the Party has lacked the 'resource' of widespread anti-immigration feeling needed to capitalise on short-term political opportunity and to overcome its organisational problems.

Certainly, this chapter has pointed to evidence that underlines the continuing importance of anti-immigration and anti-asylum seeker sentiment in Australian politics, with voters associating immigration with 'threats' of various kinds. Bi-partisan support in favour of tough asylum policies is the best evidence of the power of a solid constituency that holds these sentiments, especially when it is mobilised by political parties. However, broader shifts in attitudes across the community indicate that, at least for the time being, there is a larger constituency in favour of current immigration levels and more liberal asylum policies than there was two decades ago. Public opinion on immigration in Australia, I speculate, may have undergone a period of 'political learning' as a result of debate and protest on both sides, and as a result, it is now more contested political and policy territory. Still, it remains to be seen whether this larger pro-immigration constituency would hold together, especially if anti-immigration sentiment is stimulated by a slowdown in wages growth and related cost of living pressures.

References

Australian Bureau of Statistics (2016). Australian Demographic Statistics, September 2016. Catalogue No. 3101.0.

Australian Election Study (2016). The AES series: 1996–2016. http://www.australianelectionstudy.org/voter_studies.html.

Bohman, Andrea and Mikael Hjerm (2016). In the wake of radical right electoral success: a cross-country comparative study of anti-immigration attitudes over time. *Journal of Ethnic and Migration Studies* 42(11), 1729–47.

Cameron, Sarah M. and Ian McAllister (2016). *Trends in Australian political opinion: results from the Australian election study, 1987–2016*, ANU: School of Politics and International Relations. http://www.australianelectionstudy.org/publications.html.

Central Intelligence Agency (2016). Net migration rate. https://www.cia.gov/library/publications/the-world-factbook/rankorder/2112rank.html.

Essential Poll (2010). Federal Labor's approach to asylum seekers. 6 April. http://www.essentialvision.com.au/too-soft-or-too-tough-on-asylum-seekers-9.

Essential Poll (2011). Muslim migrants. 28 February. http://www.essentialvision.com.au/muslim-migrants.

Essential Poll (2016a). Too soft or too tough on asylum seekers. 8 November. http://www.essentialvision.com.au/too-soft-or-too-tough-on-asylum-seekers-9.

Essential Poll (2016b). 457 visas. 22 November. http://www.essentialvision.com.au/457-visas.

Essential Poll (2016c). Contribution of multiculturalism. 11 October. http://www.essentialvision.com.au/contribution-of-multiculturalism-4.

Essential Poll (2016d). Ban on Muslim immigration. 21 September. http://www.essentialvision.com.au/ban-on-muslim-immigration.

Goot, Murray and Ian Watson (2005). Immigration, multiculturalism and national identity. In *Australian social attitudes: the first report*. Shaun Wilson et al., eds. 182–203. Sydney: UNSW Press.

Goot, Murray and Ian Watson (2011). *Population, immigration and asylum seekers: patterns in Australian public opinion*, Department of Parliamentary Services (Pre-election Policy Unit). Canberra: Parliamentary Library.

Green, Antony (2016). One Nation support at the 2016 federal election. http://blogs.abc.net.au/antonygreen/2016/07/one-nation-support-at-the-2016-federal-election.html.

Hainmueller, Jens and Michael J. Hiscox (2010). Attitudes toward highly skilled and low-skilled immigration: evidence from a survey experiment. *American Political Science Review* 104(1), 61–84.

Inglehart, Ronald F. and Pippa Norris (2016). Trump, Brexit, and the rise of populism: economic have-nots and cultural backlash. Faculty Research Working Paper Series, John F. Kennedy School of Government (RWP16-026), August. https://research.hks.harvard.edu/publications/getFile.aspx?Id=1401.

ISSP Research Group (2015). International Social Survey Programme: National Identity III – ISSP 2013. GESIS Data Archive, Cologne. ZA5950 Data file Version 2.0.0 https://dbk.gesis.org/dbksearch/sdesc2.asp?ll=10&notabs=&af=&nf=&search=&search2=&db=e&no=5950.

Kelly, Paul (2017). The next populist showdown is all about immigration. *Australian*. 4 March. http://www.theaustralian.com.au/opinion/columnists/paul-kelly/next-populist-showdown-is-all-about-immigration/news-story/2bd84bdb6c3c5be77c3e67683d8dab3a.

Larsen, Gareth (2013). The subclass 457 visa: a quick guide. http://www.aph.gov.au/About_Parliament/Parliamentary_Departments/Parliamentary_Library/pubs/rp/rp1314/QG/Subclass457Visa.

Markus, Andrew (2016). *Mapping social cohesion: the Scanlon Foundation surveys 2016.* Melbourne: Monash University, ACJC, Faculty of Arts. http://scanlonfoundation.org.au/wp-content/uploads/2016/11/2016-Mapping-Social-Cohesion-Report-FINAL-with-covers.pdf.

Marr, David (2017). The white queen: One Nation and the politics of race. *Quarterly Essay* 65, 1–102.

McAllister, Ian (2003). Border protection, the 2001 Australian election and the Coalition victory. *Australian Journal of Political Science* 38(3), 445–63.

Meagher, Gabrielle and Shaun Wilson (2006). After Howard's decade, is Australia more conservative? *Australian Review of Public Affairs*. http://www.australianreview.net/digest/2006/02/meagher_wilson.html.

Morgan Poll (2016). Majority of Australians support Muslim and asylum seeker immigration. 25 October. http://www.roymorgan.com/findings/7017-australian-views-on-immigration-population-october-2016-201610241910.

Mudde, Cas (2013). Three decades of populist radical right parties in Western Europe: so what? *European Journal of Political Research* 52(1), 1–19.

Phillips, Janet (2006). Skilled migration to Australia. http://www.aph.gov.au/About_Parliament/Parliamentary_Departments/Parliamentary_Library/Publications_Archive/archive/Skilledmigration.

Phillips, Janet, Klapdor, Michael and Simon-Davies, Joanne (2010). Migration to Australia since federation: a guide to the statistics. http://www.aph.gov.au/About_Parliament/Parliamentary_Departments/Parliamentary_Library/pubs/BN/1011/MigrationPopulation#_Toc270677557.

Phillips, Janet and Harriet Spinks (2013). Immigration detention in Australia. http://www.aph.gov.au/About_Parliament/Parliamentary_Departments/Parliamentary_Library/pubs/BN/2012-2013/Detention.

Rydgren, Jens (2008). Immigration sceptics, xenophobes or racists? Radical right-wing voting in six West European countries. European Journal of Political Research 47: 737-765.

Shanahan, Dennis and Paul Kelly (2010). We must restore confidence: Tony Abbott. *Australian*, 10 August. http://www.theaustralian.com.au/national-affairs/we-must-restore-confidence-tony-abbott/news-story/400c351e9433bbb2fa4618755890b115.

Sherell, and Mares, Peter (2016). How many migrants come to Australia each year? *Inside Story*. http://insidestory.org.au/how-many-migrants-come-to-australia-each-year.

Stimson, James (2004). *Tides of Consent.* Cambridge: Cambridge University Press.

Weatherburn, Don (2016). Is crime getting worse in Australia? *The Conversation*. http://theconversation.com/election-factcheck-is-crime-getting-worse-in-australia-60119.

Williams, Richard (2005). Gologit2: a program for generalized logistic regression/partial proportional odds models for ordinal dependent variables. http://www.stata.com/meeting/4nasug/gologit2.pdf.

Williams, Richard (2016). Understanding and interpreting generalized ordered logit models, *The Journal of Mathematical Sociology* 40:1, 7–20, DOI: 10.1080/0022250X.2015.1112384.

Wilson, Shaun (2016). Labor, the Greens, and the union movement. In *How to vote progressive in Australia*, Dennis Altman and Sean Scalmer, eds. 203–29. Melbourne: Monash University Publishing.

WIN/Gallup International (2016). WIN/Gallup International's global poll shows the world is divided on immigration. http://www.wingia.com/web/files/richeditor/filemanager/ Immigration_Press_Release_EOY_2015__Finalized_Draft.pdf.

Wlezien, Chris (1995). The public as thermostat: dynamics of preferences for spending. *American Journal of Political Science* 39(4), 981–1000.

Appendix 3.1

Table 3.A1: Questions in Australian Election Studies series.

Questions/statements	Scale
All boats carrying asylum seekers should be turned back	Strongly agree – Strongly disagree (5 points)
Do you think the number of immigrants allowed into Australia nowadays should be reduced or increased?	Increased a lot – Reduced a lot (5 points)
Immigrants increase the crime rate	Strongly agree – Strongly disagree (5 points)
Immigrants are generally good for Australia's economy	Strongly agree – Strongly disagree (5 points)
Immigrants take jobs away from people who are born in Australia	Strongly agree – Strongly disagree (5 points)
Immigrants make Australia more open to new ideas and cultures	Strongly agree – Strongly disagree (5 points)
Do you approve or disapprove of the way the Liberal Party handled the leadership change in September of last year, when Malcolm Turnbull replaced Tony Abbott?	Strongly approve – Strongly disapprove (4 points)
Please say whether you think the change has gone too far, not gone far enough, or is it about right? [Aboriginal land rights/ Equal opportunities for women]	Gone much too far – Not gone nearly far enough (5 points)
Would you say the government is run by a few big interests looking out for themselves, or that it is run for the benefit of all the people?	Entirely run for the big interests – Entirely run for the benefit of all (5 points)
How does the financial situation of your household now compare with what it was 12 months ago?	A lot better – A lot worse (5 points)
On the whole, how satisfied are you with the present state of the economy in Australia?	Scale 0–10 where 0 is extremely dissatisfied and 10 is extremely satisfied
Do you personally favour or oppose same sex couples being given the same rights to marry as couples consisting of a man and a woman?	Strongly favour – Strongly oppose (4 points)
Big business in this country has too much power	Strongly agree – Strongly disagree (5 points)
If you lost your job, how easy or difficult would it be to find another job in the next 12 months?	Very easy – Very difficult (4 points)
In your community these days, how easy is it for someone who is trying to find a job to get a good job at good wages?	Very easy – Very hard (4 points)

Part 2
Politics and political participation

4

Climate scepticism in Australia and in international perspective

Bruce Tranter

The 2016 *State of the Climate* report produced by the Bureau of Meteorology and CSIRO states that 'Global average annual carbon dioxide (CO_2) levels are steadily increasing' and that 'Australia's climate has warmed in both mean surface air temperature and surrounding sea surface temperature by around 1°C since 1910'. While the rate of planetary warming remains a topic of scientific interest, estimates of the proportion of climate scientists who agree that anthropogenic climate change is occurring range between 90 and 100 per cent (Powell 2015; Cook et al. 2013; Anderegg et al. 2010; Doran and Zimmerman 2009; Oreskes 2004). A recent survey of climate researchers found that 97 per cent of published climate scientists agreed global warming has mainly anthropogenic causes (Cook et al. 2016). In Australia, the Climate Institute (2016) found that 77 per cent of Australians believe that climate change is happening, a figure that has been steadily increasing from 64 per cent in 2012. The Climate Institute (2016) also found that 60 per cent of Australians agree with the statement, 'I trust in the science that suggests the climate is changing due to human activities' – again, an increase from 46 per cent in 2013.

However, a substantial minority of people in many countries, including Australia, appear to disagree with the scientific consensus over the veracity and implications of climate change (Tranter and Booth 2015), while many tend to 'overestimate the numbers of people who reject the existence of climate change' (Leviston et al. 2013, 334). Although the proportion who reject climate change outright is relatively small (as we will see below), sceptics comprise a disproportionately vocal minority of the population in many Western nations. Opponents of the scientific consensus tend to 'exaggerate the actual degree of uncertainty in the scientific community or imply that uncertainly justifies inaction' (Lewandowsky et al. 2015). Such approaches have been labelled 'scientific certainty argumentation methods' or SCAMs (Freudenburg et al. 2008).

While trust in climate science appears to be increasing (Climate Institute 2016), deep political divisions persist over the existence of climate change and the way that Australia should respond (Tranter 2011, 2013; Tranter and Booth 2015; Fielding et al 2012). The political divide in Australia in many ways resembles that in the United States (e.g. Wood and Vedlitz 2007; Jacques et al. 2008; McCright and Dunlap 2011; Hamilton 2011), where large differences of opinion over climate change are extant between Republicans and Democrats, with the former more likely to reject anthropogenic climate change. For example, Hamilton et al. (2015, 6) found that trust in climate science in the US 'is highest among Democrats and lowest among Tea Party supporters', while among American conservatives, trust in science has declined since the mid-1970s (Gauchat 2012), and climate change has become increasingly polarised politically (e.g. Kahan et al. 2012). Divisions over climate change are not due to different levels of general scientific knowledge among climate supporters and detractors (Kahan 2015). Rather, in the US (and I suspect also in Australia), political polarisation over scientific findings arises when issues challenge particular worldviews (such as valorising free markets), but is absent when they do not (Kahan 2015; Lewandowsky et al. 2016). When it comes to attitudes on climate change in the US, political polarisation actually increases with higher levels of self-reported knowledge and education (Hamilton 2011; Hamilton et al. 2015), with political conservatives less accepting of climate change as their education level and knowledge of climate change increases, while liberals become more accepting.

In Australia, the influence of political partisanship is also strong and reflects the cues of party leaders and the policy positions of the major parties (Tranter 2013). The Australian Greens and to a lesser extent the Australian Labor Party support stronger action on climate change, while the Liberal–National Coalition's 'Direct Action' policy aims to provide incentives for industry to reduce emissions, in order to meet the 2020 target of reducing emissions by 5 per cent below 2000 levels. The direct action policy replaces the previous Labor government's carbon pricing scheme, often referred to as the 'carbon tax'. The Coalition's direct action scheme has been criticised as ineffective. When Kumarasiri, Jubb and Houghton (2016) interviewed senior managers of 'carbon-intensive listed companies', they found 'Direct Action was not as effective as a carbon tax in driving companies to act urgently and manage emissions'.

Climate scepticism in Australia

While the aim in this chapter is to examine levels of climate scepticism, it is important to recognise that climate sceptics are not a homogenous group (Poortinga et al. 2011). Some reject the notion of anthropogenic climate change altogether, arguing that while the planet may be warming, climatic changes are natural fluctuations that have occurred for millennia. Matthews (2015, 158) suggest these 'strong sceptics' may also 'express the opinion that climate activists or climate scientists are in some way dishonest or fraudulent'. For Hobson and Niemeyer (2013) this outright rejection of climate science is an example of 'deep scepticism' while it has also attracted the label 'climate change denial' (e.g. Armitage 2005; Jacques et al. 2008; Dunlap and McCright 2010).

Other sceptics agree that anthropogenic climate change is occurring, but that the rate of warming is far slower than most climate scientists claim. For Matthews (2015, 157), these are 'lukewarmers', who 'accept that human emissions of carbon dioxide have warmed the planet significantly and will continue to do so in the future. However, they believe that the level of warming will be lower than that predicted by many climate scientists, and that the global warming scare has been exaggerated.' Matthews (2015, 158) also identifies 'moderate sceptics' who are 'characterised by views that warming of the climate is not a problem, that a large proportion of past warming is due to natural processes, that the threat posed by climate change has been greatly exaggerated . . .'

The term 'neosceptic' has also emerged to describe those who, while not outright sceptics, are nonetheless opposed to policy options to limit anthropogenic climate change

(Stern et al. 2016; Perkins 2015). Stern et al. (2016) found that climate change sceptics 'offered a changing set of arguments – denying or questioning ACC's [anthropogenic climate change] existence, magnitude, and rate of progress, the risks it presents, the integrity of climate scientists, and the value of mitigation efforts'. As McCright and Dunlap (2010, 111) argue in relation to climate scepticism in the US: 'Activists in the American conservative movement have obfuscated, mis-represented, manipulated and suppressed the results of climate science research'.

When provided with a list of 12 environmental concerns and asked how urgent these were for Australia, 63 per cent of respondents to the Australian Survey of Social Attitudes (AuSSA) 2013 rated climate change as urgent, well below issues such as marine conservation, the destruction of wildlife, waste disposal, pollution, soil degradation and the logging of forests (Blunsdon 2016a).[1] Yet, when asked to *rank* the same 12 environmental issues in terms of how much they worried people in the past 12 months, climate change emerged as *the most urgent* environmental issue (Tranter and Lester 2015). While climate change may be a major environmental concern to many Australians, how do their attitudes compare to the citizens of other advanced industrialised countries? In this chapter, survey data from the International Social Survey Program (ISSP) is examined so that the level of climate change scepticism among Australians can be compared to scepticism in other advanced industrialised countries. Data from AuSSA 2014 is then drawn upon to consider Australians' knowledge of climate change, and to determine important social, political and attitudinal correlates of climate scepticism in Australia.

Major influences on attitudes to climate change

In Australia, as in many other countries, climate change attitudes have been shown to be associated with various social characteristics. These include gender, age, education, and worldviews (e.g. McCright and Dunlap 2011a; Hamilton 2010; Whitmarsh 2011; Tranter 2011). In the US, McCright and Dunlap (2011b) have shown 'conservative white males' to be more likely than others to hold sceptical positions, while in the United Kingdom sceptics are more likely to be men, to be aged over 65, to be right-of-centre, and to hold individualistic worldviews (Whitmarsh 2011). Unlike the pattern of gender differences in general scientific knowledge (Hayes 2001), McCright (2010) found that women in the US have both higher knowledge of climate change, and are more concerned about it than men are, but that women are more likely than men to underestimate their knowledge. Having low trust in governments is also associated with climate scepticism (Lorenzoni and Pidgeon 2006; Dietz et al. 2007; Tranter and Booth 2015), while in Australia, people living in rural locations tend to view politicians, government and the media as untrustworthy sources on climate change (Buys et al. 2014).

Surprisingly, Lewandowsky and Oberauer (2016, 217) argue that 'General education and scientific literacy do not mitigate rejection of science, but, rather, increase the polarisation of opinions along partisan lines'. Sceptics are claimed to assimilate information on climate change in a biased manner, with Corner et al. (2012, 463) finding newspaper editorials are evaluated differently based upon whether people accept or reject anthropogenic climate

---

1   The other environmental issues were extreme weather events, biodiversity, mining, overpopulation and nuclear power.

change. Strong sceptical views on climate change also tend to become entrenched (Hobson and Niemeyer 2013), suggesting that such beliefs are not easily swayed by evidence presented by climate scientists. Although as Whitmarsh (2011, 699) found, while 'more information will not engage the most sceptical groups, since information will tend to be interpreted in relation to existing views, and entrenched views are very hard to change. For non-sceptical and ambivalent groups . . . climate change communication – which is currently characterised by an over-reliance on hype and alarmism – can be improved'.

Attitudes on climate change vary according to the competing worldviews and values that underpin them. As Lewandowsky and Oberauer (2016, 217) put it, 'People tend to reject findings that threaten their core beliefs or worldview'. In contrast to 'collectivists', 'individualistic' worldviews are associated with rejection of anthropogenic climate change and policies to attenuate its impacts, because of perceived restrictions such action would impose upon commerce and industry (Kahan et al. 2012). In a somewhat similar vein, McCright and Dunlap (2010) posit the 'anti-reflexivity thesis' – that is 'a perspective that attributes conservatives' (and Republicans') denial of anthropogenic climate change (ACC) and other environmental problems and attacks on climate/environmental science to their staunch commitment to protecting the current system of economic production' (Dunlap 2014). As McCright, Dentzman, Charters and Dietz (2013) put it, the 'Anti-Reflexivity Thesis expects that conservatives will report significantly less trust in, and support for, science that identifies environmental and public health impacts of economic production . . . than liberals.' In the analyses that follow, I assess the influence of political ideology and political partisanship upon knowledge of climate change and attitudes toward anthropogenic climate change in Australia.

Australian attitudes on climate change – recent national and comparative data

The main focus here is on climate change attitudes and climate scepticism in Australia. I first consider how sceptical of climate change Australians are compared to the citizens of 13 other advanced industrialised countries, then focus upon the Australian case, modelling different aspects of climate scepticism. In addition to developing a profile of the social and political background of climate sceptics, I evaluate the importance of the following as predictors of climate scepticism: respondent worldviews, value orientations, trust in government and interpersonal trust, and general concern about environmental issues.

The data analysed here are from two sources, the 2010 International Social Survey Programme's Environment Module (ISSP Research Group 2012), and the 2014 Australian Survey of Social Attitudes (AuSSA; Blunsdon 2016b). Few cross-national studies examine climate scepticism. One important reason for this is that cross-national examination of climate scepticism requires appropriate international survey data. The ISSP administered the third wave of their Environment Module surveys in 2010, and in that survey a question on climate change was included for the first time. The ISSP question is: 'In general, do you think that a rise in the world's temperature caused by climate change is . . . extremely dangerous for the environment, very dangerous, somewhat dangerous, not very dangerous, or, not dangerous at all for the environment?'

For the purpose of the analyses here, climate sceptics are defined as those who respond that climate change is not very dangerous, or not dangerous at all for the environment. The ISSP survey allows cross-national comparisons to be made on climate change, although the survey does not specifically refer to human-induced (anthropogenic) climate change.

Figure 4.1 Respondents who believe that climate change is 'not very dangerous', or 'not dangerous at all' for the environment, %.

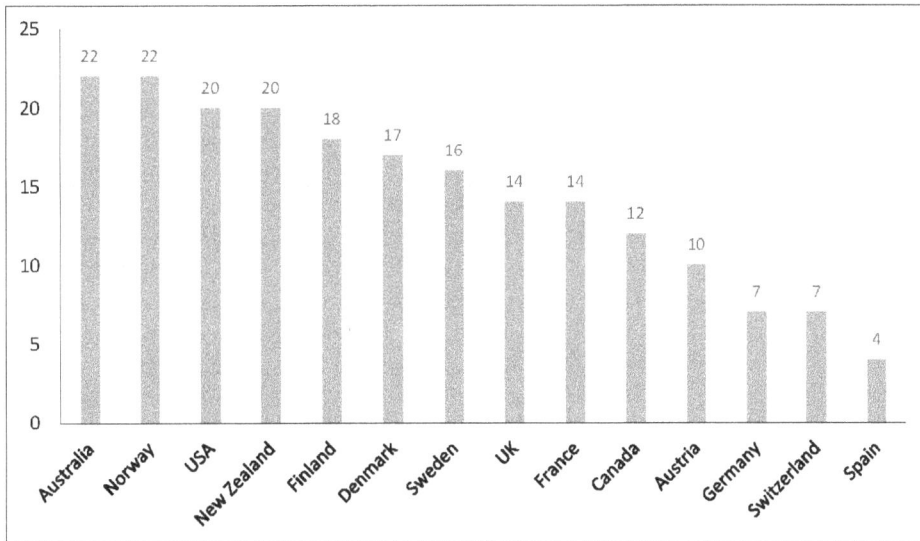

Source: International Social Survey Programme 2010.

Unfortunately, many surveys do not measure climate scepticism in a precise manner. For example, many do not refer to *anthropogenic* climate change, and as mentioned above, the vast majority of peer-reviewed climate scientists suggest that global climate change is mainly caused by anthropogenic global warming (Cook et al. 2016). The ISSP question is therefore an imprecise measure of the concept, but is a useful proxy measure of climate change for cross-national comparative purposes, because in everyday language 'climate change' tends to be associated with anthropogenic climate change. For a more detailed discussion of the ISSP questions see Tranter and Booth (2015).

Given the limitations of the ISSP data, I also examine items included in AuSSA 2014, that enable a more detailed examination of climate change attitudes. The AuSSA questions were designed specifically to measure attitudes to anthropogenic and non-anthropogenic climate change, and outright rejection of climate change, among a nationally representative sample of Australian adults.[2] Several questions from the AuSSA are used to examine climate change attitudes. The following first taps aspects of climate scepticism: 'Which of the following statements do you personally believe? 1. Climate change is happening now, and is caused mainly by human activities; 2. Climate change is happening now, but is caused mainly by natural forces; 3. Climate change is not happening now; 4. I don't know whether climate change is happening or not.'

_____

2   AuSSA 2014 is drawn from a national sample of Australian adults administered between May 2014 and February 2015. The 2014 survey was administered by mail in four waves to a systematically drawn sample of Australian adults aged 18 and above, achieving a response rate of 31 per cent (Blunsdon 2016b). The sampling frame was the Australian Electoral Roll, with analyses based upon a sample size of 1,435 cases.

AuSSA 2014 also contains a question that measures what respondents believe about the consensus position among scientists: 'Which of the following statements do you think is more accurate? 1. Most scientists agree that climate change is happening now, caused mainly by human activities. 2. There is little agreement among scientists that climate change is happening now, caused mainly by human activities.' The third question asks respondents about their knowledge of climate change: 'How much do you feel that you understand about climate change – would you say a great deal, a moderate amount, only a little, or nothing at all? 1. A great deal. 2. A moderate amount. 3. Only a little. 4. Nothing at all.'

The advantage of the AuSSA questions is that they clearly distinguish between the consensus position of climate scientists (i.e. that climate change is mainly anthropogenic), and two sceptical positions: outright rejection of climate change, and a rejection of the scientific consensus in favour of climate change that is naturally occurring. The AuSSA questions replicate survey items administered by Hamilton (2011) and Hamilton et al. (2015) in the US and therefore facilitate a comparison of attitudes in the two countries, as US data on these questions were also collected in 2014. In the next section I examine how Australia sits relative to other countries on climate scepticism, and consider how social background and other potential predictors are associated with sceptical climate change attitudes, before focusing more closely upon analysing climate scepticism in the Australian case.

Australian climate scepticism in comparative perspective

The ISSP results in Figure 4.1 show the responses of Australians and the citizens of 13 other countries on the dangers of climate change for the environment. Based upon these results, the proportion of Australians who *do not* see climate change as dangerous for the environment is 22 per cent, equal with Norway and a slightly larger proportion than that for New Zealanders and Americans. While Australians and Norwegians are very sceptical of climate change relative to other advanced countries, scepticism is relatively low among the citizens of Spain, Germany, Switzerland and Austria. These results situate Australia internationally, but we can learn more about the cross-national profile of climate sceptics by exploring their socio-demographic and political backgrounds. For example, to what extent does gender or political party allegiance shape the climate change attitudes of Australians compared to those of the citizens of other advanced countries?

Several predictors of sceptical attitudes have been operationalised drawing upon the social science literature on climate change. Table 4.1 shows the results of regression analyses (expressed as odds ratios)[3] for the 14 ISSP countries, modelling the social and political background of those who not believe that a rise in the world's temperature caused by climate change is dangerous for the environment. In other words, these results allow a comparison of the background characteristics and attitudinal dispositions of 'climate sceptics' across the 14 countries.

---

3   Odds ratios that are larger than 1 suggest the presence of a positive association between the independent and dependent variables. Odds less than 1 suggest the relationship is negative. For example, in Table 4.1, the odds for Australian men are 1.5 times that of women, and are significant at p < .01. This suggests that men are more sceptical than women that rising temperatures are dangerous for the environment.

Table 4.1: Climate change sceptics in international perspective (odds ratios).

	Australia	Austria	Canada	Denmark	Finland	France	Germany	NZ	Norway	Spain	Sweden	Switz.	UK	USA
Men	1.5**	1.5	1.5	1.7**	1.9***	1.3	1.2	1.6*	1.5*	1.8**	2.4***	1.7*	1.6*	1.1
Aged 65+	1.3*	1.3	0.93	1.6*	2.1***	1.2	1.3	1.9***	1.4	1.5	1.2	1.3	1.3	1.1
Degree	0.6***	1.4	1.1	0.7	0.8	0.8	1.2	0.8	0.6*	1.4	0.6*	1.1	0.5*	1.1
Live in large city	0.7*	0.8	0.9	0.7	0.8	1.01	1.1	1.2	0.7*	0.8	0.5*	0.9	0.4	1.1
Non-religious	0.8	0.7	1.4	1.1	1.4	1.1	1.6*	1.3	1.2	1.4	0.8	1.1	0.9	0.6*
Postmaterial (+ Post)	1.07	0.79	0.82	0.93	0.84	1.04	1.13	0.95	1.02	1.32	1.04	1.06	0.91	1.55**
Party left–right (+ right)	1.87***	1.14	1.85***	1.69***	1.37*	1.12	1.39*	1.54***	1.63***	1.22	1.22	0.99	1.51**	1.70***
Distrusts government	1.3*	0.6*	1.5	1.3	1.6**	1.3	1.2	1.4*	1.5*	1.6*	1.6	1.1	1.7*	1.5*
Science solves envir. probs.	0.98	0.99	1.3	1.1	1.4	1.5*	0.9	1.3	1.2	1.1	1.6	0.7	0.9	1.5*
Unconcerned about envir.	4.7***	2.7***	8.4***	1.5*	4.6***	2.2***	2.3**	3.7***	5.1***	2.3***	6.0***	3.9***	7.9***	3.9***
Solution to envir. problems	1.7	1.1	0.56	0.8	1.4*	0.9	0.99	1.4*	0.8	0.5	0.98	1.2	0.98	1.02
Private enterprise	1.5**	1.5	1.1	1.5*	1.2	1.5**	1.2	1.4*	1.3	1.5	1.1	1.7*	1.04	2.6***
Reduce income inequality	0.6***	1.03	0.7	0.9	1.04	0.7**	0.6*	0.7*	0.9	0.5**	0.9	0.99	1.1	0.4***
Nagelkerke R²	.25	.09	.19	.13	.17	.06	.05	.16	.24	.08	.24	.07	.24	.27
N	1,841	971	945	1,160	1,141	2,119	1,323	1,092	1,291	2,416	1,086	1,191	847	1,325

Source: ISSP 2010.

Notes: * p< .05; ** p< .01 *** p< .001. Dependent variable 'Climate Change Sceptics' =0; or 1 if 'a rise in the world's temperature caused by climate change is
. . . not dangerous or not dangerous at all for the environment'.

Comparing each independent variable (i.e. each row) across the countries, it is apparent that certain variables have a consistent and statistically significant influence on scepticism (at 95 per cent confidence). Men are more likely than women are to be sceptical about a dangerously warming climate in nine of the 14 countries, including Australia. Age is a less consistent predictor, but where the results are statistically significant, older people tend to be more sceptical than their younger counterparts. However, age is only a notable correlate for results in Australia, Denmark, Finland, and New Zealand. Tertiary educated people are *less likely* than others to be sceptical of a warming climate, but once again, this only holds for Australia and three other countries.

Postmaterial values also predict environmental concern in Western countries (Inglehart and Welzel 2005). Postmaterialists tend to prioritise quality of life issues such as the environment, to a greater extent than materialists. The latter are more likely to be concerned with economic growth and national security (Inglehart and Welzel 2005). In general, we might expect postmaterialists to be less sceptical than materialists. However, as can be seen in Table 4.1, this measure has no impact upon climate scepticism with the exception of the US, where postmaterialists are actually *more sceptical* than materialists.

A far more consistent predictor is the party left–right variable. The ISSP researchers placed respondents on a left–right scale based upon expert classification of the political party they identified with. As previous studies found in countries such as the US and Australia (e.g. McCright and Dunlap 2011a, Tranter 2011), the results show that supporters of right-wing parties are far more likely than left party supporters to be climate sceptics in nine countries. The size of the odds ratios shown in Table 4.1 suggests that the impact of the left–right scale is even stronger for Australia than the US. Low trust in government is added as a potential predictor of scepticism (Lorenzoni and Pidgeon 2006, 85). The question asks '[M]ost of the time we can trust people in government to do what is right'. Agree and Strongly agree responses are contrasted with other responses. Having low trust in government is associated with scepticism in eight countries, although Austrians who distrust government are the exception here, as they are *less* likely to be sceptical of climate change.

Another measure included in the models in Table 4.1 are beliefs in the power of scientific solutions to environmental problems. This variable measures agreement or strong agreement with the statement 'Modern science will solve our environmental problems with little change to our way of life'. Higher confidence in scientific answers to environmental problems was expected to be associated with lower climate scepticism, but has minimal impact in these results. The item 'How much do you feel you know about *solutions* to these sorts of environmental problems?' serves as a measure of self-assessed knowledge of environmental problems. The 5-point response scale ranges from 'Know nothing at all' (1) to 'Know a great deal' (5). High knowledge is measured here as answering 4 and 5 on the scale, yet once again, it is not an important predictor of climate scepticism. Higher knowledge is modelled with the expectation that understanding how to solve environmental problems should be associated with less concern about climate change. However, the results for this variable are inconclusive, with only two countries showing statistically significant results.

Two indicators from the ISSP data are also included in the models in Table 4.1 as proxies for citizen 'worldviews' (Kahan et al. 2012). These are 'Private enterprise is the best way to solve [country's] economic problems' and 'It is the responsibility of the government to reduce the differences in income between people with high incomes and those with

Figure 4.2 Australian views about the causes of climate change, %.

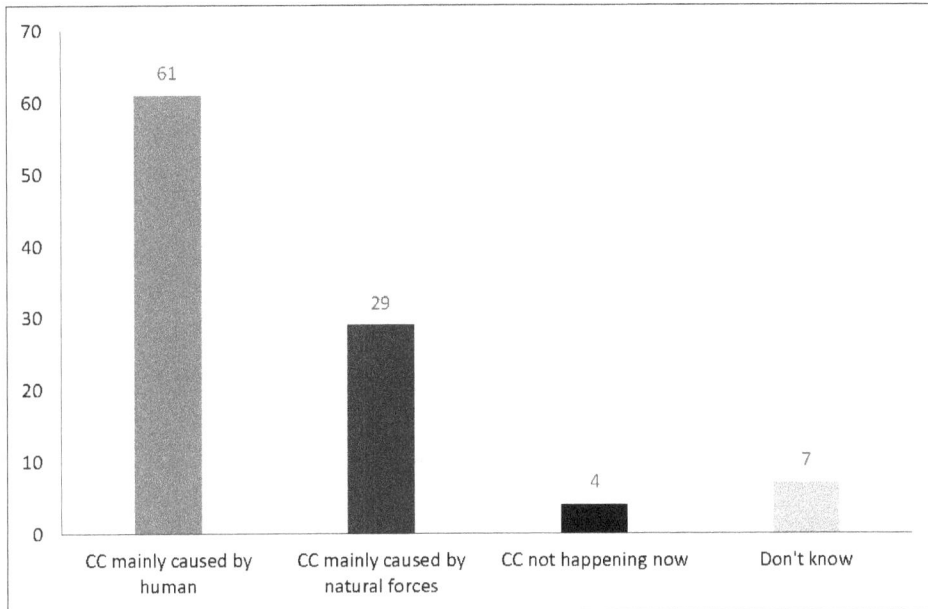

N=1,435. Source: Australian Survey of Social Attitudes (AuSSA) 2014.

low incomes' (5-point scales from Strongly agree to Strongly disagree). Strong agreement and agreement are contrasted with other responses for each question. The expectation is that 'individualistic' worldviews (i.e. those who disagree with governments redistributing income) and those who believe in the importance of private enterprise should be more sceptical than others. The results provide some evidence that 'individualists' are more sceptical than 'collectivists' on climate change among six of the 14 countries for each measure.

Low concern for environmental issues has been found to predict environmental scepticism (Engels et al. 2013). Environment concern is derived from the question 'Generally speaking, how concerned are you about environmental issues?' (Responses: 1=Not at all concerned to 5=Very concerned), with low levels of concern represented by response options 1 and 2 on the scale. In fact, being unconcerned about the environment is by far the most consistent and strongest correlate of climate scepticism. Low environmental concern is aligned with climate scepticism in all 14 countries, even after statistically adjusting for social and political background and other factors modelled here. While this finding does not necessarily mean that climate sceptics are also anti-environmentalists (Tranter and Booth 2015), this consistent cross-national finding is certainly worthy of further research.

Figure 4.3 Australian attitudes about the degree of scientific consensus about climate change, %.

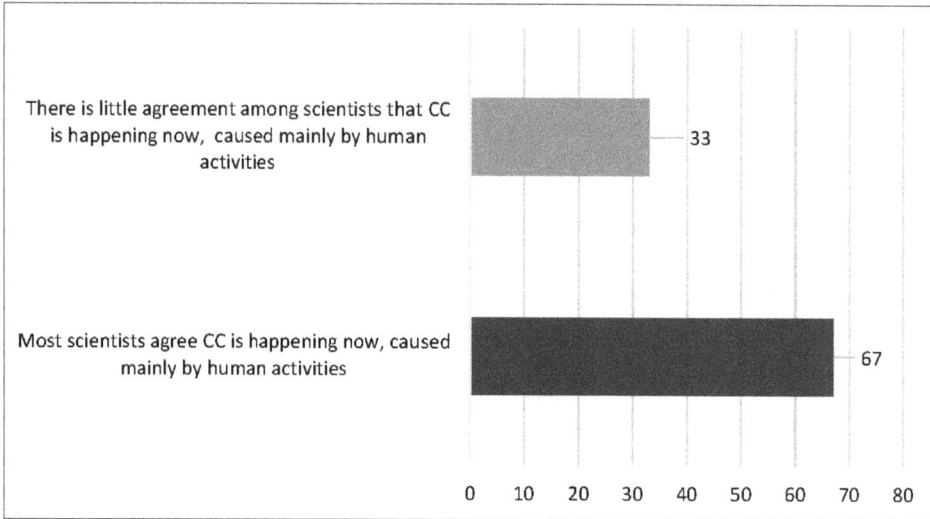

N=1,435. Source: AuSSA 2014.

Exploring climate scepticism among Australians

While the ISSP data are somewhat limited for modelling the complexity of climate change scepticism, data from the AuSSA 2014 enable a more detailed analysis of climate change attitudes among Australian adults. According to AuSSA, 61 per cent of Australians believe that climate change is occurring and is mainly caused by human activities, while 29 per cent believe climate change is happening, but is caused mainly by 'natural forces' (Figure 4.2). Only a very small minority of Australians completely reject the notion of climate change (4 per cent) while the remaining 7 per cent claim that they don't know whether it is happening or not. The Australian results can be compared with data from the US based upon the same survey question in 2014. Hamilton et al. (2015) found that 53 per cent of Americans believe in anthropogenic climate change (even less than the 61 per cent of Australians), although the proportion of Americans claiming climate change to be 'natural' was very close to the Australian estimate at 31 per cent (Hamilton et al. 2015).

Figure 4.3 shows that two thirds of Australians believe most scientists agree that climate change is happening now, and has mainly anthropogenic causes. This still leaves a large minority who are unaware of the consensus position of climate scientists (Cook et al. 2016). However, if researchers such as Cook and Lewandowsky (2016) are correct, such responses are not necessarily irrational rejections of the scientific consensus.

To what extent do social and political background characteristics differentiate climate change attitudes in Australia? To model these associations, regression analysis is again used to examine several dependent variables in Tables 4.2 and 4.3. Table 4.2 models the background characteristics and political orientations of self-assessed knowledge of climate change, while in Table 4.3, three outcomes are considered. Those who reject climate change outright are compared to all other responses, then Australians who believe that climate

Table 4.2: Self-assessed knowledge of climate change.

Social background	(odds ratios)
Men	1.9***
Aged 65+	1.4*
Degree	1.8***
Live in large city	0.98
Attitudes	
Non-trusting of government	1.2
Non-trusting of people	1.1
News from . . .	
Commercial TV/radio	0.6***
Newspapers	0.6***
Political orientations	
Left–right (0–10)	0.97
Coalition party ID	0.6**
No party ID	0.5***
Nagelkerke R^2	0.12
N	1,341

Source: AuSSA 2014.
Notes: * p< .05; ** p< .01 *** p< .001.

change has mainly natural causes are compared with people who accept that climate change is mainly human-induced. The third dependent variable in Table 4.3 models Australians' views of scientific agreement on anthropogenic climate change.

Turning first to the results in Table 4.2, it is clear that men are more likely than women to claim higher knowledge of climate change in Australia. This is consistent with McCright (2010), who found women more likely than men to understate their knowledge of climate change, although this hypothesis cannot be directly assessed because actual measures of climate change knowledge were not included in AuSSA 2014. However, the gender, age and education findings here are similar to those found using quiz questions on political processes and institutions (McAllister 1998; Tranter 2007). Given that climate change is a highly politicised issue in Australia, it is likely to be an aspect of 'political knowledge' more generally. Neither trust in government nor interpersonal trust have an impact on self-assessed climate knowledge. However, accessing news from commercial sources is associated with lower levels of knowledge, as is Coalition party identification. The politically non-aligned are also less knowledgeable on climate change than Greens or Labor identifiers, or at least they believe they are less knowledgeable.

Given that only a small proportion of respondents completely reject the notion of climate change, the resulting sub-sample is small and only strong associations are statistically significant at the 95 per cent level for the first dependent variable (Table 4.3). Those who claim to know 'nothing at all' about climate change are far more likely to claim that it is not occurring at all. Source of news is again a factor here, with reliance upon commercial TV or radio news associated with complete rejection of climate change. Identifying with the Liberal–National Coalition parties, or having no party affiliation, is also associated with outright rejection of climate change.

People who tend to reject climate change outright are unlikely to have their views swayed on the subject, even in the face of evidence from expert sources. Hobson and Niemeyer (2013, 408) found 'public climate change communication strategies or interventions can unintentionally alienate such individuals further'. Given that only 4 per cent of the AuSSA sample claim climate change is not occurring, arguably of far greater importance is the relatively large proportion of people who believe that climate change is occurring due to 'natural forces'. Some researchers suggest that such views may be shifted by the presentation of scientific evidence (e.g. Hobson and Niemeyer 2013) or exposure to the consensus view of climate scientists (e.g. Lewandowsky and Oberauer 2016). The relatively large proportion of Australians who agree that climate change is occurring mainly because of 'natural forces' is therefore more interesting from a policy perspective, as citizens with such views, at least in principle, may be more likely to shift with the provision of information or cues from political leaders (Tranter 2013).

Coalition identifiers are four times as likely as Labor and Greens party identifiers to believe in 'natural climate change'. These strong partisan results suggest that if, for example, bipartisan agreement could be reached among political leaders over appropriate approaches to addressing climate change at some time in the future, partisan attitudes may also shift. However, in practice this seems rather unlikely in the present political climate. Close to bipartisan agreement on climate change was reached in 2009 when then leader of the opposition, Malcolm Turnbull, supported then prime minister Kevin Rudd over a carbon pollution reduction scheme. Yet bipartisanship on this issue was instrumental in Turnbull's demise as leader of the Liberal Party in December 2009. This rejection of a climate change progressive reflected not only the position of elected Liberal Party members, but a larger conservative constituency who were opposed to such action on climate change. The current, politically pragmatic approach adopted by Turnbull as prime minister (i.e. having no truck with carbon taxes or emissions trading schemes) suggests that the attitudes of conservative Australians on this issue may be difficult to sway.

Believing that climate change has mainly 'natural' as opposed to anthropogenic causes is also quite strongly socially anchored. Australian men are more likely than women to be believe in natural causes, as are older Australians. Tertiary education is also a factor, with graduates more likely than non-graduates to believe in anthropogenic climate change. Unlike the ISSP results discussed above, or some previous research findings (e.g. Lorenzoni and Pidgeon 2006; Dietz et al. 2007), trust, or lack of trust in *government*, does not tend to predict climate change attitudes for these more nuanced questions. However, interpersonal or generalised trust in others does – those who have little trust in others are around twice as likely to believe in natural, rather than anthropogenic, causes.

The source of one's news is also a potential influence on climate change attitudes. People who mainly source their news from commercial television or radio, or newspapers, are far more likely to believe in natural rather than anthropogenic climate change. This to an extent reflects the influence of conservative elements of the Australian press. Those who believe that climate change is either not occurring at all, or that it is not caused by anthropogenic influences, may well gravitate to news outlets whose editors and journalists espouse similarly sceptical views. Bacon (2013) found that Australian newspapers such as the *Herald Sun* (Melbourne), the *Daily Telegraph* (Sydney) and the *Advertiser* (Adelaide) that

Table 4.3: What predicts climate scepticism among Australians? (odds ratios).

	No climate change	Natural CC vs ACC	Scientists do not agree on ACC
Social background			
Men	1.8	1.6***	1.2
Aged 65+	1.1	1.7***	1.7***
Degree	0.6	0.6**	0.7*
Live in large city	0.5	0.6	0.8
Attitudes			
Low self-assessed knowledge of CC	5.6**	0.99	3.9***
Non-trusting of government	2.2	0.8	0.96
Non-trusting of people	1.3	2.4**	1.5
News from . . .			
Commercial TV/radio	2.2*	1.9***	1.7***
Newspapers	1.6	2.1***	1.6*
Political orientations			
Left–right (0–10)	1.06	1.16***	1.15***
Coalition party ID	13.7***	4.0***	3.9***
No party ID	5.0*	1.7**	2.1***
Nagelkerke R^2	0.19	0.27	0.24
N	1,323	1,188	1,314

Source: AuSSA 2014.
Notes: * $p < .05$; ** $p < .01$; *** $p < .001$. CC refers to climate change. ACC is anthropogenic climate change.

are owned by or are subsidiaries of News Corp are most likely to 'reject' or 'express doubt' about anthropogenic climate change. Finally, in addition to the influence of Coalition party identification, a separate effect is apparent for political ideology: self-locating on the right of the political spectrum is linked to believing in natural climate change.

Comparing the impact of the independent variables upon the three dependent variables, several similarities in the direction and sizes of the effects are extant. However, one important difference is self-assessed knowledge of climate change. Low knowledge is an important predictor of rejecting climate change outright, and for the climate science dependent variable, but does not differentiate anthropogenic from 'natural' attitudes toward climate change. Based on these results, it seems that some Australians are comfortable in rejecting the science on climate change, while simultaneously acknowledging that they know 'nothing at all' about climate change.

Making sense of the climate scepticism of Australians

Australians are among the most climate sceptical of people living in advanced industrialised countries. As climate sceptics, they rank alongside Norwegians, Americans, and New Zealanders. In terms of political divisions, Australians are somewhat similar to Americans when it comes to climate scepticism. Like citizens of the US (e.g. McCright and Dunlap 2011, 2011a; Wood and Vedlitz 2007), attitudes toward climate change are deeply divided by party allegiances in Australia (Tranter 2011; Fielding et al. 2012), with National and Liberal party identifiers far more sceptical of anthropogenic climate change than Greens and Labor partisans. The politically unaligned also tend to be climate sceptics when compared to parties of the left or centre-left. This is important, as these non-partisans comprise a large proportion of Australians, around 36 per cent according to the results of AuSSA 2014. The politically unaligned seem closer to political conservatives on climate change. Like swinging voters, non-partisans may be influenced by either side of the climate debate, rather than tending to follow the cues offered by party leaders (Tranter 2013). Based on their own assessment, the politically non-aligned are less knowledgeable of climate change than those who identify with political parties, and as I have found in other analyses (not shown here), they tend to be younger than average, a known correlate of lower political knowledge (McAllister 1998; Tranter 2007). They are also located at the centre of the left–right ideology scale, while the strongest climate sceptics tend to be located on the right of the political spectrum. These factors, coupled with their lower knowledge of climate change, suggest that the views of non-partisans are not entrenched and their attitudes on climate change may potentially shift with greater knowledge of climate science.

AuSSA 2014 shows that only about 4 per cent of Australians completely reject the notion that climate change is occurring, while 29 per cent believe it is occurring but has natural causes and 7 per cent 'don't know' if it is happening or not. A majority (61 per cent) believe that anthropogenic climate change is happening, which is also the consensus position of peer-reviewed climate scientists (Cook et al. 2016). Yet one third of Australians believe there is little agreement among scientists about the anthropogenic causes of climate change. One interpretation of the latter finding is that such people are simply misinformed, unaware of 'state of the art' climate science. However, several researchers have found that when people approach highly politicised issues such as climate change, they do so through a perceptual screen mediated by their worldviews (e.g. Kahan 2015; Lewandowsky and Oberauer 2016). It may not be lack of scientific knowledge that leads many Australians to either reject anthropogenic climate change or believe that climate change is a mainly natural phenomenon (Kahan 2015), but that the implications of acting on such issues conflict with deeply held worldviews.

As Lewandowsky and Oberauer (2016) argue, rejection of science does not necessarily occur in an irrational manner; rather, it involves a process they refer to as 'rational denial'. For example, given the current state of development of renewable power sources, reducing CO_2 emissions by imposing a carbon tax, or an emissions trading scheme on high greenhouse gas emitters (or more radically, closing coal-fired power plants) would likely drive up the cost of energy, which would not only impact upon power prices for public consumers, but also create an impost upon businesses, in turn impeding economic growth. For those who place a high value upon the free market, the imposition of government regulations to achieve lower emissions is in direct conflict with their worldviews. While one may understand the findings of climate scientists, the implication of taking action to reduce climate change can cause cognitive dissonance that results in reduced trust in climate scientists (Lewandowsky and Oberauer 2016). Cook and Lewandowsky (2016 in Lewandowsky and Oberauer 2016, 4) found that 'participants who strongly supported free market economics lowered their acceptance of human-caused global warming in response to information about the climate consensus … people adjusted their trust in climate scientists downward, thereby not only avoiding an adjustment of their belief in the science but also safe-guarding their endorsement of free-market economics'.

In addition to political divisions, scepticism tends to be higher among Australian men than among women, a case resembling the 'conservative white male' effect in the US (McCright and Dunlap 2011b). The similarities with the US do not end there. For example, both countries have a substantial conservative mass media hostile to the consensus position on climate science. In the US, right-wing talkback radio and Rupert Murdoch-owned media outlets such as FOX News 'consistently denigrate climate change … providing frequent opportunities for contrarian scientists and CTT representative to disparage climate change, the IPCC, and climate scientists' (Dunlap and McCright 2011, 152). The editorial pages of newspapers such as the *Wall Street Journal* feature 'a regular forum for climate change denial' (Dunlap and McCright 2011, 152).

In Australia, a somewhat similar situation exists where climate sceptics are given greater media coverage relative to the consensus position of climate scientists in certain media, for example Murdoch's News Corp-owned television, and commercial radio stations (Bacon 2013). The results presented in this chapter are supportive of such claims. Compared to those who favour public broadcasters (i.e. the Australian Broadcasting Corporation and the Special Broadcasting Service), Australians who rely upon commercial TV or commercial radio for their news and information tend to reject climate change outright, to be more sceptical of the consensus position of climate scientists, or to believe that climate change has natural causes.

Changing the attitudes of at least some sceptical Australians on climate change is a precursor to changing behaviour and will provide an impetus for changes to government policy toward stronger action to reduce greenhouse gas emissions. This brings us to the importance of a bipartisan political stance on climate change (Donald 2017). Political agreement between the major parties is a necessary, although perhaps not sufficient condition for real change to occur. Bipartisanship needs to be accompanied by dissemination of climate science research in a way that reflects the consensus position of climate scientists who publish research in peer-reviewed journals, rather than over-representing the numerically small but extremely vocal opinions of climate sceptics who are so prominent in right-wing media (e.g. McCright and Dunlap 2011; Bacon 2013).

In experimental research, Ranney and Clark (2016) found that explaining how the greenhouse effect operates increases acceptance of climate science across the political divide. Cook and Lewandowsky (2016, 160) also found that 'among Australians, consensus information partially neutralized the influence of worldview, with free-market supporters showing a greater increase in acceptance of human-caused global warming relative to free-market opponents'. However, importantly, the climate change message needs to be framed in a way that is compatible with the views of political and economic conservatives, yet in a way that does not challenge or conflict with their more sceptical worldviews (Kahan 2015). For example, by highlighting the economic opportunities that will accompany the growth of the renewable energy sector if this sector is encouraged to grow. These should be seen as challenges to be overcome, rather than insurmountable obstacles. The alternative, continuing on the path of inadequate action, moving too slowly to address *the* most important global problem, will see our wide brown land and 'bronzed Aussies' turn into burnt offerings on the BBQ of climate change, an outcome that Direct Action policies and even Slip, Slop, Slap will prove ineffective to prevent.

References

Anderegg, William, James Prall, Jacob Harold and Stephen Schneider (2010). Expert credibility in climate change. *Proceedings of the National Academy of Sciences of the United States of America* 107(27), 12107–2109. doi: 10.1073/pnas.1003187107.

Armitage, Kevin C. (2005). State of denial: the United States and the politics of global warming. *Globalisations* 2(3), 417–27.

Bacon, Wendy (2013). *Sceptical climate part 2: climate science in Australian newspapers.* Australian Centre for Independent Journalism. https://www.uts.edu.au/sites/default/files/Sceptical-Climate-Part-2-Climate-Science-in-Australian-Newspapers.pdf.

Blunsdon, Betsy (2016a). *Australian survey of social attitudes, 2013.* Canberra: Australian Data Archive, Australian National University.

Blunsdon, Betsy (2016b). *Australian survey of social attitudes, 2014.* Canberra: Australian Data Archive, Australian National University.

Buys, L., R. Aird, K. van Megen, E. Miller and J. Sommerfeld (2014). Perceptions of climate change and trust in information providers in rural Australia. *Public Understanding of Science* 23(2): 170–88.

Climate Institute (2016). *Climate of the nation 2016: Australian attitudes on climate change.* http://www.climateinstitute.org.au/articles/publications/con-2016-report-page.html/section/478.

Cook, John and Stephan Lewandowsy (2016). Rational irrationality: Modeling climate change belief polarization using Bayesian networks. *Topics in Cognitive Science* 8, 160–79.

Cook, John, Naomi Oreskes, Peter Doran, William Anderegg, Bart Verheggen, Ed Maibach, J. Stuart Carlton, Stephan Lewandowsky, Andrew Skuce, Sarah Green, Dana Nuccitelli, Peter Jacobs, Mark Richardson, Bärbel Winkler, Rob Painting and Ken Rice (2016). Consensus on consensus: a synthesis of consensus estimates on human-caused global warming. *Environmental Research Letters* 11. doi:10.1088/1748-9326/11/4/048002.

Cook, John, Dana Nuccitelli, Sarah Green, Mark Richardson, Bärbel Winkler, Rob Painting, Robert Way, Peter Jacobs and Andrew Skuce (2013). Quantifying the consensus on anthropogenic global warming in the scientific literature. *Environmental Research Letters* 8(2). doi:10.1088/1748-9326/8/2/024024.

Corner, Adam, Lorraine Whitmarsh and Dimitrios Xenias, D. (2012). Uncertainty, scepticism and attitudes towards climate change: Biased assimilation and attitude polarisation. *Climatic Change* 114, 463–78.

CSIRO and Bureau of Meteorology (2016). *State of the Climate.* http://www.csiro.au/en/SOTC-2016.

Dietz, Thomas, Amy Dan and Rachael Shwom (2007). Support for climate change policy: social psychological and social structural influences. *Rural Sociology* 72(2), 185–214.

Donald, Peta (2017). Industry, environment, community groups demand bipartisan energy policy. *ABC News,* 13 February. http://www.abc.net.au/news/2017-02-13/industry-groups-demand-bipartisan-energy-policy/8263928.

Doran, Peter and Maggie Zimmerman (2009). Examining the scientific consensus on climate change. *EOS* 90(3), 22–23.

Dunlap, Riley (2014). Clarifying anti-reflexivity: conservative opposition to impact science and scientific evidence. *Environmental Research Letters* 9. doi:10.1088/1748-9326/9/2/021001.

Dunlap, Riley and Aaron McCright (2011). Organized climate change denial. In *The Oxford handbook of climate change and society*. J. Dryzek, R. Nrgoaard, R. and D. Schlosberg, eds. New York: Oxford University Press.

Engels, Anita, Otto Hüther, Mike Schäfer and Hermann Held (2013). Public climate-change scepticism, energy preferences and political participation. *Global Environmental Change* 23, 1018–27.

Fielding, Kelly, Brian Head, Warren Laffan, Mark Western and Ove Hoegh-Guldberg (2012). Australian politicians' beliefs about climate change: political partisanship and political ideology. *Environmental Politics* 21(5), 712–33.

Freudenburg, William, Robert Gramling and Debra Davidson (2008). Scientific certainty argumentation methods (SCAMs): science and the politics of doubt. *Sociological Inquiry* 78(1), 2–38.

Gauchat, Gordon (2012). Politicization of science in the public sphere: a study of public trust in the United States, 1974 to 2010. *American Sociological Review* 77(2), 167–87.

Hamilton, Lawrence (2011). Do you believe the climate is changing? *Carsey Institute Issue Brief No. 40*. Durham: University of New Hampshire.

Hamilton, Lawrence (2010). Education, politics and opinions about climate change: evidence for interaction effects. *Climatic Change* 104(2), 231–42. doi: 10.1007/s10584-010-9957-8.

Hamilton, Lawrence C., Joel Hartter, Mary Lemcke-Stampone, David W. Moore and Thomas G. Safford (2015). Tracking public beliefs about anthropogenic climate change. *PLOS One* 10(9): e0138208. https://doi.org/10.1371/journal.pone.0138208.

Hayes, Bernadette C. (2001). Gender, scientific knowledge, and attitudes toward the environment. *Political Research Quarterly* 54(3), 657–71.

Hobson, Kersty and Simon Niemeyer (2013). What sceptics believe: the effects of information and deliberation on climate change scepticism. *Public Understanding of Science* 22(4), 396–41.

Inglehart, Ronald and Christian Welzel (2005). *Modernization, cultural change and democracy: The human development sequence,* New York: Cambridge University Press.

ISSP Research Group (2012). International Social Survey Programme: Environment III–ISSP 2010. GESIS Data Archive, Cologne. ZA5500 data file version 2.0.0. doi: 10.4232/1.11418.

Jacques, Peter, Riley Dunlap and Mark Freeman (2008). The organisation of denial: conservative think tanks and environmental scepticism. *Environmental Politics* 17(3), 349–85.

Kahan, Dan (2015). Climate science communication and the measurement problem. *Political Psychology* 32, 1–43.

Kahan, Dan, Ellen Peters, Maggie Wittlin, Paul Slovic, Lisa Ouellette, Donald Braman and Gregory Mandel (2012). The polarizing impact of science literacy and numeracy on perceived climate change risks. *Nature Climate Change* 2, 732–35.

Kumarasiri, Jayanthi, Christine Jubb and Keith Houghton (2016). Direct action not as motivating as carbon tax say some of Australia's biggest emitters. *The Conversation*. https://theconversation.com/direct-action-not-as-motivating-as-carbon-tax-say-some-of-australias-biggest-emitters-64562.

Leviston, Zoe, Iain Walker and Morwinski, S. (2013). Your opinion on climate change might not be as common as you think. *Nature Climate Change* 3, 334–37.

Lewandowsky, Stephan and Klaus Oberauer (2016). Motivated rejection of science. *Current Directions in Psychological Science* 25(4), 217–22.

Lewandowsky, Stephan, Naomi Oreskes, James Risbey, Ben Newell and Michael Smithson (2015). Seepage: Climate change denial and its effect on the scientific community. *Global Environmental Change* 33, 1–13.

Lorenzoni, Irene and Nick Pidgeon (2006). Public views on climate change: European and USA perspectives. *Climatic Change* 77(1–2), 73–95.

Matthews, Paul (2015). Why are people skeptical about climate change? Some insights from blog comments. *Environmental Communication* 9(2), 153–68.

McAllister, Ian (1998). Civic education and political knowledge in Australia. *Australian Journal of Political Science* 33(1), 7–23.

McCright, Aaron (2010). The effects of gender on climate change knowledge and concern in the American public. *Population and Environment* 32(1), 66–87.

McCright, Aaron, Katherine Dentzman, Meghan Charters and Thomas Dietz (2013). The influence of political ideology on trust in science. *Environmental Research Letters* 8. doi:10.1088/1748-9326/8/4/044029.

McCright, Aaron and Riley Dunlap (2010). Anti-reflexivity. The American conservative movement's success in undermining climate science and policy. *Theory, Culture & Society* 27(2–3), 100–33.

McCright, Aaron and Riley Dunlap (2011a). The politicization of climate change and polarization in the American public's views of global warming, 2001–2010. *The Sociological Quarterly* 52, 155–94.

McCright, Aaron and Riley Dunlap (2011b). Cool dudes: the denial of climate change among conservative white males in the United States. *Global Environmental Change* 21(4), 1163–72.

Oreskes, Naomi (2004). The scientific consensus on climate change. *Science* 306(5702), 1686.

Perkins, John (2015). Mitigation measures: Beware climate neo-scepticism. *Nature* 522(287). doi:10.1038/522287c.

Poortinga, Wouter, Alexa Spence, Lorraine Whitmarsh, Stuart Capstick and Nick Pidgeon (2011). Uncertain climate: an investigation into public scepticism about anthropocentric climate change. *Global Environmental Change* 21, 1015–24.

Powell, James (2015). The consensus on human-caused global warming. *Skeptical Inquirer* 39: 42.

Ranney, Michael and Dav Clark (2016). Climate change conceptual change: scientific information can transform attitudes. *Topics in Cognitive Science* 8(1), 49–75.

Stern, Paul, John Perkins, Richard Sparks and Robert Knox (2016). The challenge of climate-change neoskepticism. *Science* 353(6300), 653–54.

Tranter, Bruce (2007). Political knowledge and its partisan consequences. *Australian Journal of Political Science* 42(1), 73–88.

Tranter, Bruce (2011). Political divisions over climate change. *Environmental Politics* 20(1), 78–96.

Tranter, Bruce (2013). The great divide: political candidate and voter polarisation over global warming in Australia. *Australian Journal of Politics and History* 59(3), 397–413.

Tranter, Bruce and Kate Booth (2015). Scepticism in a changing climate: a cross-national study. *Global Environmental Change* 33, 154–64.

Tranter, Bruce and Libby Lester (2015). Climate patriots? Concern over climate change and other environmental issues in Australia. *Public Understanding of Science*. doi: 10.1177/0963662515618553.

Whitmarsh, Lorraine (2011). Scepticism and uncertainty about climate change: dimensions, determinants and change over time. *Global Environmental Change* 21(2), 690–700.

Wood, Dan and Arnold Vedlitz (2007). Issue definition, information processing and the politics of global warming. *American Journal of Political Science* 51(3), 552–68.

5

Gender, voting, and women's representation in the 2016 Australian election

Katrine Beauregard

Historically, there has been an underrepresentation of women in Australian politics. Despite Australia being one of the pioneers with New Zealand in granting women the right to vote in 1902 (1893 for New Zealand) (Inter-Parliamentary Union 2017), the first women were not elected to the federal parliament until 1943 and still today women constitute less than half of elected representatives. In February 2017, women were 28.7 per cent of members of the House of Representatives and 41.9 per cent of senators (Parliamentary Library 2017). Still, according to McAllister (2011), the increase from a handful of women to an average of 33 per cent representation in Australian parliaments has been one of the most significant changes in legislative recruitment in Australia. The greater presence of women in politics has mirrored important changes in Australian society in the past half-century regarding gender roles. Women have a greater presence in the labour force and higher levels of education. These changes in women's lives and in their presence in formal political institutions have been a common phenomenon among established democracies, leading to expectations concerning their impact on voter behaviour.

Indeed, the women's vote has been important to understanding electoral behaviour since women gained the right to vote. Early electoral studies found that women's voting patterns differed from those of men. Ever since, the question of whether women constitute a voting bloc and how political parties can take advantage of this bloc has been a scholarly concern but also a puzzle for the media and politicians. As women constitute half of the voting population, small gender differences in vote choice can have great consequences. In other words, when elections can be won by a few votes, securing an advantage among a large demographic group could influence electoral success positively.

Gender patterns in vote choice have not been consistent around the world or in Australia. As mentioned above, changes in women's roles in politics and society have influenced women's vote and what is being described as the gender gap – that is, the percentage-point difference between women and men in support for a political party. Traditionally, women have voted for centre-right political parties in a greater proportion than men, but as their roles have changed, so has their behaviour. But the slow disappearance of the gender voting gap has not stayed still for long in Australia. As I show below, the gender gap in vote choice has transformed over the years so that, in the 2016 election, women were more likely to vote for a centre-left political party – the Australian Labor Party (ALP) or the Australian Greens – than men. This movement seems to be part of a global trend towards realignment where women in established democracies have moved from the right of men to the left of men (Inglehart and Norris 2003).

This chapter investigates the gender gap in vote-choice evidence in the Australian federal election of 2016 by situating this gap in its historical context. Multiple explanations have been offered to understand why women are now more likely to support left-wing political parties in established democracies. They tend to fall into two broad categories capturing structural and cultural explanations. This chapter will investigate how well these explanations allow us to understand why Australian women favoured the Labor Party to a greater extent than men in 2016. Australian women were also more likely than men to vote for the Australian Greens in 2016. If we were to combine votes for both the Labor and Greens parties, the impact of women tending toward the centre-left would produce an even larger gender gap. This chapter, however, only focuses on the gender gap in favour of the Labor Party as it is one of the major two political parties in Australia. Also, the factors that explain the gender gap for the Labor Party might not be the same as the explanations for the Greens vote. Morever, since the Australian Greens are a smaller political party, the smaller number of respondents in the Australian Election Study who have voted for this party makes it difficult to investigate the gender gap in vote choice for the Greens.

Using data from the Australian Election Study (AES) 2016, this chapter investigates the gender gap in vote choice but also across the characteristics and attitudes that have been commonly used to explain women's and men's different voting behaviour. The first section examines the evolution of the gender gap in vote choice in Australia since 1967. Second, this gender gap is explored by analysing the influence of a series of individual characteristics and socio-demographic factors. Third, the importance of political issues in understanding vote choice is analysed. Fourth, a section identifies the state of gender differences in political values and support for increasing the number of women MPs. The final section reports on a regression analysis comprising the possible factors explaining the gender voting gap in Australia to determine which are the most important.

The gender gap in vote choice

Gender differences in vote choice have been the subject of multiple investigations over the years. Early on, the literature on vote choice identified women as more likely to vote for centre-right political parties, although the differences with men's rates of support were small (Duverger 1955; Butler and Stokes 1974; Campbell et al. 1960). Inglehart and Norris (2003) refer to this gender difference as the 'traditional gender gap' (77, emphasis in the original text). This traditional gender gap was found in multiple established democracies such as France, Britain, the United States, Italy, and Germany, starting in the 1950s and continuing until the 1970s (Inglehart 1977). Australia was not exempt from this trend, as shown by Figure 5.1. In 1967, the gender gap was 9 percentage points with men more likely than women to vote for the Labor Party. In the 1970s, Australian women remained slightly more conservative than men with the gender gap declining to 6 percentage points in 1979. However, as Aitkin (1982) stipulated, this gender gap in vote choice was rather small and less important than differences caused by other factors such as occupation or income.

Explanations for this traditional gender gap in vote choice tend to focus on the role of religion and values in women's lives (Inglehart and Norris 2003). Since women were more likely than men to be religious and to have more conservative values and

Figure 5.1 Gender gap in vote choice, 1967–2016.

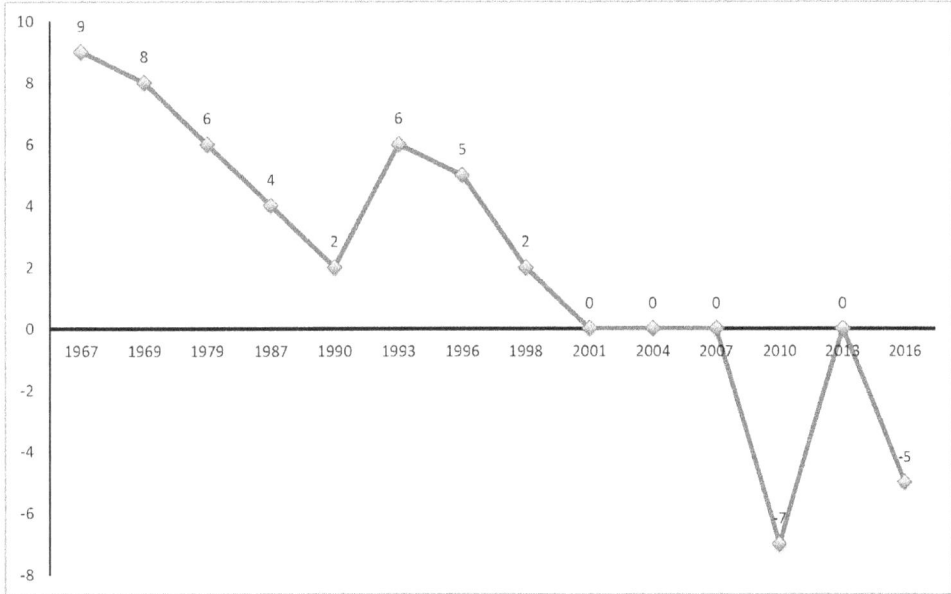

Sources: Australian National Political Attitudes Survey (ANPAS) 1967–79; Australian Election Study (AES) 1987–2016.

Note: Updated from McAllister (2011). The figure shows the percentage of men voting Labor minus the percentage of women voting Labor.

political attitudes, they favoured political parties associated with these attitudes. On the other hand, Goot and Reid (1975) emphasise that early voting studies tend to ignore important factors that may explain women's voting behaviour such as income, job security, and mobility. Consequently, women's greater religiosity and conservatism may have been overrepresented as explanations for the traditional gender gap. McAllister (2011) adds that in the Australian context, this tendency of women to support conservative parties contributed to the dominance of the Liberal–Country Coalition in government at the federal level between 1949 and 1972.

As Figure 5.1 demonstrates, this traditional gender gap in vote choice declined in the 1980s to reach 2 percentage points in 1990. This pattern was also found in other established democracies (Inglehart and Norris 2003). Women were found still to be more conservative than men; however, this gap was smaller and would sometimes disappear when controls for religiosity and labour force participation were included (DeVaus and McAllister 1989). The literature on the gender gap in vote choice then started to discuss the '*modern* gender gap' (Norris and Inglehart 2003, 78, emphasis in the original text), where women are more likely than men to support left-wing political parties. Australia in the 1990s, however, did not fit into this pattern of realignment.

In Canada, for instance, a modern gender gap in vote choice emerged in the 1990s, with women more likely to vote for the centre-left New Democratic Party (Erickson and O'Neill 2002). This pattern is only found outside the province of Québec. In Québec, the party system was not organised around left–right issues, preventing the emergence of a modern gender gap. A different party system, however, cannot explain why Australia was late in experiencing the rise of a modern gender gap since the party system is organised around the traditional left–right axis. While the gender gap had decreased to 2 percentage points in 1990 (see Figure 5.1), it increased to 6 percentage points in 1993. McAllister (2011) explains this result by the unpopularity of Paul Keating, the Labor prime minister, among women. He argues that Keating's adversarial style was not well received among women, leading to a larger gender gap with women more likely to favour the Coalition. Consequently, leader selection is possibly one of the reasons explaining Australia's lack of a modern gender gap in the 1990s. Another possible explanation might be found in the role of cultural values. As noted by Erickson and O'Neill (2002), cultural values are important in understanding the shift from a traditional gender gap to a modern gender gap. One possibility is that Australian women might have remained more conservative in their values than men for a longer period of time than women in other established democracies, explaining Australia's lag when it comes to the emergence of a modern gender gap in vote choice.

After 1993, the gender gap in vote choice started to decline again until it disappeared in 2001 (see Figure 5.1). The difference between women's and men's vote choice was also negligible at the 2004 and 2007 elections. McAllister (2011) argues that men and women increasingly experience similar lives, 'so that the factors that once led women to be more politically conservative than men have gradually disappeared' (113) (see also Hayes and McAllister 1997; Studlar et al. 1998). Considering the most important factors explaining the decline in the size of the gender gap, McAllister (2011) notes that women are now more likely to participate in the labour force than they were in the 1960s and 1970s, and women are now more likely than men to obtain a university degree. Inglehart and Norris (2003) add that industrial Western societies underwent cultural change where attitudes toward women's roles shifted – a greater acceptance toward women participating in the labour force and in politics emerged. All these factors combined to create a convergence in men's and women's experiences, leading to the decline and disappearance of the gender gap in vote choice.

However, Figure 5.1 shows that the gender gap in vote choice did not merely close. Indeed, in 2010, the gender difference was -7 percentage points, indicating that women were more likely than men to vote Labor. McAllister (2011) explains this result by arguing that Australia's first female prime minister, Julia Gillard, had an important impact on women's vote choice. Julia Gillard was more popular among women than among men while the then Liberal leader, Tony Abbott, was more popular among men than among women. This interpretation of the 2010 results seems to be confirmed by the absence of a gender gap in the 2013 election, where the gender difference in vote choice returned to zero. Commercial polls, on the other hand, show that the gender gap remained for the whole 2010 to 2013 period, with women more likely to support the Labor Party (Newspoll and the *Australian* 2013). It is consequently possible that the modern gender gap never fully disappeared after the 2010 election.

Voting patterns in the 2016 election suggest a return to a modern gender gap pattern, with women voting in greater proportion than men for the Labor Party. This has occurred without a woman heading the Labor Party, indicating that Australia's gender gap in vote choice might be changing more permanently – as opposed to being the result of leadership choices. That women are more likely to support a centre-left political party than men has been a common phenomenon in established democracies (Studlar et al. 1998; Inglehart and Norris 2003). Inglehart and Norris (2003) highlight two broad sets of factors that can explain this modern gender gap – structural and cultural explanations.

Structural explanations emphasise women's position in society. Inglehart and Norris (2003) argue that increases in labour force participation and education levels for women have pushed them to the left. Moreover, since women are concentrated in particular industries, lower-paying employment, and the public sector, women may be more likely to vote for political parties that emphasise support for social programs and the presence of a large public sector (see also Klein 1984). Additionally, Inglehart and Norris (2003) note that marital status and the presence of children are important structural factors explaining women's more left-wing vote choices. As women are traditionally the ones responsible for the wellbeing of their children, for instance, the presence of children may emphasise to women the need for welfare programs such as health care, child care, and education. Differences in marital status are related to differences in lifestyles, which in turn can influence preferences toward political issues and vote choice (Plutzer 1998).

Cultural explanations of the modern gender gap in vote choice, on the other hand, highlight the role of values such as attitudes towards the role of government and gender equality. Inglehart and Norris (2003) argue that post-industrial democracies develop a set of values that prioritises quality of life, individual self-expression, environmental protection, and direct participation in political decisions. More specifically, in countries such as Australia, citizens develop greater support for gender equality. Furthermore, since women are especially likely to benefit from this cultural transformation, they will be more likely to support gender equality and government intervention to secure this equality, leading women to support parties to the left of centre. In sum, cultural explanations should be reflected in different policy priorities, different attitudes toward government intervention and equality, and different levels of support for intervention addressing women's underrepresentation among women and men. The following sections of this chapter investigate how the gender gap in the 2016 Australian election is affected by structural and cultural factors.

The gender gap and demographic characteristics of voters

This section reviews how the gender gap in vote choice in the 2016 Australian election is affected by structural characteristics. First, Table 5.1 shows how the gender gap for the 2016 federal election (presented in Figure 5.1) varies across age groups. Inglehart and Norris (2003) argue that the modern gender gap is more likely to occur among younger citizens while the traditional gender gap should persist among older citizens. Younger women should be more likely to vote for left-wing political parties than younger men since they are the ones more likely to have benefited from the structural changes in women's roles and conditions (Inglehart and Norris 2003). On the other hand, older women should be more likely to conserve their traditional voting behaviour and remain more likely to support right-wing parties than older men. As the table shows, the gender gap in vote choice is largest among respondents aged between 18 and 34 years and is the smallest among those aged 65 years and over. In all age groups, women are more likely to favour the Labor Party; however, gender differences are not significant for either the 50–64 years or 65 years and over age group. Consequently, it seems that the emergence of a modern gender gap in Australian politics is the result of a younger generation of female voters moving to the centre-left.

Table 5.1: Gender gap in the Labor vote across socio-demographic and individual characteristic groups, %.

	Vote Labor		
	Men	Women	Gap
Age			
18–34	30.1	37.3	-7.2***
35–49	30.6	36.3	-5.7***
50–64	30.6	36.4	-5.8
65 and over	25.8	29.4	-3.6
N	1,236	1,316	
Education			
No uni degree	31.4	34.3	-2.9**
Uni degree	26.7	36.6	-9.9***
N	1,237	1,301	
Employment			
Not full-time	31.4	35.0	-3.6***
Full-time	27.4	35.7	-8.3***
N	1,244	1,325	
Income			
First quartile	33.5	33.6	-0.1
Second quartile	32.5	34.5	-2.0*
Third quartile	28.2	35.6	-7.4*
Fourth quartile	24.3	35.3	-11.0***
N	1,204	1,244	
Marital status			
Single	31.1	40.4	-9.3**
Married/partner	28.7	33.3	-4.6***
Widowed/divorced	29.3	35.9	-6.6
N	1,239	1,318	

Source: AES 2016.
Notes: The gap is calculated by subtracting the percentage of women who voted Labor from the percentage of men. Chi-square tests are conducted to assess the statistical significance of gender gaps. *: $p < 0.05$; **: $p < 0.01$; ***: $p < 0.001$.

Second, Table 5.1 compares the gender gap in vote choice for citizens with and without a university degree. Women's greater access to higher education has been one of the major changes to women's lives in the last 50 years. McAllister (2011) argues that this trend of women obtaining a university education in greater proportions than men should lead to changes in women's levels of political interest and the involvement of women in politics. Thus, education levels should influence the gender gap in vote choice. As Table 5.1 demonstrates, gender differences in voting for the Labor Party are larger among citizens holding a university degree than among those without. The gap is 9.9 percentage points among the former and is 2.9 percentage points in the latter. For both groups, the gender gap is significant at the $p < 0.05$ level. Women with a university degree are more likely to vote for the Labor Party while men with a university degree are less likely to vote for the same party.

Third, the gender gap in voting for the Labor Party is larger for citizens employed full-time. For these citizens, the gap is 8.3 percentage points ($p < 0.001$), where women are significantly more likely than men to vote Labor. The gender gap is still present, in the same direction, among citizens without full-time employment, but smaller at 3.6 percentage points ($p < 0.001$). This result supports the previous discussion on women's participation in the labour force as an explanation for the modern gender gap. When women are employed full-time, they tend to occupy 'pink collar' jobs that are lower paid, or they are employed by the public sector (Burns et al. 2001; Workplace Gender Equity Agency 2016). Because of their employment, women may be more reliant on welfare programs, which lead them to support the Labor Party to a greater extent than men.

Fourth, Table 5.1 shows that as the income quartile of respondents increases, the size of the gender gap also increases. These gender gaps are significant ($p < 0.05$) for the three highest income quartiles, with women being more likely than men to vote for the Labor Party. For men, as their income increases, they are less likely to vote for the Labor Party. This is in line with McAllister's (2011) findings that higher-income earners are more likely to vote for the Liberal–National Coalition and less likely to vote Labor. On the other hand, the percentage of women voting for the Labor Party does not change much across income quartile – it varies between 33.6 per cent for the first quartile and 35.3 for the fourth quartile. Women with a higher income may have a higher education level and be employed, both factors that should lead them to vote for the Labor Party, counterbalancing the factors that should lead high earners to vote for the Liberal–National.

Finally, Table 5.1 demonstrates that the gender gap also varies by respondent marital status. The largest gap occurs for single individuals where women are more likely to vote Labor ($p < 0.01$) and the smallest gap is among married or partnered individuals, although women are still more likely than men to vote Labor ($p < 0.001$). For widowed or divorced individuals, the gender gap in vote choice is in the middle; however, it is not significant, which means that for this group of citizens, men and women are equally likely to vote for the Labor Party. Single women's greater likelihood of voting for the Labor Party may be a reflection of their different lifestyles than married women. Single women may be younger and more likely to be employed or to be studying for a higher degree, all factors that should lead them to support centre-left parties.

Political issues and the gender gap

The previous section demonstrates that the gender gap in vote choice in the 2016 federal election varies across a range of socio-demographic characteristics. As discussed, a possible explanation for women being more likely than men to vote for the Labor Party resides in women's greater support for welfare. Due to the differences identified between women and men that were explored in the previous section, we have identified reasons why the former are more likely to support and prioritise government programs. This section investigates the importance of different political issues in explaining men's and women's vote choice.

Table 5.2: Most important issues during the 2016 election campaign by vote choice and gender, %.

	All	Liberal–National			Labor		
		Men	Women	Gap	Men	Women	Gap
1 Health and Medicare	24.1	11.8	17.5	-5.7	30.4	40.6	-10.2
2 Management of the economy	20.0	34.1	25.4	8.7	10.4	9.2	1.2
3 Education	12.1	2.9	10.3	-7.4	20.3	19.7	0.6
4 Taxation	10.5	14.3	11.0	3.3	13.2	6.4	6.8
5 Government debt	7.2	16.5	11.6	4.9	3.3	0.9	2.4
6 Superannuation	6.3	6.9	7.3	-0.4	6.3	5.8	0.5
7 Refugees and asylum seekers	6.1	4.0	5.8	-1.8	3.0	5.1	-2.1
8 Environment	5.5	1.3	1.7	-0.4	2.5	7.1	-4.6
9 Immigration	4.2	5.3	5.8	-0.5	2.7	1.3	1.4
10 Global warming	4.1	1.3	1.7	-0.4	4.7	1.9	2.8
Chi-square		40.2383***			29.6878***		
N	2,690	552	464		365	468	

Source: AES 2016.

Notes: The gap is calculated by subtracting the percentage of women from the percentage of men. ***: p < 0.001. The chi-square assesses the statistical significance of the overall relationship between issue priorities and gender. The small sample size for each combination of vote choice, issue, and gender makes it difficult to assess the significance of each gap. Indeed, difference proportion tests indicate that each gender difference is not significant at p < 0.05. However, the chi-square indicates that the overall differences between women and men are significant at p < 0.001 for both Liberal–National and Labor voters.

The AES 2016 includes a question asking respondents: 'which of these issues was most important to you and your family during the election campaign?' Ten policy areas were given: taxation, immigration, education, the environment, government debt, health and Medicare, refugees and asylum seekers, global warming, superannuation, and management of the economy. Table 5.2 presents responses to this question for both men and women as well as for Labor and Liberal–National voters (that is, those voters who selected either Labor or the Liberal–National parties first in the House of Representatives). As one would expect, social policy issues were more important to Labor voters while Liberal–National voters selected economic issues. Citizens who prioritised education and health and Medicare were more likely to vote for the Labor Party while citizens who agreed that immigration, government debt and the management of the economy were the most important issues voted for the Liberal–National parties. These results are in line with previous findings (McAllister 2011).

Moreover, gender differences occurred for the most important issue of the electoral campaign. One of the largest gaps emerged for citizens agreeing that health and Medicare is the most important issue. For both Liberal–National and Labor voters, women are more likely than men to mention this issue as the most important; however, the gender gap is larger among Labor voters (10.2 percentage points for the latter compared to 5.7 percentage points for the former). Overall, 24.1 per cent of Australians identify this issue as the most important, but among Labor voters, 40.6 per cent of women responded that health and Medicare was the most important issue compared to 30.4 per cent of men. As discussed above, women may be more 'structurally' reliant on welfare programs and thus more likely to support parties defending such programs. Women are more likely to prioritise welfare issues such as health since they are more likely to be employed in this sector and women are also more likely to have responsibility for taking care of their children and elderly relatives. In the 2016 election, the Labor Party heavily campaigned on health and Medicare, and it seems the party was able to attract women voters who believed that this was the main issue of the election.

A large gender gap also occurs for citizens who chose the management of the economy as the most important issue, but only for Liberal–National voters. Men were more likely than women to mention this response (34.1 and 25.4 per cent respectively, for an 8.7 percentage points gap) while a similar percentage of female and male Labor voters selected this option (the gender gap is 1.2 percentage points). Additionally, for both Labor and Liberal–National voters, men were more likely than women to answer that taxation was the most important issue; however, a similar percentage of both party supporters mentioned this answer. The gender gap, however, is larger among Labor voters (6.8 percentage points compared to 3.3 percentage points). Men were also more likely than women to agree that government debt was the most important issue, with the gender gap being larger for Liberal–National voters (4.9 percentage points).

Education is also another policy area associated with a gender gap, but only for Liberal–National voters. For Liberal–National voters only, women are more likely than men to respond that this was the most important issue of the campaign, with a gender gap of 7.4 percentage points. Female Labor voters were more likely to mention the environment than their male counterparts by 4.6 percentage points – a gender gap that is not reproduced for Liberal–National voters. Finally, men were more likely than women to respond that global warming was the most important issue; however the gender gap is small for both Labor and Liberal–National voters (2.8 and 1.7 percentage points respectively).

Overall, women are more likely to favour social policy issues while men give a higher priority to economic issues. If we were to combine *welfare issues* (health and Medicare and education) and *economic issues* (management of the economy, taxation, and government debt), the gender gap in issue priorities would be even larger (13.1 percentage points for Liberal–National voters and 10.8 percentage points for Labor voters on welfare issues, and 16.9 percentage points for Liberal–National voters and 10.4 percentage points for Labor voters on economic issues). This is in line with Gidengil's (1995) findings that when men and women are making political decisions they use different considerations. Men evaluate political decisions based on economic considerations while women's evaluations of the same political decisions are based on social considerations. Thus, when deciding on which party to vote for, a greater reliance on social issues may lead women to support the Labor Party as this party has emphasised these issues in its campaign.

Gender, values, and attitudes toward women's representation

The next set of factors to explore in understanding women's greater support for the Labor Party is political values. As discussed above, women's greater propensity to vote for centre-left and left-wing political parties can be explained by their different political values.

Women should be more likely to support gender equality as they are the main beneficiaries of greater support of such equality (Inglehart and Norris 2003). Additionally, women tend to be more likely to attribute gender inequality to structural barriers such as discrimination than to blame women's personal choices (Cassese et al. 2015; Gurin 1985). Consequently, women will be more likely to favour government intervention to resolve inequality. These attitudes complement the previous discussion on why women might favour welfare issues. In sum, it is expected that women's attitudes and values toward government intervention and equality should differ from those of men. As well, women should be more likely to support governmental action aiming at redressing inequalities.

Table 5.3 presents gender differences for various political attitudes. The first part of the table shows gaps in opinions toward government intervention. For most of these attitudes women are significantly different from men. Since income tax is necessary for government policies and intervention, women are less likely than men to agree that high income tax makes people less willing to work hard; the gender gap is 8 percentage points (p < 0.01). Women also disagree with men on the role of trade unions. As women are more likely to work for the public sector, and more likely to depend on welfare programs, they may be more likely to support trade unions. Moreover, Australian union density is now slightly higher among women than men (see Australian Bureau of Statistics 2014), possibly contributing to women's more favourable opinion of unions. Table 5.3 also indicates that fewer women than men agree that trade unions have too much power (a 16.1-percentage-point gap; p < 0.001) and women are less likely than men to agree there should be stricter laws to regulate the activities of trade unions (a 10.7-percentage-point gap; p < 0.001). On the other hand, women and men agree on the role of business in society, with similar percentages of both sexes agreeing that big business has too much power. Thus, it seems that gender differences are located in the role of government and trade unions.

The second part of Table 5.3 reports on attitudes toward equality. The first two questions asked Australians about their attitudes toward income redistribution and government's role in ensuring such redistribution. For both questions, women are slightly more likely than men to favour redistribution of income and government intervention; both gender gaps are small (2.2 and 2.6 percentage points respectively) and not significant. The next questions in Table 5.3 ask respondents whether equality for specific groups has gone too far. Men are more likely than women to agree that equal opportunities for migrants and Aboriginal land rights have gone too far. The gender gap is only significant for the latter question (p < 0.01).

The last three questions in Table 5.3 assess the differences between women and men in attitudes toward gender equality. As expected, women are more likely than men to favour gender equality. Women are less likely to agree that equal opportunities for women have gone too far (9-percentage-point gap; p < 0.01); women are also more likely to agree that they should be given preferential treatment when applying for jobs and promotions (4-percentage-point gap; not significant); and finally, women are more likely to respond that the government should increase opportunities for them in business and industry (21.2-percentage-point gap; p < 0.001).

These gender differences in values have been linked to gaps in support for specific governmental interventions to increase the presence of women in politics (Gidengil 1996). One important avenue for increasing women's representation in the legislature has been the introduction of gender quotas. Both major parties have discussed this method in relation to the issue of women's underrepresentation in Australian politics. This discussion

Table 5.3: Gender differences in political attitudes toward government intervention and equality, %.

	Women	Men	Gap
Role of government			
High income tax makes people less willing to work hard	41.2	49.2	-8.0**
The trade unions in this country have too much power	38.8	54.9	-16.1***
There should be stricter laws to regulate the activities of trade unions	49.2	59.9	-10.7***
Big business in this country has too much power	73.3	75.1	-1.8
Equality			
Income and wealth should be redistributed towards ordinary working people	56.2	54.0	2.2
The government should take measures to reduce differences in income levels	56.2	53.6	2.6
Equal opportunities for migrants have gone too far	33.1	35.9	-2.8
Aboriginal land rights have gone too far	23.3	32.9	-9.6**
Equal opportunities for women have gone too far	5.5	14.5	-9.0*
Women should be given preferential treatment when applying for jobs and promotions	10.8	6.8	4.0
The government should increase opportunities for women in business and industry	60.2	39.0	21.2***

N=2,668. Source: AES 2016.
Notes: The gender gap is calculated by subtracting the percentage of men from the percentage of women. Difference of proportion tests are conducted to assess the statistical significance of gender gaps. *: $p < 0.05$; **: $p < 0.01$; ***: $p < 0.001$.

has been informed by the gender division among elected representatives, which varies across political parties. As reported by Table 5.4, both the Labor and Liberal parties elected a similar percentage of women in the House of Representatives and the Senate until early 2000. After this point, the Labor Party started electing more women than the Liberal Party; indeed, the Labor Party elected 41 and 54 per cent of women in the House and Senate respectively while the Liberal Party elected 20 per cent of women in the House and 25 per cent in the Senate. Overall, Australia ranks 50th internationally for the representation of women in the national legislature (Inter-Parliamentary Union, 2017). Top established democracies such as Sweden and Finland have elected legislatures that are over 40 per cent women – consequently, Australia would achieve a higher position in the global ranking if the Liberal Party elected a similar number of women as Labor.

In recent years, the discrepancy in women's parliamentary representation has been the object of debate. As prime minister, Tony Abbott was criticised for initially including only one woman and later two women in his Cabinet. This low Cabinet representation, combined with the Liberal Party's representation in Parliament being less than 30 per cent women, has led some female Liberals to call for gender targets, if not full quotas.[1] Notably, in 2010, Liberal Senator Judith Troeth released a policy paper arguing in favour of a party quota for candidate preselection (Troeth 2010). The latest call for targets has emerged after the Labor

---

1   After ousting Tony Abbott as the leader of the Liberal Party, the new prime minister Malcolm Turnbull nominated an increased number of women – five – to his Cabinet.

Table 5.4: Women's representation in federal parliament by party, %.

	House			Senate		
	ALP	Liberal	Gap	ALP	Liberal	Gap
1977	0	0	0	15	14	1
1980	6	0	6	23	17	6
1983	8	0	8	20	18	2
1984	9	2	7	18	18	0
1987	9	2	7	16	26	-10
1990	9	6	3	16	24	-8
1993	11	8	3	13	23	-10
1996	8	22	-14	31	26	5
1998	24	23	1	31	29	2
2001	31	24	7	39	26	13
2004	33	20	13	46	24	22
2007	33	22	11	44	28	16
2010	32	22	10	44	29	15
2013	38	22	16	56	19	37
2016	41	20	21	54	25	29

Source: Parliamentary Handbook of the Commonwealth of Australia, multiple years.
Note: The gap is calculated by subtracting the percentage of Liberal women from the percentage of ALP women.

Party adopted such a rule, in 2015, to ensure the party election of 50 per cent women in Parliament by 2025 (Crowe 2015). The Liberal Party, however, has always rejected gender quotas, arguing that they run against the merit-based system of candidate selection. On the other hand, the Labor Party has been more open to the idea of a gender quota. Since 1981, there are party quotas for internal positions. The Labor Party's first candidate quotas with effective sanctions for non-compliance were adopted in 1994: they stipulated that 35 per cent of candidates be women (Quota Project 2017). In 2002, the quota was increased to 40 per cent and in 2015 to 50 per cent (by 2025). McAllister (2012) mentions that this gender quota was a major factor in increasing women's representation in the Labor Party, since the policy takes into account selection for winnable seats when nominating women. In sum, the lack of a target or quota in the selection of candidates for the Liberal Party is one of the main explanations for the current ceiling on the number of women elected to federal parliament.

AES 2016 includes a question asking respondents 'should there be more efforts to increase the number of women MPs? If so, what means would you prefer?' Five possible response options were given: 1) No, there is no need to increase the number of women MPs; 2) No, nothing needs to be done, it will happen naturally; 3) Yes, by legally requiring all political parties to select more women candidates by means of a quota; 4) Yes, the political parties should make their own voluntary commitments to increase the number of women MPs; and 5) Yes, by encouraging more women to participate in politics. Table 5.5 presents the responses according to gender and which party citizens voted first for in the House of Representatives.

Table 5.5: Gender differences in support for increasing the number of women MPs, %.

	Liberal–National			Labor		
	Men	Women	Gap	Men	Women	Gap
No, there is no need to increase the number of women MPs	10.5	7.0	3.5	9.6	3.2	6.4
No, nothing needs to be done, it will happen naturally	50.4	37.7	12.7**	29.3	21.7	7.6
Yes, by legally requiring all political parties to select more women candidates by means of a quota	4.4	6.8	-2.4	15.3	15.5	-0.2
Yes, the political parties should make their own voluntary commitments to increase the number of women MPs	9.9	18.1	-8.2	19.2	22.1	-2.9
Yes, by encouraging more women to participate in politics	24.8	30.5	-5.7	26.6	32.7	-6.1[+]
Chi-square	26.3038***			24.6127***		
N	544	459		365	466	

Source: AES 2016.
Notes: The gender gap is calculated by subtracting the percentage of women from the percentage of men. Difference of proportion tests are used to assess the significance of the gender gap. [+]: p < 0.10; **: p < 0.01.

According to Table 5.5, overall gender differences are significant – that is, men and women have different opinions about the necessity of increasing the number of women MPs. Men are more likely than women to answer 'no' on the question of whether increasing the number of women MPs is necessary, and this occurs for both Liberal–National and Labor voters. Among Liberal–National voters, the opinion that women's representation will increase 'naturally' is the most frequently chosen answer, but men are significantly more likely (p < 0.01) than women to agree with this option (a 12.7-percentage-point gap). Labor men are also more likely than women to select this answer, but the gender gap is smaller and not significant (7.6 percentage points). Women are slightly more likely than men to support legislative gender quotas – that is, legislation requiring political parties to nominate a certain percentage of women candidates where failure to follow the legislation would result in penalties for political parties. However the difference on this proposition is nearly non-existent for Labor voters (0.2-percentage-point gap compared to 2.4-percentage-point difference for Liberal–National voters). Larger gender gaps for both groups of voters appear for support for voluntary measures – that is, measures that are not enforced by the government, but within the parties – i.e. voluntary commitments by political parties that encourage women to participate in politics. Women are more likely than men to support both of these options, with encouraging women being the most popular answer among female Labor voters. The only significant difference, however, is for encouraging women to participate in politics among Labor voters (p < 0.10).

How do Australian attitudes on ways to increase women's representation compare globally? One recent study conducted in Latin America demonstrates that the average support for legislative quotas is about 5 points on a 1 to 7 scale (where 7 indicates that the respondent strongly agrees with gender quotas) (Barnes and Córdova 2016). An older study of Canadian opinions shows that 32 per cent of men and 45 per cent of women favour gender quotas in varying strength (Gidengil 1996). Consequently, Australians' support for gender quotas seems somewhat lower than in Latin American countries despite the different question used to measure attitudes toward gender quotas. This different level of support can be explained by the wider adoption of gender quotas in Latin America. Like Australia, Canada does not have gender quotas and Australians exhibit a similar level of support for quotas as Canadians.

Interestingly, 32.7 per cent of female Labor voters and 30.5 per cent of female Liberal–National voters answered that encouraging women to participate in politics is necessary. For the two types of quotas – legislative and voluntary party quotas – female Labor voters are more likely to support these options than either men or female Liberal–National voters. This result may be explained by the ideology of supporters of the respective parties. A stronger adherence to 'liberal' individualism principles among Liberal–National voters might lead them to believe that individuals are responsible for the present inequalities between women and men (Krook et al. 2009); consequently, they will prefer non-state intervention that ensures equality of opportunities to solve these issues. That, in turn, leads to an opposition to legislative measures imposed by the government aimed at correcting the imbalance between the sexes. By contrast, centre-left ideologies reflected in the Labor Party might favour structural explanations for the inequality between women and men, resulting in greater support for methods such as gender quotas.

In sum, Australian women are more likely than men to favour government intervention, equality, and measures aiming at increasing the number of women MPs. The results presented in this section tend to confirm cross-national research on the different values and opinions held by women and men (Inglehart and Norris 2003). A greater commitment to the policies of gender equality as well as increased representation of women in politics are encouraging more women to support centre-left political parties.

Bringing it all together

This final section evaluates the contribution of all four different sets of explanations explored above to better understand the gender gap in vote choice in the 2016 federal election. To achieve this, a logistic regression is performed with voting for the Labor Party over the ALP as the outcome variable. A logistic regression is necessary since the outcome takes the form of a dichotomous indicator where respondents who voted for the Labor Party are coded '1' and otherwise is indicated with '0'. In the first model presented below, gender is measured with a dummy indicator where women are coded '1' and men '0'. Socio-demographic and individual characteristics included in the model are: respondents' age, level of education, employment status, income level, and marital status.

Issue priorities are recoded into two indicators according to the answers where the largest gender gaps occurred in Table 5.2. Respondents prioritising management of the economy, taxation, and government spending are grouped into a single indicator where giving priority to one of these issue is coded '1' and otherwise '0'. The second category consists of respondents who indicated that welfare issues (education and health and Medicare) were the most important priority; again, welfare priorities are coded '1' while other answers are coded '0'.

Six indicators are employed to assess the impact of political attitudes toward government intervention and equality on voting for the Labor Party. The first indicator assesses support for the statement that tax makes people less willing to work hard. Second, attitudes toward unions are measured by combining opinions on whether trade unions have too much power and on whether there should be stricter laws to regulate the activities of trade unions. Third, opinions on whether big business has too much power are used. Four, the indicator for attitudes toward redistribution is created by combining responses on support for income and wealth redistribution toward ordinary people, and for government taking measures to reduce differences in income levels. Five, opinions on whether equal opportunities for migrants and Aboriginal land rights have gone too far are added to build the indicator for attitudes toward minorities. Six, attitudes toward equality for women combine responses to statements on equal opportunities for women, preferential treatment for women when applying for jobs and promotions, and government involvement to increase opportunities for women in business and industry.

The final set of factors included in the model is support for increasing the number of women MPs. Three dichotomous indicators are used: supporting legally requiring political parties to select more women candidates by means of a quota, supporting political parties making their own voluntary commitments to increase the number of women MPs, and encouraging women to participate in politics.

Results are presented in Table 5.6. Model 1 of this table displays findings for the whole sample and includes a coefficient for women. This latter coefficient shows that women are no more or less likely to vote for the Labor Party once controls for socio-demographic status, issue priorities, political attitudes, and support for increasing the number of women MPs are included. Moreover, only one of the socio-demographic characteristics is significantly associated with voting for the Labor Party at the $p < 0.05$ level. As respondents get older, they are significantly less likely to choose Labor over the Liberal Party. Issue priorities and attitudes are better predictors of voting Labor. Selecting economic issues as the main priority is significantly and negatively associated with voting Labor. Moreover, there is a positive and significant relationship between respondents prioritising welfare issues and voting for the Labor Party. Positive attitudes toward unions, redistribution and minorities are also significantly linked with voting for the Labor Party. Agreeing that big business has too much power is also linked with a greater likelihood of voting Labor over Liberal. Finally, citizens supporting legislative quotas are significantly more likely to vote for the Labor Party. Overall, these results highlight a clear left–right divide in Australian politics: respondents favouring centre-left priorities and attitudes are more likely to vote for the Labor Party.

Models 2 and 3 in Table 5.6 show the results for the same logistic regression, but for women and men respectively. This allows for an investigation of whether the same factors explain women's and men's votes for the Labor Party. For both men and women, socio-demographic characteristics are not significantly linked with voting for this party, with the exception of age, which is significant at a lower level ($p < 0.10$) for women. Similarly, both women and men indicating a priority for welfare issues are significantly more likely to vote for Labor – it appears that welfare issues play an equally important role for both sexes.

Economic issues priority and political attitudes appear to make a difference to gender patterns in the Labor vote. Male respondents who agreed that economic issues were the most important issues of the electoral campaign are significantly less likely to vote Labor while the same relationship is not significant at the $p < 0.05$ level for women. Another difference in models 2 and 3 is on the role of attitudes toward minorities. Women agreeing that equal opportunities for migrants have gone too far are significantly less likely to vote for the Labor Party. This relationship, however, is not significant for men. The impact

Table 5.6: Gender and voting for the Labor Party in 2016.

	All	Women	Men
Women	-0.199 (0.179)		
Socio-demographic			
Age	-0.014* (0.007)	-0.017[+] (0.009)	-0.012 (0.011)
Education	0.008 (0.042)	0.066 (0.057)	-0.074 (0.063)
Employment	0.065 (0.202)	0.325 (0.278)	-0.323 (0.334)
Income	-0.120 (0.109)	-0.262[+] (0.144)	0.112 (0.168)
Married	0.125 (0.284)	0.336 (0.360)	-0.017 (0.476)
Divorced	0.230 (0.315)	0.533 (0.421)	-0.063 (0.484)
Issue priority			
Economic	-0.606** (0.210)	-0.538[+] (0.312)	-0.704* (0.281)
Welfare	0.665*** (0.205)	0.622* (0.281)	0.719* (0.306)
Attitudes			
Tax	-0.004 (0.080)	0.048 (0.122)	-0.019 (0.112)
Unions	0.672*** (0.052)	0.678*** (0.075)	0.719*** (0.083)
Business	0.708*** (0.118)	0.498** (0.158)	0.918*** (0.190)
Redistribution	0.241*** (0.058)	0.301*** (0.081)	0.215** (0.081)
Minorities	-0.140* (0.059)	-0.180* (0.070)	-0.108 (0.098)
Women	0.059 (0.054)	0.060 (0.078)	0.055 (0.082)
Support women MPs			
Legislative quotas	0.800* (0.334)	0.703[+] (0.406)	1.010[+] (0.523)
Party quotas	0.273 (0.254)	0.147 (0.351)	0.439 (0.370)
Encouraging women	0.216 (0.220)	0.295 (0.310)	-0.001 (0.325)
Constant	-6.796*** (1.059)	-6.518*** (1.405)	-7.802*** (1.733)
N	1,564	760	804

Source: AES 2016.
Notes: Cell entries are logistic coefficients (from regression models) with standard errors in parentheses.
[+]: $p < 0.1$, *: $p < 0.05$, **: $p < 0.01$, ***: $p < 0.001$.

of other political attitudes – such as opinions on unions, business, and redistribution – in explaining men's and women's likelihood of voting Labor is similar for both sexes. In sum, with the exception of attitudes toward minorities and economic priorities, men and women do not differ in the attitudes that lead them to vote for the Labor Party.

The final group of explanatory variables assesses support for increasing the number of women MPs. Results in Table 5.5 demonstrate that for both women and men, such opinions are not significantly related to voting for the Labor Party. The only exception is support for legislative quotas, where supporting such options is linked with voting for the Labor Party over Liberal; however, the relationships only reach the p < 0.10 level of significance.

Conclusion

For a long time, the role of gender in Australian politics has been discussed in the media and by politicians of both major parties. Despite their greater presence in the labour force and rising levels of education, women are still underrepresented in politics. Political parties play a role in maintaining the dominance of men in the highest offices of politics. They also play a role in possible solutions to this problem, such as gender quotas. Moreover, the discussion of gender has occurred during and after the election of the first female prime minister of Australia, Julia Gillard. As discussed above, Gillard's election to the highest office has coincided with the emergence of a new gender gap in vote choice – one where women are more likely than men to vote for the Labor Party. Gender has long been a salient issue in Australian politics and the emergence and endurance of a gender gap in favour of Labor is one of its latest consequences.

This chapter has tested structural and cultural explanations to understand why Australian women are now more likely than men to favour the Labor Party. Once a series of socio-demographic and individual characteristics are taken into account, the gender gap in voting remains. In other words, women with the same characteristics as men (such as age or education level) are more likely than men to vote Labor. This finding may indicate that structural explanations are not enough to explain the modern gender gap. The contributing factor to the modern gender gap in Australia may be more likely to be found in the different values held by women and men. Women's greater emphasis on welfare may lead them to be more likely than men to vote for the Labor Party. By positioning themselves as the defenders of health policies and Medicare, the Labor Party may have been able to attract a larger share of the women's vote since the Labor Party favours government intervention to a greater extent. In brief, these gender differences in values and policy preferences may indicate a more permanent shift, with more women voting Labor and more men voting Coalition. If women's preferences are deeply held, then the gender gap as observed in 2016 may be here to stay.

References

Aikin, Don (1982). *Stability and change in Australian politics*. Canberra: ANU Press.

Australian Bureau of Statistics (2014). *Characteristics of employment, Australia, August 2014*. Canberra: ABS.

Australian Election Study (2016). The AES series: 2016. australianelectionstudy.org.

Barnes, Tiffany D. and Abby Córdova (2016). Making space for women: explaining citizen support for legislative gender quotas in Latin America. *The Journal of Politics* 78(3), 670–86.

Burns, Nancy, Kay Lehmann Schlozman and Sidney Verba, (2001). *The private roots of public action: gender, equality, and political participation*. Cambridge, Mass.: Harvard University Press.

Butler, David and Donald E. Stokes (1974). *Political change in Britain*. New York: St Martin's Press.

Campbell, Angus, Philip E. Converse, Warren E. Miller and Donald E. Stokes (1960). *The American voter*. New York: Wiley.

Cassese, Erin C., Tiffany D. Barnes and Regina P. Branton (2015). Racializing gender: Public opinion at the intersection. *Politics and Gender* 11(1), 1–15.

Crowe, David (2015). Liberal MP Sharman Stone backs quotas for women. *Australian*, 28 July. http://bit.ly/2uRAscM.

DeVaus, David and Ian McAllister (1989). The changing politics of women: gender and political alignments in 11 nations. *European Journal of Political Research* 17(3), 241–62.

Duverger, Maurice (1955). *The political role of women*. Paris: UNESCO.

Erickson, Lynda and Brenda O'Neill (2002). The gender gap and the changing woman voter in Canada. *International Political Science Review* 23(4), 373–92.

Gidengil, Elisabeth (1995). Economic man – social woman? The case of the gender gap in support for the Canada–United States free trade agreement. *Comparative Political Studies* 28(3), 384–408.

Gidengil, Elisabeth (1996). Gender and attitudes toward quotas for women candidates in Canada. *Women and Politics* 16(4), 21–44.

Goot, Murray and Elizabeth Reid (1975). *Women and voting studies: mindless matrons or sexist scientism?* Beverly Hills, CA: Sage.

Gurin, Patricia (1985). Women's gender consciousness. *Public Opinion Quarterly* 49(2), 143–63.

Hayes, Bernadette and Ian McAllister (1997). Gender, party leaders, and electoral outcomes in Australia, Britain and the United States. *Comparative Political Studies* 30(1), 3–26.

Inglehart, Ronald (1977). *The silent revolution: changing values and political styles among Western publics.* Princeton, NJ: Princeton University Press.

Inglehart, Ronald and Pippa Norris (2003). *Rising tide: gender equality and cultural change around the world*. Cambridge: Cambridge University Press.

Interparliamentary Union (2017). Statistical archive: women in national parliaments (1 March). www.ipu.org/wmn-e/classif-arc.htm.

Klein, Ethel (1984). *Gender politics*. Cambridge, Mass.: Harvard University Press.

Krook, Mona Lena, Joni Lovenduski and Judith Squires (2009). Gender quotas and models of political citizenship. *British Journal of Political Science* 39(4), 781–803.

McAllister, Ian (2012). Early promise unfulfilled: the electoral representation of women in Australia. In *Women and legislative representation: electoral systems, political parties, and sex quotas*. Manon Tremblay, ed., 101–12. New York: Palgrave.

McAllister, Ian (2011). *The Australian voter*. Sydney: UNSW Press.

Norris, Pippa (2004). *Electoral engineering: voting rules and political behavior*. Cambridge: Cambridge University Press.

Norris, Pippa and Marc N. Franklin (1997). Social representation. *European Journal of Political Research* 32(2), 185–210.

Parliamentary Library (2017). *Composition of Australian parliaments by party and gender: a quick guide*. Canberra: Parliament of Australia, Department of Parliamentary Services.

Plutzer, Eric (1988). Work life, family life and women's support for feminism. *American Sociological Review* 53(4), 640–49.

Quota Project (2017). Global database of quotas for women. quotaproject.org.

Studlar, Donley T., Ian McAllister and Bernadette Hayes (1998). Explaining the gender gap in voting: a cross-national analysis. *Social Science Quarterly* 79(4), 779–98.

Troeth, Judith (2010). Modernising the parliamentary Liberal Party by adopting the organisational wing's quota system for preselections. Policy Paper. 23 June. http://apo.org.au/system/files/57011/apo-nid57011-98866.pdf.

Workplace Gender Equality Agency (2016). *Australia's gender equality scorecard*. Canberra: Australian Government. https://www.wgea.gov.au/sites/default/files/80653_2015-16-gender-equality-scorecard.pdf.

6

Battlers and aspirationals: the Liberal Party and the median voter

Ian McAllister and Toni Makkai

Major political parties are perennially seeking the middle ground of politics, where electoral success or failure is often thought to reside. The search for the median voter – the person with middle-of-the-road opinions and concerns and who is open to changing her vote – has occupied considerable time and effort from parties, candidates and their large followings of advisers. Crafting policies that appeal to this group is considered to be crucial to winning an election. Indeed, the median voter model has come to assume such importance in theories of electoral behaviour that it has been referred to as 'a fundamental property of democracy' (Congelton 2004, 707).

Identifying the median voter and the demographic group that she belongs to has given rise to a minor public relations industry. In Britain, various terms have been used to denote this stereotypical voter, most recently with 'Holby City Woman' and 'Motorway Man' in the 2010 general election. The former was described as a female public sector employee in her 30s or 40s concerned about education and the cost of childcare (Aaronovitch 2009); the latter was seen as 'aspirational, materialistic and car-dependent' (Pickard 2010). Both were regarded as representing key demographic groups which could decide the outcome of the election. In the United States, the equivalent of 'Holby City Woman' is the 'Soccer Mom', a term that emerged in the mid-1990s, and her successor, 'Hockey Mom', who was associated with Sarah Palin's vice-presidential candidature in the 2008 presidential election (Burns, Eberhardt and Merolla 2013).

Australia has generated its fair share of these median voter stereotypes. Most commonly used are the terms 'aspirational voter' and 'battler'. The former term was added to the *Australian National Dictionary* in 2016, where it is defined as 'a voter who is mainly concerned with material improvement or gain.'[1] In the same edition, the Dictionary also added the term '*Howard's battler*', which it defined as 'a person (especially working-class), traditionally regarded as a Labor voter, who was instrumental in electing John Howard's conservative Coalition to power in the 1996 federal election; such a person who continues to vote for the Coalition.' Like their international counterparts, these terms epitomise the concept of the floating voter, who comes from a key demographic group and whose support is crucial for electoral success.[2]

---

1 The OED defines an aspirational voter as 'A voter whose primary concern is the achievement of personal success and material gain.'

2 Another new entry in the 2016 edition relevant here is '*mortgage belt*', which is defined as 'an area where many people are paying off a mortgage on their home, regarded as electorally volatile.' These themes are

This chapter examines the extent to which the terms 'aspirational' and 'battler' represent identifiable social groups with distinctive political leanings, as opposed to catchy media phrases that serve to summarise the prevailing public mood and have few electoral implications. If such groups are identifiable, has their voting behaviour been as pivotal as is often alleged, most notably in the 1996 election? And perhaps most importantly, have any changes that are evident been permanent, or is the party loyalty of these voters continually open to change at each election? This chapter seeks to answer these questions using the 1993 to 2016 Australian Election Study (AES) surveys, which are national public opinion surveys conducted after each federal election using a common set of questions.

The first section examines the emergence of the median voter as a key demographic in Australia, and compares this experience with that of Britain. The second section outlines the theory that underpins the median voter and the assumptions on which the theory is based, while the third section uses the 1993–2016 surveys to identify various types of voters within the electorate and estimates their relative size. The fourth section seeks to identify the social groups that most characterise the median voter, while the fifth section examines their electoral support. Finally, the conclusion places the results in the context of international research on the policy implications of the median voter.

The emergence of the median voter

The terms 'aspirational voters' and 'battlers' are now widely used in Australian politics, and they are increasingly used internationally as well. The terms are often assumed to identify the groups of voters that the major parties must win over in order to gain office. They have their origins in the 1996 election victory by the Liberal Party led by John Howard, which ended 13 years of Labor government. Compared to the 1993 election, the Coalition gained 29 seats to give it a total of 94 seats, the largest number of seats the Coalition has secured in any federal election before or since.[3] The scale of the victory led to the widespread belief that a key demographic group – previously supporting Labor – had shifted its support to the Coalition (Singleton, Martyn and Ward 1998). The fact that the 1996 win presaged three further election successes appeared to confirm the belief that this change had become permanent.

In theory, 'aspirational voters' and 'battlers' are distinct groups, but in practice there is considerable overlap. Both terms conflate occupational status, patterns of consumption, and political attitudes, as well as current and prior voting behaviour. The net effect of this conflation is that arriving at agreed definitions is problematic. Scalmer (2005, 5), for example, notes that aspirational 'defies easy definition', while Goot and Watson (2006, 4) talk of 'conceptual confusion'. Brent (2004, 4) suggests that battlers are distinguished not just by their defection to the Liberals in 1996, but by their prior long-term loyalty to Labor. Haydon Manning (2014, 228) adopts a more precise definition: 'battlers are taken to be those survey respondents who were blue collar or in lower-paid white collar employment and who believed that their household was a little or a lot worse off financially than 12 months previously.'

---

also explored in relation to the 1996 federal election in McAllister (2017). The current chapter also draws on parts of this work.

3 The Coalition gained 91 seats in the 1975 election, based on a total of 127 seats, which represents a larger proportion of the total. Labor lost 5.1 per cent of its two-party vote in 1996 and recorded its lowest primary vote since 1934.

The definitions that appear in the *Australian National Dictionary* suggest that aspirationals are those who strive for material gain and by implication would normally regard the Liberals as most able to deliver that goal. Such voters could be more or less prosperous in terms of their economic position; the core point is that they seek to improve their current situation. In contrast, battlers are identified mainly by their defection from Labor to Liberal in the 1996 election with the goal of significantly improving their economic position; they are assumed to be much less prosperous than the general population. The common themes in these definitions are, first, the desire for material gain and/or upward social mobility and, second, a preference for the Liberals as the party most likely to create the conditions that will achieve those goals.

'Battler' resonates with an earlier term that gained much currency in conservative politics in the mid-twentieth century – 'the forgotten people' (Dryenfurth 2005). This term was first used by Robert Menzies in a 1942 radio speech following the fall of Singapore. In the speech, Menzies characterised the 'forgotten people' as 'those people who are constantly in danger of being ground between the upper and the nether millstones of the false class war; the middle class who, properly regarded, represent the backbone of the country' (quoted in Brett 1984, 255). The parallels between the 'forgotten people' and the 'battler' are obvious; both imply that there is an existential political threat to the economic position of these citizens, and that the opportunity to achieve material prosperity through hard work and skill may be denied to them.

Similar terms have also been widely used in British politics, starting with 'Selsdon Man' in 1970. This term was coined by the Labour prime minister Harold Wilson following a workshop for the Conservative shadow cabinet held in the Selsdon Park Hotel, London. The outcome of the workshop was a policy agenda based on free-market economic policies, and the venue gave its name to a free-market pressure group formed in 1973. Wilson used the term to disparage free-market policies, but in fact they appealed to many voters seeking upward social mobility and the Conservatives won the subsequent general election.[4] Since 1970, there has been a long list of terms used to identify what have been thought to be key demographic groups in British politics.

Most of these British stereotypes have been used to identify demographic groups which it was thought would defect from Labour to the Conservatives, but several have canvassed defection in the opposite direction. One of the most important of these was 'Mondeo Man', which was seen by Tony Blair as the key demographic that Labour had to win in the 1997 election in order to end the long period of Conservative government. Blair launched the term at the 1996 Labour conference, when he spoke of meeting a self-employed electrician who was polishing his car: 'his instincts were to get on in life and he thought our instincts were to stop him' (quoted in Moran 2005, 237). Another key Labour demographic was 'Worcester Woman', 'a middle class mother in her 40s or 50s who had previously voted for the Conservatives, but was swayed by Tony Blair's charismatic and youthful energy and his policies targeted to woo the middle class' (Christophersen 2010, 17).

While stereotypical labels of voters change, the idea that a voter should be free to improve her economic position and that government should assist in this process has underpinned all of these ideas. The idea also appears to be gaining momentum, at least

---

4   'Selsdon Man is designing a system of society for the ruthless and the pushing, the uncaring. His message to the rest is "you're out on your own."' http://www.bbc.com/news/election-2015-england-32212380.

Figure 6.1 Mentions of 'aspirations voters' in Australia and Britain, 1992–2016.

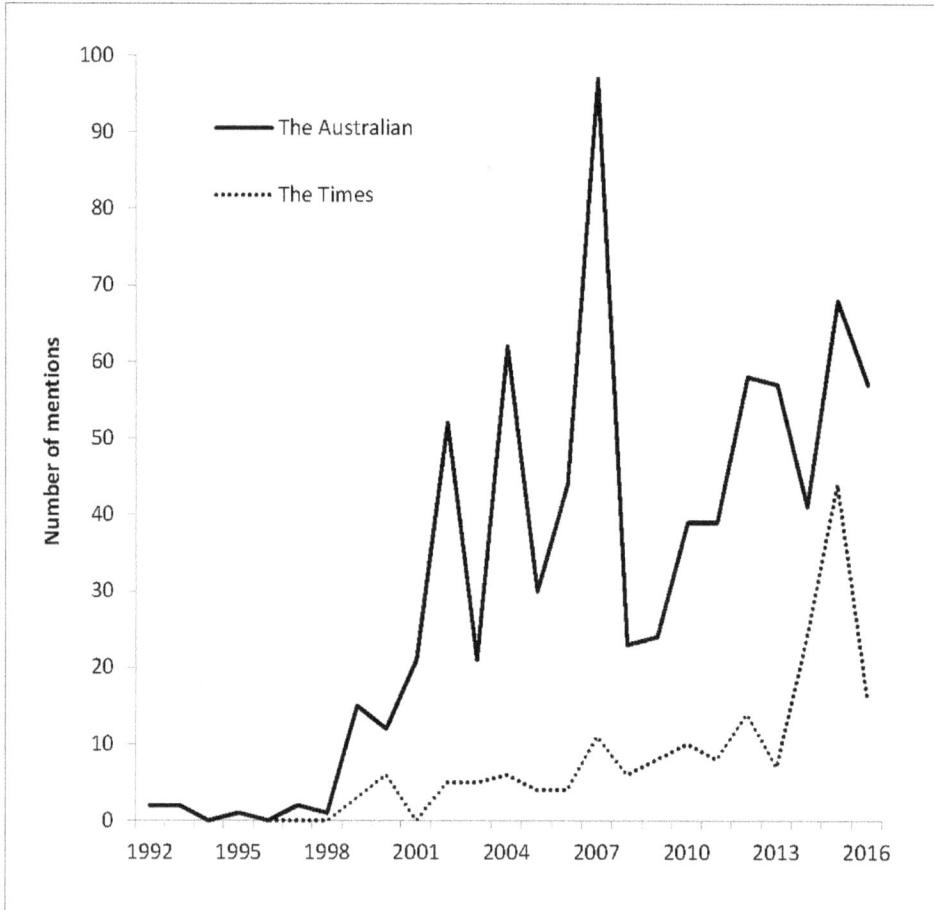

Note: The figures are the number of mentions of 'aspirational voter' or 'aspirational voters' in the two newspapers for the period for which data is available.

as it is reflected in newspaper mentions. Figure 6.1 shows the number of mentions of 'aspirational voter' in the *Australian* and the *London Times* newspapers.[5] The first mentions of the term appear in the early 1990s and their frequency in the *Australian* climbs steadily with each election, peaking at 86 mentions in the 2007 election. In the 2010 election there were just 29 mentions, but rising to 50 in 2013 before declining slightly to 41 in 2016. The frequency of mentions in the *London Times* is lower, but it is notable that there is a sharp increase, to 44 mentions, during the 2015 general election.

---

5   Goot and Watson (2006, 2; see also Goot and Watson 2007) present similar data from 1999 to 2004 using the term 'aspirational' in conjunction with the terms 'Latham' and 'Howard.' They show a steady increase in the use of the term, particularly for Howard. The term 'battler' is rarely used in Britain, hence the graph is restricted to estimating the frequency of 'aspirational.'

In Australia, 'aspirational voters' and 'battlers' have come to epitomise the concept of the floating voter, and the idea that government should assist rather that impede individuals who wish to achieve material gain through hard work and effort. In Britain, the concept has progressed further, with places, consumer goods and even television programs being used to identify the key demographic group to which these individuals are thought to belong. Underpinning this interpretation is the view that elections are won or lost in the centre-ground and that a normal distribution of public opinion encourages centripetal party competition. The next section examines the theoretical background to this claim.

The median voter theory

First applied to politics by Anthony Downs in 1957, the median voter theory predicts that parties will shift their appeals to the political centre in order to win votes, since this area is assumed to contain the largest proportion of uncommitted voters. The model is based on three assumptions. First, it assumes that there is a plurality electoral system and a two-party system. If, for example, there is a proportional electoral system and/or a multiparty system, the main parties will have less incentive to appeal to the centre. Instead, they may seek alliances with the parties that occupy the political space closest to themselves. Second, the model assumes that voters' opinions are distributed along a single continuum, such as left versus right. If there is a second cross-cutting continuum, such as freedom versus authority, then the assumption of linearity does not apply. In this case, what constitutes the political centre becomes blurred and the optimum party strategy is unclear. And third, the model assumes a unimodal distribution of opinion. If public opinion is bimodal then there is no identifiable political centre.

The median voter model rapidly gained prominence in voting research, and has been widely applied to many countries with highly varied institutional arrangements (for a review, see Holcombe 1989). It soon became clear that the model was highly sensitive to a country's institutional design characteristics, and if specific characteristics were not present, the model would not behave as predicted. However, empirical research has demonstrated that if the three conditions noted earlier are met, then two-party convergence is indeed likely to occur. While party candidates will tend to be closer to the median voter in their own party, it does appear that their views will also shift towards appealing to uncommitted voters who occupy the centre (Grofman 2004, 40).

In Australia, the Liberal and Labor parties' pursuit of the median voter is encouraged by three factors. First, while partisanship has remained relatively stable since 1996, with about one in six voters not identifying with a political party, the extent of voting volatility has increased consistently. In 1967 almost three in every four voters said that they had always voted for the same party in federal elections; by 2016 that figure had declined to 40 per cent (Cameron and McAllister 2016, 21), although in the vast majority of cases, voters will defect from their partisanship only once or twice during a voting lifetime. Second, the vote gap that separates the two political parties is consistently small. In the 28 federal elections conducted since 1945, the mean vote difference between the parties, based on the two-party preferred vote, was just 4.4 per cent, meaning that little more than 2 per cent of the electorate would need to change their vote in order to alter the election outcome. Third, compulsory voting brings to the polls around one in seven voters who would not attend under a voluntary voting system.[6] These voters are more likely to be uncommitted, thus increasing the pool of voters potentially occupying the centre-ground of politics (Mackerras and McAllister 1999).

The pursuit of the median voter has obvious attractions for the major political parties. Institutional design provides a strong incentive for the major parties to seek the support of the uncommitted median voter, and to largely take their own supporters for granted since they have few other alternatives. Where support for minor parties has periodically posed a potential threat – for Labor, from the Australian Democrats and latterly the Greens, and for the Liberals, from One Nation – the operation of the preferential electoral system for the House of Representatives ensures that the major parties regain the bulk of the minor party vote through the distribution of preferences. The trend towards two-party convergence in Australia corresponds very closely to the predictions of the median vote theory.

Identifying the median voter

The confusion over defining an aspirational voter and a battler makes operationalising the concept of the median voter using public opinion surveys difficult. Past research has used a variety of measures covering occupation, political attitudes, and voting behaviour. Manning (2014, 228; see also Manning 2005) identifies battlers as those in blue-collar or lower-paid white-collar employment who considered their household to have become worse off financially over the previous year. Using this definition, Manning estimates battlers to represent around 17 per cent of the electorate in 1996. Goot and Watson (2006, 5) use two definitions for aspirational: a narrow occupational definition based on self-employment; and a broader definition that includes attitudes towards getting ahead in one's job and achieving a high income, among other things. According to this latter definition, around 7 per cent of the electorate are aspirational.[7]

Building on this previous research, the approach used here is to identify aspirational voters by their attitudes to government policies that may either encourage or impede their ability to achieve material gain. Using a subjective rather than an objective measure is based on the logic that aspiration is more a state of mind than a consequence of a person's position in the employment structure. By contrast, being a battler is less attitudinally based and is more likely to stem from a person's objective economic situation; in this case, a battler is defined by her gross family income and by her evaluation of the performance of the household's income over the past year.

In order to identify aspiration, two broad issues are used: attitudes towards the direction of government spending, and views of trade union regulation. How government approaches both issues has the potential to affect a person's ability to achieve material gain through public policy, the first by choosing between more government spending towards social services or tax cuts, and the second by whether or not to increase the level of trade union regulation.[8] In principle, reducing taxes and weakening trade union influence should increase the opportunities for material gain, especially for the self-employed. Both

---

6   This estimate is based on the question: 'Would you have voted in the election if voting had not been compulsory?' In 2013, 14 per cent of the respondents said that they 'probably' or 'definitely' would not have voted under a voluntary system.

7   The estimate is based on the 2005 Australian Survey of Social Attitudes.

the level of government spending and trade union laws have been major issues in most of the elections conducted over the 1993 to 2016 period. Both therefore focus on how government policies can shape a voter's level of economic prosperity.

In 1993 and 1996 the electorate's views were strongly in favour of regulating the activities of trade unions. Figure 6.2 shows that around six out of every ten respondents took this view. The proportion in favour of more regulation has declined consistently since then, to a low of 42 per cent in 2007, when the Liberal government's industrial relations policy called WorkChoices was a major issue. Support for regulation has gradually increased since 2007, to 55 per cent in 2016 when the Liberal government made union activities in the building industry an election issue. Attitudes towards less tax as opposed to greater government spending on social services shows a similar pattern. In 1993 and 1996 just under six in every ten respondents favoured less tax, but that proportion has declined consistently, reaching its lowest figure – 34 per cent – again in 2007. Since then, the proportion in favour of less tax has remained at around one in three of the electorate, about the same proportion who favour more spending on social services.[9]

In contrast to using attitudes towards public policy to define aspirational voters, battlers are defined by the perceived condition of their household economy. More specifically, a battler is considered to be someone whose family income falls into either the fourth or fifth quintile in the survey in question, together with an assessment that the financial situation of the household has become either 'a little worse' or 'a lot worse' over the previous year. This definition therefore identifies someone who has a relatively low income, at the same time as feeling that their household income is under pressure and shows little sign of improving.

Although battlers and aspirationals are based on different definitions, in practice there is necessarily some overlap between them. A battler trying to cope with the difficulties caused by a low income can also be aspirational, insofar as she sees a remedy to her situation in terms of changes in government policy. However, in 1996 just 17 per cent of aspirational voters were also battlers, little different from the population figure of 16 per cent.[10] For the purposes of classification, then, battlers are considered as a discrete group, while aspirationals are those who have the political views outlined above but who are not battlers. At the other end of the spectrum, the responses to the two attitude questions enable us to identify those who are broadly collectivist in their views, by favouring more government spending on social services and by opposing more union regulation.[11] Those who do not fall into any of these three categories are classified as indifferent.

It is also important to bear in mind that in an over-time analysis such as that presented here, these groups will be composed of different people at different points in time. For example, an individual may improve her economic position over time, and while being classified as

8   The AES has consistently asked another question on support for the redistribution of wealth. However, this does not include any reference to the role of government in achieving redistribution.

9   Around one in three of the electorate take an intermediate position. (See Cameron and McAllister 2016.)

10   The correlation between the two items is also negligible, r = .051 (p = .034).

11   The categories are defined as follows. Strongly aspirational: strongly favours reducing tax, and strongly agrees with stricter union laws. Aspirational: strongly favours reducing tax and agrees with stricter union laws, or mildly favours reducing tax and strongly favours stricter union laws, or mildly favours reducing tax and favours stricter laws. Collectivist: strongly or mildly favours reducing tax and strongly disagrees or disagrees on stricter union laws. Indifferent: all others who do not fall into the three categories above.

Figure 6.2 Attitudes towards unions and taxation, 1993–2016.

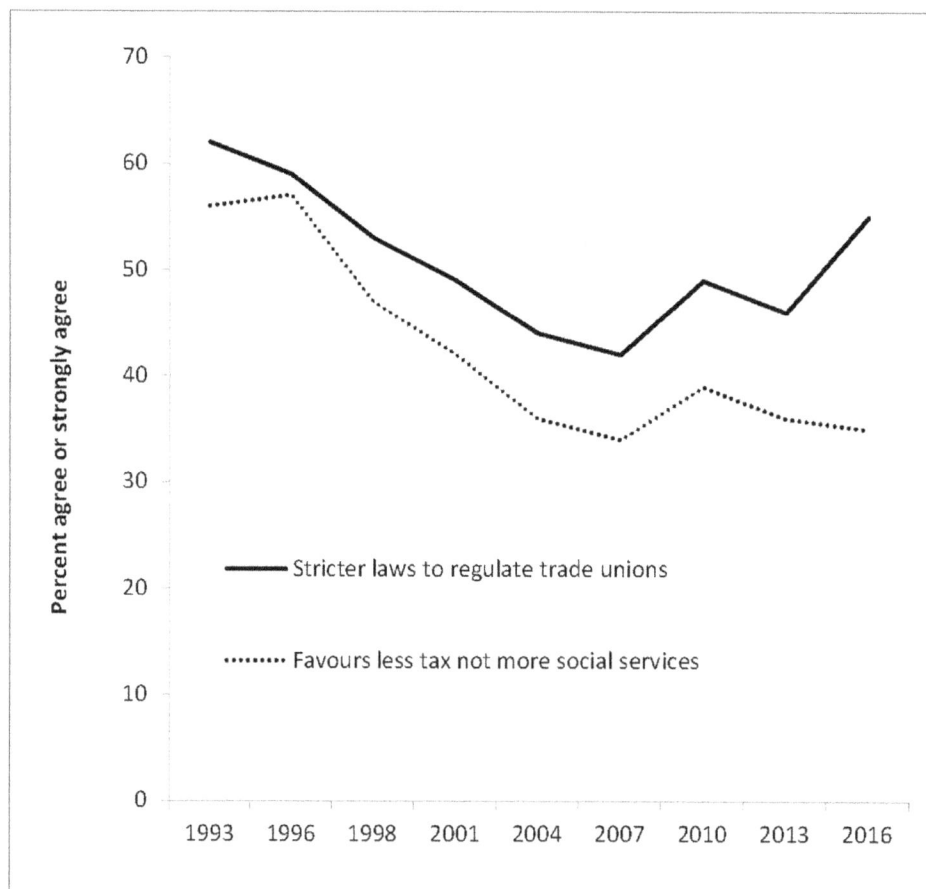

Source: Australian Election Study (AES), 1993–2016.

a low-income battler in the 1990s, could be a relatively prosperous aspirational voter in the 2000s. In other words, underlying the trends examined in this chapter is a dynamic which involves a degree of fluidity in the individuals who occupy the various categories.

These four groups of voters have varied considerably in size from 1993 through to 2016 (Figure 6.3). In 1993, the first year for which we can make an estimate,[12] battlers constituted one in five of the electorate. This estimate comes in the wake of the 1990–91 recession, when unemployment peaked at 10.8 per cent and interest rates at just over 16 per cent. With improving economic conditions, the proportion of battlers declined to 15 per cent in 1996 and 1998, only to increase again to 18 per cent in 2001 following the economic slowdown of 2000. Since then battlers have declined in size; in 2016 they

---

12   The 1990 AES did not include a family income question, and the 1987 survey did not include the trade union question. Hence the starting year for the analysis is 1993.

Figure 6.3 Types of voters, 1993–2016.

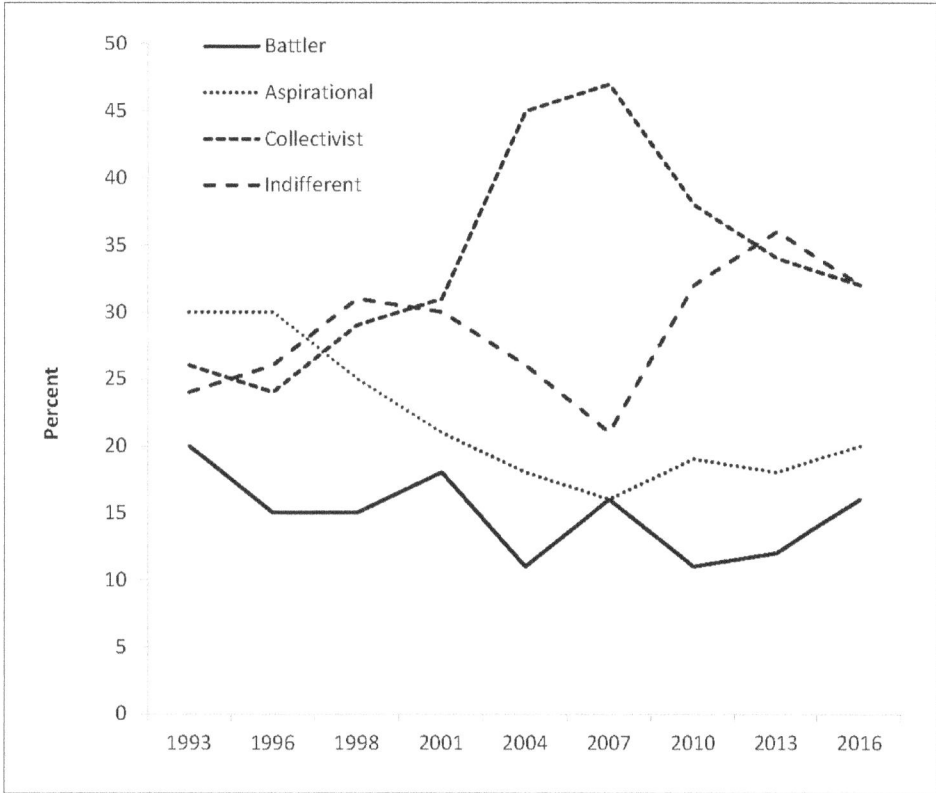

Source: AES 1993–2016.

represented 16 per cent of the electorate. The proportion of aspirational voters has also declined over the period, from three in every ten voters in both 1993 and 1996, to just 20 per cent in 2016. At the other end of the political spectrum, collectivist voters numbered just over one in four voters in 1993, but by 2007 this had increased to almost half of the electorate. In 2013 and 2016 collectivists numbered around one in every three voters.

The patterns in Figure 6.3 emphasise the declining size of the two groups that are taken to represent the median voter. In 1993 and 1996 battlers and aspirationals together accounted for 50 per cent and 45 per cent of the electorate, respectively. However, by 2016 they together accounted for 36 per cent. This decline has been driven by the relative economic prosperity generated by the mining boom that occurred between the mid-2000s and 2011–12. Prosperity has changed attitudes to government spending as well as towards trade unions, and generated improved living standards. At the same time, collectivists have grown substantially in size and were most prevalent at the time of the 2007 election, which brought the election of the Rudd Labor government following 11 years of Coalition government.

Table 6.1: Socioeconomic characteristics of types of voters, 1996 and 2016.

	1996				2016			
	Battler	Aspirational	Collectivist	Indifferent	Battler	Aspirational	Collectivist	Indifferent
Social background								
Gender (per cent male)	45	51	53	43	44	61*	48	45
Age (mean years)	50.6*	45.8	46.6	43.8	55.1*	51.3*	46.2	46.1
Urban resident (per cent)	37*	54	55	50	40*	54*	67	52*
Education and occupation								
University degree (per cent)	10*	23*	34	23*	18*	41*	48	33*
Trade qualification (per cent)	27*	22	16	16	22*	18*	11	14
Employed (per cent)	30*	51	50	49	34*	69	63	58
Non-manual worker (per cent)	39*	58	60	56	63	40*	60	57
Government employee (per cent)	10*	17*	28	20*	23	18*	26	18*
Self-employed (per cent)	26*	30*	11	14	17	32*	15	18
Economic status								
Family income (mean, '000s)	13.5*	45.5*	38.9	38.0	32.0*	103.0	102.0	94.3*
Union member (per cent)	24*	18*	39	23*	13*	10*	24	17*
Middle-class image (per cent)	30*	57*	45	47	29*	61	59	49*
(N)	(273)	(539)	(435)	(471)	(435)	(523)	(854)	(840)

* significantly different from collectivist at p<.01, two-tailed. Ns for individual items vary due to missing values.

Source: AES 1996, 120=2016.

Who is the median voter?

Accurately identifying the social composition of the four groups is the first step to understanding their potential importance in shaping electoral outcomes over an extended period. If the groups that represent the median voter can be readily identified, then the parties can craft individual appeals to try and win their support. To see how socially distinctive the groups are, three broad categories of background characteristics – social background, education and occupation, and economic status – are examined across the four groups of voters (Table 6.1). The 1996 election is chosen as the baseline for the analysis as it has been identified as the election in which the battlers first became electorally important.

Judged against collectivists, there are relatively few differences in terms of social background across both elections among battlers and aspirationals, the only significant differences being that battlers are more likely to be older and non-metropolitan residents. There are, however, very substantial differences between the groups in terms of their education and occupation which are replicated in each election. Aspirational voters and especially battlers are less likely to have a university education, less likely to be employed, and more likely to have a trade qualification. In addition, aspirational voters are consistently more likely to be self-employed.

Important differences between the groups also emerge on economic status. Income is not a relevant point of comparison for battlers since that is one of the two criteria by which they are measured. However, income was important for aspirationals in 1996, who had a significantly higher family income than the other groups, but not in 2016. Nevertheless, aspirationals have the highest family income of any of the four groups. Aspirationals were also more likely than anyone else to regard themselves as being middle class. And they are also significantly less likely in both elections, along with battlers, to be trade union members.

The median voter – either battler or aspirational – can therefore be identified with a high degree of precision by their socioeconomic characteristics. This enables the political parties to target these groups, and to develop policies designed specifically to try and win their votes. Battlers and aspirationals are similar in many of their background characteristics, with the crucial exceptions that battlers have much lower incomes, do not see themselves as middle class, and are older and less urban-based. In principle, then, policies aimed at the redistribution of wealth and support for social welfare should appeal to battlers to a greater extent than aspirationals, who prioritise retaining as much of their wealth as possible. We return to the policy implications of this interpretation in the conclusion.

The electoral impact

Following each federal election, the Liberal Party federal director and the Labor Party national secretary traditionally give a National Press Club speech reassessing their election campaign, and explaining the reasons for their success or failure. In 1996 the Liberal federal director, Andrew Robb, attributed Liberal success to a fundamental shift in votes to the Coalition from a specific demographic group. Using an exit poll based on 52 electorates, Robb argued that these votes had come 'from workers and their families –

Howard's battlers'. This change, he argued, had come about because Labor had decided 'to chase the votes of the socially progressive, often highly educated, affluent end of middle Australia'.[13]

Robb's speech is often cited as the genesis of the view that the Coalition's four successive electoral successes starting in 1996 were attributable almost solely to the support of 'Howard's battlers' (Brent 2004). Without the key support of this group, it was argued, this unbroken run of election successes would have been impossible. The idea of the 'battler', engaged in an unequal fight against an uncaring corporate elite, fitted the populism of the times (Greenfield and Williams 2001). It has entered the lexicon of the political class, and is regularly used as a convenient shorthand label to identify working-class conservatives. The term was also soon part of the media's election rhetoric, and there have been numerous stories since 1996 purporting to identify the archetypal 'Howard battler' and to trace her views of the contemporary political scene.

Identifying the four types of voters allows us to trace their vote over the 1993 to 2016 period (Figure 6.4) and to test this argument empirically. The evidence suggests that whilst battlers did support the Coalition in large numbers in 1996, they deserted them almost as rapidly in 1998. In 1996 almost two in three battlers voted for the Coalition, but in 1998 the proportion voting for the Coalition was just one in four – a massive shift in support in a short period of time. Moreover, battlers remained consistently unlikely to vote for the Coalition through the 2000s until 2010, when their support shifted back to the Coalition, although not in the numbers seen in 1996. Moreover, by 2016 battler support for the Coalition had returned to the levels found between 1998 and 2007. The evidence would suggest, then, that the idea of Howard's battlers defecting from Labor to Liberal in 1996 and continuing their support after 1996 is a myth. These voters did defect from Labor to Liberal in 1996, but the Liberals did not retain their loyalty.

If the battlers were unlikely to vote for the Coalition between 1998 and 2007, who did they vote for? The main beneficiary of the defection of the battlers from the Coalition after 1996 was Labor. In 1998, 54 per cent of battlers voted Labor, as did 53 per cent in 2001. This proportion gradually increased to 60 per cent in 2004 and peaked at 65 per cent in 2007. The defection of the battlers from the Coalition in 1998 has two main explanations. First, the rise of One Nation proved attractive to a significant minority of battlers, with 11 per cent of them voting for the party. Second, concerns about the impact of the introduction of a goods and services tax on their household economy caused many battlers to return to Labor. Among battlers, 59 per cent preferred Labor policy on the new tax compared to 42 per cent of the general population.

The surge in battler support for the Coalition in 2010 was equally temporary. That appears to have been driven by the twin concerns of declining economic performance following the Global Financial Crisis and the high numbers of refugee arrivals by boat following Labor's changes to border protection policy. By 2016 battler support for the Coalition had again dissipated. Labor was once again the main beneficiary, but not at the level they experienced in 1998 and 2001. In 2016, 39 per cent of battlers voted Labor, but one in four voted for minor parties – the highest proportion doing so among any of the four voter groups. While the numbers in the survey are small, particular beneficiaries of this move away from both major parties in 2016 appear to have been One Nation and the Nick Xenophon Team.

---

13 http://australianpolitics.com/1996/03/13/andrew-robb-the-1996-federal-election.html.

Figure 6.4 Coalition voting among battlers and aspirationals, 1993–2016.

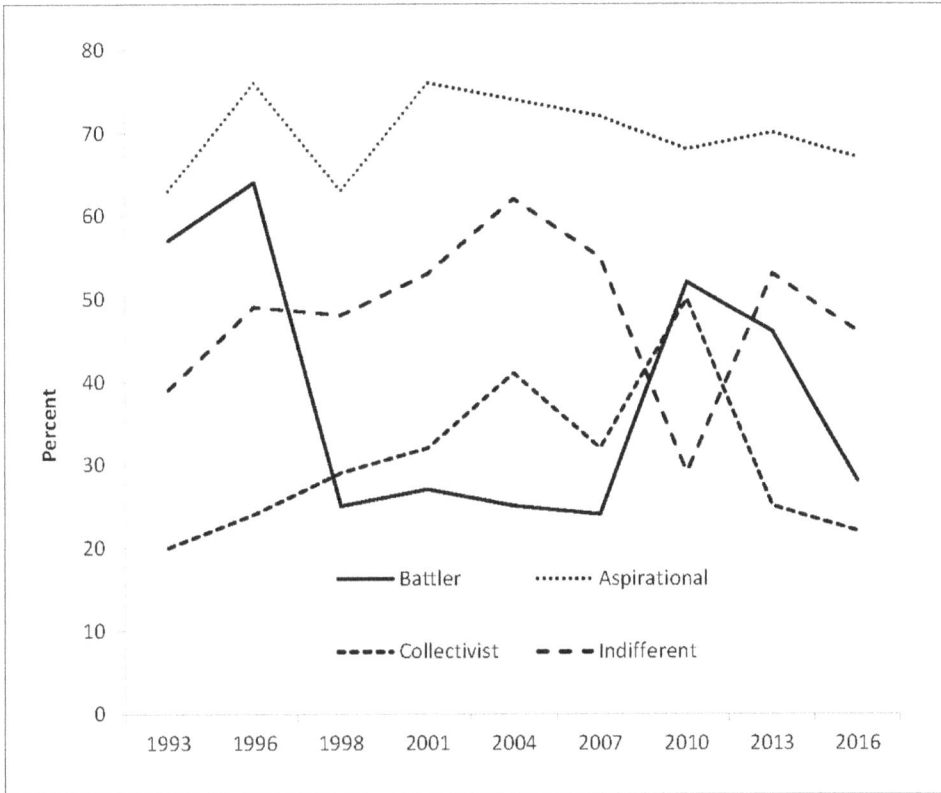

Source: AES 1993–2016.

In contrast to the battlers, aspirational voters have remained consistently supportive of the Coalition throughout the 1993 to 2016 period. Figure 6.4 shows that around seven in every ten aspirational voters have supported the Coalition with peaks of 76 per cent in both 1996 and 2001. The only partial exception to this pattern occurs in the 1998 election when 63 per cent voted for the Coalition, the same figure as in 1993. For all practical purposes, then, aspirational voters are a core part of the Coalition's electoral support. However, because the proportion of aspirationals within the population is declining, their overall contribution to the Coalition vote has also declined, from 45 per cent of the Coalition vote in 1993, to a low of 25 per cent in 2004. In the 2016 election, 34 per cent of the total Coalition vote came from aspirational voters.

The evidence would suggest, then, that the majority of battlers who defected from Labor to Liberal in 1996 simply returned to Labor in 1998. Moreover, throughout the period of the Howard Liberal government they remained staunch Labor voters, only again turning their backs on Labor after the experience of the dysfunctional 2007–10 Rudd–Gillard government. There is some survey evidence from the 2007 AES that this shift among the battlers away from Labor may have been driven by disapproval of Julia Gillard's replacement of Kevin Rudd.[14] The belief that 'Howard's battlers' were a distinct group who permanently shifted their support from Labor to Liberal therefore has no empirical evidence to support it. Between 1998 and 2007, battlers were much more likely to see their interests being served by Labor rather than by the Liberals.

Conclusion

The pursuit of the median voter has come to occupy much time and effort among party professionals. The narrowness of the vote gap between the major parties, with typically a 1 to 2 per cent shift in votes delivering success or failure, has given added urgency to this search. But does the median voter exist? If the median voter does exist, who is she, and what drives her defection between the major parties? The evidence presented here, relying on national election studies conducted immediately after each federal election since 1993 and using exactly comparable measures, has suggested that there is a median voter, but that she owes no loyalty to one or other party. Moreover, the stereotypical Howard battler invented by Andrew Robb in 1996 just as rapidly defected from the Liberals in 1998 and did not return for another five elections.

To a large extent the myth of the median voter has been driven by the mass media, for whom the appeal of a catchy phrase to symbolise the times outweighs the requirement to test it against the evidence. Indeed, it would seem that the *Australian National Dictionary* is wrong to define 'Howard's battlers' as an identifiable group that remained loyal to the Liberals after 1996. Not unsurprisingly, the battlers took the view that the introduction of a goods and services tax in 1998 would not be in their economic interests and largely shifted their support back to Labor. They only returned to the Liberals in 2010, again temporarily, and then not in the proportions seen in 1996. By 2016 they had moved to Labor, as well as supporting several of the more prominent minor parties.

The other median voter group, the aspirationals, have consistently remained loyal to the Coalition, and their importance to the Liberal vote has diminished not because of any change in their partisan loyalty but as a consequence of the decline in their absolute size within the electorate. But the support of aspirational voters for the Liberals has been gradually declining since the peak in 2001. Among this older and more prosperous demographic group, concerns about the changes introduced by the Coalition government in 2015–16 to superannuation, pensions, and aged care have served to erode Liberal support.

Median voters have the potential to decide election outcomes, but they can also shape policies. Since the parties identify them as key groups to appeal to, they are more likely to develop policies that the groups will find attractive. And if they win the election, then the party will implement the policies that the median voter favours. Kang and Powell (2010), for example, show that welfare policies are shaped by the preferences of voters, so that a shift to the left among voters will result in government policies aimed at bolstering social welfare, while a shift to the right will result in an opposite effect. In this way, the median voter may not only affect party strategy; she may affect the direction of public policy as well.

---

14   In the 2010 AES, battlers were more likely to rank Rudd higher than Gillard (4.7 and 4.3 on the 0 to 10 thermometer scale, respectively). In turn, just 17 per cent of battlers approved of Rudd's replacement by Gillard, compared to 18 per cent of aspirationals and 33 per cent of collectivists.

References

Aaronovitch, David (2009). Can Tories win over Holby Woman? *Times*, 28 July.

Australian Election Study (2016).*The AES studies: 1993–2016*. http://www.australianelectionstudy.org/voter_studies.html.

Brent, Peter (2004). *Howard's battlers: the electoral evidence*. Paper presented to the Australasian Political Studies Association Conference, University of Adelaide, 29 September–1 October 2004.

Brett, Judith (1984). Menzies' forgotten people. *Meanjin* 43(2), 253–65.

Burns, Sarah, Lindsay Eberhardt and Jennifer F. Merolla (2013). What is the difference between a hockey mom and a pit bull? Presentations of Palin and gender stereotypes in the 2008 presidential election. *Political Research Quarterly* 66(4), 687–701.

Cameron, Sarah and Ian McAllister (2016). *Trends in Australian political opinion, 1987–2016*. Canberra: ANU. http://australianelectionstudy.org.

Christophersen, Mariette (2010). David Cameron's electoral strategy: a winning formula? *British Politics Review* 5, 7–8.

Congleton, Roger D. (2004). The median voter model. In *The encyclopedia of public choice*. Charles K. Rowley and Friedrich Schneider, eds. 25–42. London: Springer.

Downs, Anthony (1957). *An economic theory of democracy*. New York: Harper.

Dyrenfurth, Nick (2005). Battlers, refugees and the republic: John Howard's language of citizenship. *Journal of Australian Studies* 28(1), 183–96.

Goot, Murray and Ian Watson (2006). *Are aspirationals different?* Paper presented to the Australasian Political Studies Association Conference, University of Newcastle, 25–27 September 2006.

Goot, Murray and Ian Watson (2007). Explaining Howard's success: social structure, issue agendas and party support, 1993–2004. *Australian Journal of Political Science* 42(2), 253–76.

Greenfield, Cathy and Peter Williams (2001). 'Howardism' and the media rhetoric of 'battlers' vs 'elites'. *Southern Review* 34(1), 32–44.

Grofman, Bernard (2004). Downs and two party convergence. *Annual Review of Political Science* 7, 25–46.

Holcombe, Randall G. (1989). The median voter model in public choice theory. *Public Choice* 61(1), 115–25.

Kang, Sin-Goo and G. Bingham Powell (2010). Representation and policy responsiveness: the median voter, election rules, and redistributive welfare spending. *Journal of Politics* 72(4), 1014–28.

Mackerras, Malcolm and Ian McAllister (1999). Compulsory voting, party stability and electoral advantage in Australia. *Electoral Studies* 18(2), 217–33.

Manning, Haydon (2005). 'Aspirational voters' and the 2004 federal election. *Australian Review of Public Affairs*. http://www.australianreview.net/digest/2005/07/manning.html.

Manning, Haydon (2014). Voters and voting. In *Government and politics in Australia*. Alan Fenna, Jane Robbins and John Summers, eds. 79–97. Sydney: Pearson.

McAllister, Ian (2017). Howard's battlers and the 1996 election. In *The ascent to power, 1996: the Howard government, vol. 1*. Tom Frame, ed. 80–95. Sydney: UNSW Press.

Moran, Joe (2005). The strange birth of middle England. *Political Quarterly* 76(2), 232–40.

Pickard, Jim (2010). British parties in election drive to track down Motorway Man. *Financial Times*, 22 January. Available at http://on.ft.com/2x6w6ze.

Scalmer, Sean (2005). Searching for the aspirationals. *Overland* 180, 5–9.

Singleton, Jeff, Paul Martyn and Ian Ward (1998). Did the 1996 federal election see a blue-collar revolt against Labor? A Queensland case-study. *Australian Journal of Political Science* 33(1), 117–30.

7

No steps further! Australian attitudes to 'the right of free assembly' in comparative perspective

Markus Hadler and Anja Eder

> The right of peaceful assembly shall be recognized. No restrictions may be placed on the exercise of this right other than those imposed in conformity with the law and which are necessary in a democratic society in the interests of national security or public safety, public order (*ordre public*), the protection of public health or morals or the protection of the rights and freedoms of others.
>
> Article 21, *International Covenant on Civil and Political Rights*

After the experiences of the atrocities of the Second World War committed by totalitarian regimes, the United Nations came together and declared several basic human rights. This Human Rights Charter includes the freedom to express one's opinion and the freedom of assembly and association. These rights were re-enforced in 1966 in the International Covenant on Civil and Political Rights, which was signed by Australia in 1972 and ratified in 1980 (see https://bit.ly/1lEGjfc). In total, this treaty is now ratified by 168 countries and signed by another seven. Only 22 states have not signed, a group that includes countries such as Saudi Arabia, Malaysia and South Sudan.

The freedom of assembly and speech is a human, political, and civil right (Barendt 2005). Yet, one of the big questions in comparative sociology is if the content of such institutions is also reflected in the public attitudes and views of citizens. What do individuals think about public protesters who express extreme opinions? What are the boundaries of the freedom of assembly and freedom of speech in people's views? Such questions are not only of academic interest, but are also of immediate relevance for politics, given that many countries have seen a resurgence of protests by religious extremists, racists and totalitarian groups.

Recently, Australia has seen a number of protests from groups that oppose an 'Islamisation' of the country and try to reclaim a 'white' Australia. Among the supporters of this movement is the street protest group United Patriots Front and the voters of the right-wing political parties One Nation and Rise Up Australia. These rallies were frequently accompanied by counter-protests from various anti-racism groups, which have led to some violent conflicts (for example in June 2016 in Melbourne[1]). At the same time, the

---

1   See, for example, 'Violence breaks out after anti-immigration, anti-racist rallies in Melbourne' on ABC news, 26 June, 2016: https://ab.co/290tOuq.

20-year-old Section 18C of the Racial Discrimination Act came under discussion because liberal politicians considered it a threat to free speech in Australia. Section 18C aims to protect people and particularly minorities from public humiliation and thus penalises 'racial vilification' or 'hate speech' (McNamara 2016).

Given these developments, this chapter investigates to what extent Australians are open to protests of extremist groups and also compares their attitudes to public opinion in other countries. We use the 2014 Citizenship Module fielded as part of the International Social Survey Programme (ISSP) (see ISSP Research Group 2016) which was fielded in Australia as part of the Australian Survey of Social Attitudes (2014) and in similar general social surveys in a total of 34 countries. It includes three questions on the right of assembly of three groups: religious extremists, people who want to overthrow the government, and groups who are prejudiced against any racial or ethnic group. These three items are at the centre of our analysis and we refer to them collectively as the 'acceptance of the freedom of assembly'.

When considering possible influences on this 'acceptance' of the freedom of assembly, we draw on the closely related literature on social and political tolerance and further consider the impact of economic and social-psychological factors. These include institutional arrangements such as democratic experience, the effect of international civil society, and political rhetoric, as well as economic circumstances and group threat. The next section thus offers an overview of these various theoretical backdrops, which is then followed by a description of our data sources, variables, and analytical strategy. The results section starts with a comparison of the acceptance of the freedom of assembly of extremists in Australia to that in other countries. This international overview is followed by an Australia-specific analysis that shows which social groups are particularly opposed or in favour of these rights. The discussion and conclusion section then relates our findings to the existing literature.

Political and social tolerance

Political tolerance is a fundamental precondition of liberal democracies and implies that political minorities 'must be given the means of contestation – the right to try to convince others of the rightness of their positions' (Gibson 2013). From this point of view citizens should tolerate the freedom of assembly for extremist groups. However, philosophers such as Karl Popper (1945) emphasised the paradox of tolerance, namely that limitless 'tolerance of intolerance' in the long run will lead to the disappearance of tolerance.

When considering the literature on political and social tolerance, we can distinguish a more 'materialistic' and a more 'cultural/ideational' conceptualisation of this question (see Figure 7.1). While the former emphasises social and psychological forces such as economic circumstances and threat from different groups, the latter focuses upon the role of institutions such as democratisation, party positions, and international ideas. Our review starts with a brief summary of the former.

Group threat and economic circumstances

At a very basic level, the role of economic development and affluence is considered in the postmaterialism thesis (Inglehart and Baker 2000; Inglehart and Welzel 2005). This thesis

Figure 7.1 Explanatory approaches to social and political tolerance.

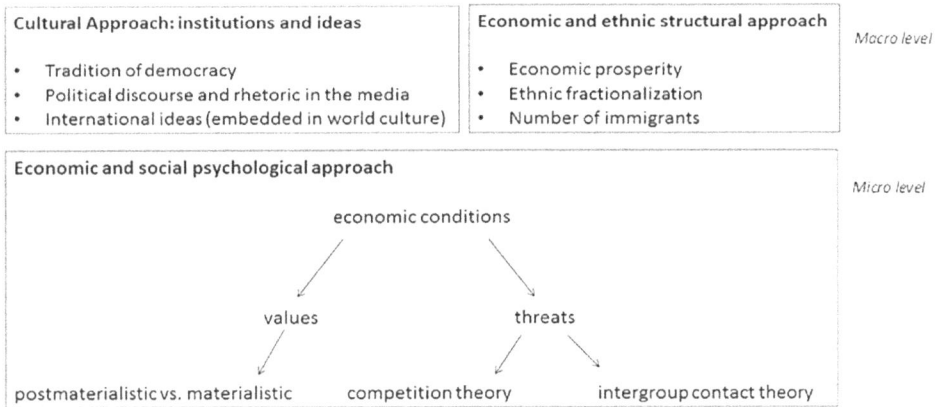

Cultural Approach: institutions and ideas	Economic and ethnic structural approach	
• Tradition of democracy • Political discourse and rhetoric in the media • International ideas (embedded in world culture)	• Economic prosperity • Ethnic fractionalization • Number of immigrants	*Macro level*

Economic and social psychological approach

Micro level

economic conditions

values   threats

postmaterialistic vs. materialistic   competition theory   intergroup contact theory

asserts that individuals develop postmaterialist values once a sufficient level of economic security is achieved, whereas individuals who experience scarcity maintain materialistic values. Inglehart (1999) considers this economic insecurity conducive to xenophobia and authoritarian attitudes, while postmaterialists value diversity and emphasise self-expression. Social and political tolerance as well as acceptance of democratic norms are thus supposed to be more common among postmaterialists.

The role of economic circumstances is also considered within the approaches emphasising group threat. Group threat theory and competition theory in the field of ethnic and racial relations point out that antagonism is more likely when different groups rival for limited resources (Blumer 1958; Quillian 1995). The perceived threat depends on the size of the other group; further, other groups are more likely to be seen as a threat during periods of economic hardship (Persell, Green and Gurevich 2001).

Alternatively, intergroup contact theory postulates positive effects of intergroup contact on tolerance. These effects, however, occur only if, among other conditions, intergroup interaction is sanctioned by authorities, law, or custom (Allport 1954; Pettigrew 1998; Pettigrew and Tropp 2011). Both prejudices against racial or ethnic groups and social interactions with people from other ethnicities are more likely in ethnically heterogeneous societies. In this regard previous research has shown that social interactions of people from diverse ethnicities contribute to an increase in interpersonal trust (Stolle et al. 2008).

In sum, we can expect that affluence fosters the acceptance of the freedom of assembly while economic hardship will result in less acceptance. As for contact with other groups, two contrary effects have been postulated within group threat and intergroup contact theory. As will be pointed out in the following section, political rhetoric and ideas might be intervening factors that shape individual reactions to the presence of other groups and their activities.

The role of institutional and ideational factors

The most basic institutional factor in creating political tolerance is the level of democratisation. Democracies are built on the idea of free speech and expression of opinion. In a democracy, individuals are thus constantly exposed to varying views and opinions. Following Peffley and Rohrschneider (2003), such exposure can result in learning effects and attitudinal change, and will lead to a higher level of tolerance and greater acceptance of opposing opinions and possibly political actions.

Within democracies, political players, and here, particularly parties and mass media, are said to influence group relations (Allport 1954; Blumer 1958). Political rhetoric may affect normative conceptions in three ways (Bohmann 2011): it may reinforce or mitigate symbolic boundaries arising from longer-standing institutional frameworks or exogenous processes such as economic prosperity; it may increase the visibility of diversity; and it may bring ethnocentric views into the sphere of acceptance. Party rhetoric thus may make things acceptable to say, e.g. due to freedom of speech, due to protection of minorities, or due to concerns about safety or public order. In addition, we would also expect that individuals in countries with more political rhetoric on issues of diversity are more likely to show more openness and thus are also accepting of meetings of extremists. However, depending on how groups are portrayed, media reports may also reinforce existing stereotypes and lead to divisions within societies.

Finally, we also need to consider the international environment. As pointed out in the introduction, human rights, among them the right of free assembly, became increasingly important after 1945. This intergovernmental network has been accompanied by a more influential civil society of NGOs and various other groups (Boli and Thomas 1999). Together, they form an institutional skeleton, which furthers the spread of global ideas such as human rights. The underlying rationale across these different realms is that rights are extended to individual actors and not assigned to specific social groups. Local actors then more frequently align with the associated cultural models (Meyer et al. 1997; Hafner-Burton and Tsutsui 2005) – through this process, there is an increasing emphasis on individual rights such as freedom of opinion. Given that such international models are diffused through international associations, we would expect that individuals who are more exposed to global cultural models, through individual characteristics or by residing in a country that has greater linkages to international society, should be more accepting of assembly rights.

Methods and data

The empirical analysis is based on public opinion data collected by the International Social Survey Programme (ISSP) in 2014 (ISSP Research Group 2016). Data was gathered in 34 countries (when distinguishing between East and West Germany), resulting in a total sample size of 49,807 respondents (see Table 7.1 for an overview). The surveys are random samples, were collected in face-to-face or mail interviews, and are representative for the adult population of each country.

Our dependent variable – the acceptance of the freedom of assembly – is derived from a battery of questions on political tolerance towards three different groups. Respondents were asked:

- Should religious extremists be allowed to hold public meetings?
- Should people who want to overthrow the government by force be allowed to hold public meetings?

- Should people prejudiced against any racial or ethnic group be allowed to hold public meetings?

The response categories are: Should definitely be allowed; Should probably be allowed; Should probably not be allowed; Should definitely not be allowed; and Cannot decide.

Independent variables for the entire sample

We considered the following items as independent variables:

- Aspects of group threat and economic position are considered by the following items: a) respondent income (in various brackets, plus a dummy variable for those who do not have any income or didn't report their income); b) work status (working for pay, unemployed, disabled, in training or mandatory services, retired, housemaker, and others); and c) immigration background, which considers the place of birth of the respondents and their parents (Australia, English-speaking countries, and non-English-speaking countries or being Aboriginal or Torres Strait Islander).
- Religious denomination is also included, and measured by subjective belonging to the major religious groups.
- The number of contacts is captured by an item asking respondents how many people they are in contact with each day, with answer possibilities 0–4, 5–9, 10–19, 20–49, and 50 or more. This 'social contact' is an indicator of social trust and might relate to a higher level of tolerance.
- Education can be related to group threats, as the type and degree of threats change with educational attainment. Education, however, is also a proxy for exposure to global cultural models. It is measured in the various national degrees. The other indicators of exposure to world society are age and residency due to the stronger exposure to global cultural models among younger groups and urban dwellers. Age is measured in years and residence captured by categories ranging from a large city to a rural area and the state (or territory) of residency. As the rhetoric of parties differs vastly between left- and right-wing parties, we also consider the respondents' reported party preference at the last federal election. Finally, gender is included as an additional control variable.

Independent variables at the country level

Economic circumstances and 'threat' due to immigration are captured by the level of prosperity and the size of the immigrant population. National prosperity is captured by GDP (in US$1,000) drawn from the World Bank (2016). Immigration numbers are based on UN-collected data at the time or shortly before the ISSP surveys were conducted (United Nations, Department of Economic and Social Affairs 2015). Immigration levels are measured as the size of the immigrant population as a percentage of the country's whole population. Immigration numbers for Taiwan were taken from the webpage of the National Immigration Agency (Ministry of Health and Welfare 2016).

We measure multicultural policies with the Multiculturalism Policy Index (MCP) by Banting and Kymlicka (2013), which captures several important conceptions of citizenship. The MCP provides a measure of multiculturalist accommodation policies 'designed to recognize, accommodate and support the cultural differences of minority groups' (Banting and Kymlicka 2013, 583). To construct the index, the authors scored and aggregated indicators of multicultural policies across areas such as education, media, and culture as either 0 (no such policy), 0.5 (partial) or 1 (clear policy).

A country's ethnic 'fractionalisation' was captured by an index developed from James D. Fearon, who identifies 822 ethnic groups in 160 countries (2003, 204). He defines ethnic fractionalisation as 'the probability that two individuals selected at random from a country will be from different ethnic groups' (Fearon 2003, 208). If a country is ethnically homogeneous, the value of the index will be 0; if there are two groups, one makes up 95 per cent and the other 5 per cent of the population, the value will be 0.10; if there are three groups, each with 33 per cent, the index is 0.67, and so forth. Thus, the index of ethnic fractionalisation covers the population shares of ethnic groups and not only the number of groups. Analogous to the measure of ethnic fractionalisation, Fearon provides a measure of *cultural* fractionalisation that focuses on the 'cultural proximity' of the spoken languages within a country. 'In a country with a large number of groups that speak structurally unrelated languages, the expected resemblance will be closer to zero' (Fearon 2003, 212).

In order to measure a country's tradition of democracy we used data from the Polity IV Project (Marshall et al. 2010). The project 'examines concomitant qualities of democratic and autocratic authority in governing institutions, rather than discrete and mutually exclusive forms of governance'. In order to account for the diverse traditions of democratisation, or, more concretely for first, second and third waves of democratisation (Huntington 2012), we consider a country's democratic experience in the course of the last 50 years. Thus, a country's democratic tradition includes the number of years between 1960 and 2010 in which it was democratic or autocratic with the underlying scale ranging from -10 to +10. We transformed the data into a ten-point scale (1 means autocratic and 10 means democratic).

Complementary to a country's democratic tradition in the broader sense, the degree of non-institutionalised participation in the narrower sense was included in the analysis. Non-institutional participation regards the number of people who indicate 'having signed petitions' and 'attended lawful demonstrations'. Data stems from the Democracy Barometer (Merkel et al. 2016) which uses weighted survey data from different sources (e.g. European Social Survey, Comparative Study of Electoral Systems, International Social Survey).

As for political rhetoric, we use data from the Comparative Manifesto Project (CMP, Volkens et al. 2015), which codes quasi-sentences of party manifestos for negative/positive stances towards a variety of policy dimensions. Civic rhetoric is captured by manifestos' positive references to equality (category 503), civic mindedness (606), and multiculturalism (607). Ethnic rhetoric covers positive references to national way of life (601) and traditional morality (603) as well as negative references to multiculturalism (608). We calculated the average salience per party for the respective elections before 2014 for civic and ethnic rhetoric and the combined index considering both dimensions.

Ties to world society are measured by 'the number of organizations of which a country or territory is a member, whether directly or through the presence of members in that country' (UIA 2014, 45). World society scholars consider this variable a proxy for embedding in a world culture. It was taken from the *Yearbook of International Organizations* (Union of International Associations various years) and logged.

Results

Table 7.1 presents an overview of attitudes towards the freedom of assembly for our three different groups and the overall measure of an index considering all three items for all countries that fielded the 2014 ISSP survey. Table 7.1 also presents the level of acceptance in the previous survey of 2004, and the change over the subsequent ten years, for those countries that took part in both waves. The countries are sorted according to the overall level of political acceptance in 2014 (or 2004 in case the 2014 data is not available).

The mean values represent the average answer to the question of whether or not these groups are supposed to be allowed to hold public meetings, with a reversed order so that 4 represents 'definitely allowed', 3 'probably allowed', 2 'probably not allowed', and 1 'definitely not allowed'. A higher value represents more acceptance of such assemblies. Considering the three different extremist groups and the averages across countries, people who would like to overthrow the government are the least tolerated, followed by racists and religious extremists. The averages are around 2, closest to the answer 'probably not allowed'.

Considering the ranking of our countries in Table 7.1, the lowest level of acceptance can be found in Russia, followed by the Netherlands, Turkey and Belgium. The highest level of acceptance can be reported for the United States, followed by Israel, the Philippines and Iceland. Australia lies in the middle of all considered countries, with an average value of 1.8 in 2014. Comparing the acceptance of the freedom of assembly for the three different social groups in Australia, people who would like to overthrow the government are the *least* tolerated, followed by racists and religious extremists. As for the change over time, comparing the overall level of acceptance in 2014 and 2004 indicates a small shift towards more tolerance. The average across country means is 1.77 in 2014 (1.75 when considering only countries that took part in both waves) and 1.70 in 2004. The change is thus a minor shift towards more tolerance of 0.05. Yet, a paired sample t-Test using the country means indicates that this change is significant. With a mean change of 0.12 in this period, the acceptance of the freedom of assembly increased by an above-average amount in Australia. Australians thus have become *more* tolerant over time than the average respondent in most other countries.

This descriptive overview raises a few further questions. Our basic idea that political tolerance and the acceptance of the right of assembly should be higher in consolidated democracies is certainly not supported. Some Western democracies such as the US, Iceland and Denmark are among the most open societies, but the populaces of the Netherlands, Belgium and Austria are among the least supportive, as far as the freedom of assembly for extremist groups is concerned. A possible explanation is differences in the inclusion of individuals in their polities (Schofer and Fourcade 2001). While the US places a lot of emphasis on individual participation, demands and actions, the latter countries are rather state-centred societies, with little preference for individual demands and actions. This fundamental difference might also affect the tolerance towards individual actions such as protests.

Further, considering the changes over time in the least accepting European countries, the level of rejection of these freedoms was high in 2004 as well; only in the Netherlands did it improve over the last decade. This stability points to the influence of more steady societal characteristics such as the aforementioned differences in the integration of the individual into the polity. It also shows that explanations pointing to the influence of recent

Table 7.1: Acceptance of the freedom of assembly across countries and over time (higher score=more accepting).

Country	Religious extremists	Overthrow govt	Racists	Overall 2014	Overall 2004	Change in overall
US-USA	3.00	2.09	2.21	2.41	2.35	0.06
IL-Israel	2.64	1.91	1.98	2.18	2.15	0.03
PH-Philippines	2.85	1.79	1.77	2.13	1.92	0.21
IS-Iceland	2.16	2.31	1.96	2.13	NA	NA
IN-India	2.71	1.79	1.83	2.12	NA	NA
ZA-Sth Africa	2.45	1.92	1.96	2.11	1.90	0.21
SE-Sweden	2.41	1.71	2.11	2.06	1.78	0.28
GE-Georgia	1.99	1.95	1.92	1.96	NA	NA
DK-Denmark	2.05	1.77	1.95	1.92	1.81	0.11
VE-Venezuela	2.65	1.59	1.48	1.90	1.82	0.08
NO-Norway	1.96	1.67	2.04	1.89	1.94	-0.05
CZ-Czech Republic	1.92	1.84	1.80	1.85	1.74	0.11
FI-Finland	2.24	1.34	2.01	1.80	1.86	-0.06
KR-Korea (Sth)	1.87	1.71	1.82	1.80	1.84	-0.04
AU-Australia	1.91	1.60	1.88	1.80	1.68	0.12
TW-Taiwan	2.03	1.56	1.75	1.78	1.73	0.05
PL-Poland	1.78	1.88	1.63	1.78	1.78	0
SK-Slovak Rep	1.65	1.93	1.73	1.77	1.71	0.06
LT-Lithuania	1.75	2.00	1.48	1.75	NA	NA
HU-Hungary	1.81	1.73	1.68	1.74	1.46	0.28
GB-Great Britain	1.79	1.63	1.76	1.73	1.84	-0.11
HR-Croatia	1.62	1.83	1.52	1.66	NA	NA
FR-France	1.65	1.64	1.62	1.64	1.63	0.01
SI-Slovenia	1.60	1.72	1.46	1.61	1.82	-0.21
CH-Switzerland	1.64	1.50	1.58	1.58	1.52	0.06
ES-Spain	1.78	1.46	1.41	1.55	1.55	0.00
CL-Chile	1.74	1.40	1.43	1.52	1.41	0.11
DE-Germany	1.53	1.38	1.56	1.50	1.41**	0.09
JP-Japan	1.51	1.37	1.53	1.47	1.41	0.06
AT-Austria	1.32	1.34	1.56	1.41	1.32	0.09
BE-Belgium	1.38	1.36	1.46	1.40	1.39	0.01
TR-Turkey	1.49	1.35	1.35	1.40	NA	NA
NL-Netherlands	1.50	1.19	1.48	1.39	1.48	-0.09
RU-Russia	1.37	1.34	1.37	1.36	1.48	-0.12
Total	1.93	1.66	1.71	1.77 (1.75*)	1.70	0.05

2014: Total N= 49,807; Australia: N=1,432; Sample range: N=899 (Sweden) to N=3,124 (South Africa).
2004: Total N=52,550; Australia: N=1,914, Sample range: N=853 (Great Britain) to N=2,784 (South Africa).
Source: International Social Survey Programme (ISSP) 2014.
Notes: * countries that took part in both waves, ** average of East and West Germany.
1=Definitely not allowed to have a meeting to 4=Definitely allowed to have a meeting.

Table 7.2: Correlation between the average national acceptance of freedom of assembly for extremist groups in 2014 and country characteristics.

Acceptance 2014	Acceptance 2004	Affluence (GDP)	Immigration	INGOs*	Democracy score	Non-institutional participation**
1.00	0.90	-0.13	0.00	-0.24	0.07	0.03
Multicultural policy	Ethnic rhetoric	Civic rhetoric	Overall rhetoric	Ethnic fractionalisation	Cultural fractionalisation	
0.28	-0.08	0.15	0.03	0.31	0.18	

N=34. Source: ISSP 2014.
Notes: * International Non-Governmental Organisation, ** Non-institutional participation includes 'having signed petitions' and 'attended lawful demonstrations'.

political developments and terror threats in Europe as a cause of a high scepticism towards public protesters who express extreme opinions do not seem to apply.

Given these questions, the following analysis considers other influences on public opinion in this area, particularly the role of institutions and social structures (such as the level of immigration, economic circumstances, political rhetoric, etc.) that might have an influence on citizens' attitudes toward the freedom of assembly. For the purposes of simplicity, only the overall acceptance index averaging all three groups and the latest wave from 2014 are considered. Table 7.2 displays the results of this analysis as correlations between the average level of acceptance and the societal characteristics related to the theories we discussed in the first section of this chapter.

The strongest effects can be found among indicators that are related to societal *heterogeneity* such as ethnic fractionalisation. The correlation between these factors and the acceptance of the freedom of assembly for extremist groups is around a moderate -0.3. Therefore, acceptance is higher in societies which are characterised by strong ethnic fractionalisation. This result supports the intergroup contact theory. Multicultural policies, and to a lesser extent a civic rhetoric in party programs, foster the acceptance of the freedom of assembly for extremist groups. However, the size of the immigrant population does not have any verifiable effect. Hence, attitudes toward freedom of assembly for extremist groups seem to depend on the proportion of ethnic groups within societies as well as on the concrete policies addressing multicultural issues and the political discourse within countries.

The findings further indicate that a country's democratic experience has no verifiable effect on people's acceptance of the freedom of assembly for extremist groups. However, *non-institutionalised* forms of democracy do explain country differences. The acceptance of freedom of assembly for extremists is higher the more common non-typical forms of participation are. Thus, the classical institutional approach of the tradition of democracy

Table 7.3: Structural and cultural characteristics of Australia compared to 33 countries.

	Australia	Other countries minimum value	Other countries maximum value
Affluence (GDP per capita)	65,400	5,500	67,300
International Non-Governmental Organisation (number)	6,167	1287	11,754
Democracy score (10-point scale)	10	2	10
Non-institutional participation (%)	84.1	-2.2	92.4
Immigration (%)	23	0.2	26.5
Multicultural policy (0 to 1)	8	0	8
Ethnic rhetoric (0–15)	11.8	0.1	15.2
Civic rhetoric (0–18)	11.4	3.3	14.8
Overall rhetoric (0–26)	23.3	3.7	26.1
Ethnic fractionalisation (0 to 1)	0.15	0	0.9
Cultural fractionalisation (0 to 1)	0.15	0	0.7

Source: See methods and data section.

fails to explain cross-country differences, whereas a wider practice of non-institutional forms of democracy ('having signed petitions' and 'attended lawful demonstrations') goes hand in hand with a higher acceptance of the freedom of assembly for extremist groups. Moreover, the refusal of the freedom of assembly for extremists is somewhat lower in less affluent societies, a result that contradicts the general assumptions of the competition theory on the macro-level. Also contrary to expectations, a stronger integration in global cultural models is associated with lower acceptance of public meetings by extremists.

Before we continue with the analysis of the internal dynamics in Australia, we briefly summarise the country's relative position in terms of its structural and cultural characteristics (see Table 7.3). Australia is an affluent, democratic, and multicultural society with a distinct ethnic and civic rhetoric in party programs. Although the number of immigrants in Australia is high, ethnic and cultural distance between the major social groups is rather low according to the used index. Finally, the number of people signing petitions and attending lawful demonstrations is very high in Australia.

After considering the associations at the country level, we now turn to the differences among Australians. These further analyses of micro-factors are needed to understand to what extent competition theory and/or intergroup contact theory explain differences in the acceptance of the freedom of assembly for extremist groups. Also, in face of the distinct effect of multicultural policy, the impact of political orientations on the micro-level should contribute to a deeper understanding of the country-comparative findings.

Acceptance of the freedom of assembly among Australians

After situating Australia in a global context and a brief consideration of potentially influential country-level factors, this section now turns towards differences among Australians. For this

Table 7.4: Effects of individual characteristics on the acceptance of the freedon of assembly (Australia only, Generalized Linear Model, Maximum Likelihood estimation).

Parameter	B	Std Error	Sig.
Socio-demographics			
Female	-.18	.05	.00
Highest completed degree of education	.03	.01	.01
Aboriginal or Torres Strait Islander (ATSI)	.39	.18	.03
Born in non-English speaking country	.19	.07	.01
Australian-born #	Ref	.	.
Politics			
Liberal Party	-.16	.15	.28
National Party	-.26	.19	.16
Labor Party	-.11	.15	.44
Independent candidate	.46	.22	.04
Greens	.32	.15	.04
No party preference ##	Ref	.	.
Location			
Farm	-.18	.10	.06
Village	-.11	.10	.26
Town	-.18	.07	.02
Suburbs	-.19	.07	.00
Big city	Ref	.	.

Source: ISSP 2014, Australian cross-section only (fielded as part of Australian Survey of Social Attitudes 2014).

Notes: Dependent variable: mean index on acceptance of freedom of assembly.

Variables also included, but not significant: country-specific regions (states and territories), religious affiliation, work status, income, age, and contact with other people: Australia.

'No information on parents', 'born in English-speaking country', and 'born in Australia but parents from abroad' do not differ from reference group and are not shown.

All other party preferences do not differ from reference group (with exception of negative effect of Animal Justice Party, but only a single respondent) and are not shown.

purpose, the sample was limited to Australian respondents and analysed using a general linear regression. The dependent variable is a mean index of the three different items on the freedom of assembly. It includes a total of 1,112 respondents out of 1,432, due to missing responses for some of our core variables.

The independent variables included all the variables mentioned in the methods section. However, it turns out that the model effects are not significant for residency in the different Australian states and territories, religious denomination, work status, age, income and the frequency of contact with other people. For the sake of brevity, these variables are only mentioned at the bottom of Table 7.4, whereas the significant effects are reported in more detail.

Migration background, party preference, gender, education, and location (urban versus rural) all have a significant effect on the acceptance of the freedom of assembly for extremist groups. Respondents who were born outside Australia in a non-English speaking country, as well as Aboriginal and Torres Strait Islander peoples, report being *more* accepting of assemblies than the reference group of Australian-born (excluding Aboriginal and Torres Strait Islander peoples). Party preference also matters – those respondents who voted for an independent candidate, as well as Green voters, are also more accepting than voters for the Liberals, the National Party, and Labor, with differences between these three main parties not significant when compared to the reference group of 'no party preference'. In addition, women are less accepting of extremists, whereas better-educated respondents and those who live in urban areas are more willing to allow assemblies of such groups.

These findings point to two distinctive reasons for tolerance. On the one hand, *underrepresented* groups are more open to the freedom of assembly, possibly due to their own lack of political efficacy and the need to use this means of protest for their own cause. On the other hand, individuals in *privileged* social positions – such as highly educated respondents – are more open to the freedom of assembly as well. Here, ideological commitment to freedom, rather than a lack of efficacy, may be at work.

Conclusion

This chapter considers political tolerance in the form of accepting assemblies of religious extremists, people who want to overthrow the government, and groups who are prejudiced against racial or ethnic groups. It thus touches on an important social philosophical problem: the tension between the democratic toleration of extremists and showing too much tolerance towards groups who would like to abandon democracy itself. In the introduction we emphasised the supremacy of the freedom of assembly as expressed in the International Covenant on Civil and Political Rights. In reality, most countries have set limits to this freedom, such as in case of criminal associations or when protests are violent. Yet there are clear cross-national differences in the extent and nature of regulation in this area.

The United States is among the most liberal countries and puts heavy emphasis on the right of assembly. This kind of tolerance is illustrated in the decision in *National Socialist Party of America v Village of Skokie*, where the Supreme Court ruled that the swastika did not constitute 'fighting words' and that the National Socialist Party was allowed to march through a Jewish neighbourhood. Another well-known group, the Ku Klux Klan, also often has public assemblies – in fact, right after the presidential election in 2016, it announced a parade to celebrate president-elect Donald Trump's victory (Kaleem 2016). In line with this legal emphasis on freedom of assembly, our analysis has shown that US respondents are the most accepting when it comes to public meetings of extremist groups.

In Austria, by contrast, due to its fascist past, any public expression of pro-Nazi views or the public display of Nazi symbols is against the law ('re-engagement in National Socialist activities') and can lead to arrest. Yet, right-wing protests and assemblies do occur and are legal. Recently, however, the former Secretary of the Interior proposed to limit the right of assembly, for example, if protests interfere with economic interests. These few examples highlight some of the differences between Austria and the US, and help to explain why Austria is among the countries with the least acceptance of the right to free assembly. Beyond these specific circumstances, Austria also has low ethnic heterogeneity and non-institutional political participation, both factors that are associated with more tolerance towards assemblies.

Multicultural Australia, which has recently experienced numerous violent anti-immigration and anti-racist street protests, is placed in the middle in terms of political tolerance. Acceptance of the freedom of assembly for extremist groups is less pronounced in Australia compared to the US, but this freedom is more accepted in Australia than in, say, Austria or the Netherlands. On the one hand, recent calls to repeal laws on racial vilification and hate speech, as well as the electoral success of right-wing movements in Australia, indicate that freedom of assembly and speech are controversial issues. On the other hand, the results of this chapter show a slight increase in tolerance in Australia since 2004 as well as in the strength of policies addressing multicultural issues and the number of people who sign petitions and attend lawful demonstrations. Hence, the political and civic negotiation processes for 'tolerating intolerance' differ from other countries and provide interesting insights into Australian society. Further analyses (beyond this chapter) indicate the high priority that Australians place on the protection of minority rights, which are considered more important than the right to civil disobedience.

Noting Australia's overall position in the middle of our survey group, there are still important differences among Australian respondents about these assemblies. Respondents who identify as Aboriginal or Torres Strait Islander, male respondents, better-educated individuals, urban dwellers, and Greens voters are all more in favour of allowing public assemblies of extremists. These findings indicate that underrepresented groups and groups following an ideology of political tolerance are least opposed to the freedom of assembly for extremists in Australia. Further results, beyond the analyses presented in this chapter, show that respondents who report to counter-act an unjust or harmful law by trend are more tolerant toward the freedom of assembly for extremist groups.

In sum, our international comparison of the acceptance of the freedom of assembly for extremist groups shows pronounced refusal in most countries, where a narrow line of 'No steps further!' is drawn, whereas a few countries are more open. The divide between countries seems, at first, erratic, given that classic indicators of affluence or duration of democracy do not explain cross-country variation. However, the degree of ethnic heterogeneity (and thus internal differences within countries) as well as the degree of use of non-institutionalised forms of democratic action turn out to be influential, and these factors offer more generalisable explanations than the local idiosyncrasies mentioned before. In short, ethnically heterogeneous countries in which policies directly address multicultural issues, and in which people are more prone to sign petitions and attend demonstrations, are also more willing to accept the freedom of assembly for extremist groups.

References

Allport, Gordon W. (1954). *The nature of prejudice*. Cambridge: Addison-Wesley Publishing Company.
Banting, Keith and Will Kymlicka (2013). Is there really a retreat from multiculturalism policies? New evidence from the multiculturalism policy index. *Comparative European Politics* 11(5), 577–98.
Barendt, Eric (2005). *Freedom of speech*. Oxford: Oxford University Press.
Blumer, Herbert (1958). Race prejudice as a sense of group position. *The Pacific Sociological Review* 1(1), 3–7.
Bohmann, Andrea (2011). Articulated antipathies: Political influence on anti-immigrant attitudes. *International Journal of Comparative Sociology* 52(6), 457–77.

Boli, John, and George M. Thomas (1999). *Constructing world culture: international nongovernmental organizations since 1875*. Stanford: Stanford University Press.

Fearon, James D. (2003). Ethnic structure and cultural diversity by country. *Journal of Economic Growth* 8(2), 195–222. doi: 10.1023/A:1024419522867.

Gibson, James L. (2013). Political tolerance in the context of democratic theory. *The Oxford handbook of political science online*. doi: 10.1093/oxfordhb/9780199604456.013.0021.

Hafner-Burton, Emilie and Kiyoteru Tsutsui. (2005). Human rights in a globalizing world: the paradox of empty promises. *American Journal of Sociology* 110(5), 1373–411.

Huntington, Samuel P. (2012). *The third wave: democratization in the late 20th century*. Vol. 4. Norman: University of Oklahoma Press.

Inglehart, Ronald (1999). Postmodernization brings declining respect for authority but rising support for democracy. In *Critical citizens: global support for democratic government*. Pippa Norris, ed. 236–56. Oxford: Oxford University Press.

Inglehart, Ronald and Wayne E. Baker (2000). Modernization, cultural change, and the persistence of traditional values. *American Sociological Review* 65(1), 19–51.

Inglehart, Ronald and Christian Welzel (2005). *Modernization, cultural change, and democracy: the human development sequence*. Cambridge: Cambridge University Press.

ISSP Research Group. 2016. International social survey programme: Citizenship II – ISSP 2014. GESIS Data Archive, Cologne. ZA6670 Data file Version 2.0.0, doi:10.4232/1.12590.

Kaleem, Jaweed (2016). The Ku Klux Klan says it will hold a Trump victory parade in North Carolina. *Los Angeles Times*, 10 November. http://www.latimes.com/nation/politics/trailguide/la-na-updates-trail-guide-kkk-trump-north-carolina-1478822255-htmlstory.html.

Marshall, Monty G., Keith Jaggers and Ted R. Gurr. (2010). *Polity IV project: dataset. Political regime characteristics and transitions, 1800–2009*. Vienna: Center for Systemic Peace.

McNamara, Luke (2016). What is Section 18C and why do some politicians want it changed? *ABC News*, 1 September. http://abc.net.au/news/2016-09-01/what-is-section-18c-and-why-do-some-politicians-want-it-changed/7806240.

Merkel, Wolfgang and Daniel Bochsler (project leaders); Karima Bousbah, Marc Bühlmann, Heiko Giebler, Miriam Hänni, Lea Heyne, Lisa Müller, Saskia Ruth and Bernhard Wessels (2016). *Democracy barometer: codebook*. Version 5. Aarau, Switzerland: Center for Democracy.

Meyer, John W., John Boli, George M. Thomas and Francisco O. Ramirez (1997). World society and the nation-state. *American Journal of Sociology* 103(1), 144–81.

Ministry of Health and Welfare (2016). *Statistical yearbook of the interior: immigration*. http://sowf.moi.gov.tw/stat/year/elist.htm#7.

Peffley, Mark and Robert Rohrschneider (2003). Democratization and political tolerance in seventeen countries: a multi-level model of democratic learning. *Political Research Quarterly* 56(3), 243–57.

Persell, Caroline Hodges, adam Green, and Liena Gurevich (2001). Civil society, economic distress, and social tolerance. *Sociological Forum* 16(2).

Pettigrew, Thomas F. (1998). Intergroup contact theory. *Annual Review of Psychology* 49, 65–95.

Pettigrew, Thomas F. and Linda R. Tropp (2011). *When groups meet: the dynamics of intergroup contact*. New York: Psychology Press.

Popper, Karl (1945). *The open society and its enemies*. London: Routledge & Sons.

Quillian, Lincoln (1995). Prejudice as a response to perceived group threat: population composition and anti-immigrant and racial prejudice in Europe. *American Sociological Review* 60, 586–611.

Schofer, Evan and Marion Fourcade-Gourinchas (2001). The structural contexts of civic engagement: voluntary association membership in comparative perspective. *American Sociological Review* 66, 806–28.

Stolle, Dietlind, Stuart Soroka and Richard Johnston (2008). When does diversity erode trust? Neighborhood diversity, interpersonal trust and the mediating effect of social interactions. *Political Studies* 56(1), 57–75.

Union of International Associations (various years). *Yearbook of international organizations*. Munich: K. G. Saur.

United Nations, Department of Economic and Social Affairs (2015). *Trends in international migrant stock: migrants by destination and origin*. United Nations database (POP/DB/MIG/Stock/Rev.2015).

Volkens, Andrea, Pola Lehmann, Theres Matthieß, Nicolas Merz, Sven Regel and Annika Werner (2015). *The manifesto data collection: Manifesto project (MRG / CMP / MARPOR)*. Version 2015a. Berlin: Wissenschaftszentrum Berlin für Sozialforschung (WZB).

World Bank (2016). *World development indicators*. http://data.worldbank.org/data-catalog/world-development-indicators.

8

The collapse of polling as a way of asking about policy preferences: campaign polls in Australia and Britain

Murray Goot

The development of opinion polls, George Gallup argued in defence of polling, opened the way to a new 'stage of democracy': the continuous assessment of 'public opinion on all the major issues of the day' (Gallup and Rae 1940, 125). During campaigns, polls were never about issues alone, of course, 'major' or otherwise; they were also about how respondents would vote, what they thought of the party leaders, and a number of other things. But the position of respondents on some of the political issues of the day was a substantial part of the mix. This was true from the earliest years of polling in the United States, in Britain (see Goot 2017, 108, for the 1945 election) and especially in Australia (see APOP 1943a, 1943b, for the 1943 election).

How large a presence do questions about issues have in the pre-election polls now? To answer this question, this chapter asks three others. What sorts of things did the opinion polls ask about during the 2016 Australian election campaign and the 2015 British election campaign? How did the agendas of the Australian polls differ from the agendas of the British polls? And how different were the preoccupations of the various polling organisations in Australia and how did they vary in Britain?

While the focus is on the polls published during the Australian campaign, this chapter documents considerable variation not only in what polling companies in Australia concentrated on but also in the preoccupations of polling companies in Britain. If some concentrated on issues of public policy, most did not; a greater number gave little, if any, attention to issues of this kind. Moreover, when issues of public policy were raised, the questions weren't necessarily designed to ascertain where respondents stood, Gallup's hope; for the most part they were intended to establish which party or which party leader respondents most trusted or thought best able to handle the issue, something by which Gallup set much less store. The newspapers that commissioned relatively few questions about issues included elite papers – the *Australian*; and in Britain, the *Guardian* and *Observer* – not just the tabloids. What the pollsters polled was a function of who (if anyone) commissioned the polls, the markets those commissioning the polls operated in (including their assessment of what their audiences wanted), and the technology deployed.

During the Australian campaign, all but one of the seven polling firms reported how respondents intended to vote. All but one reported respondents' views of the party leaders. All but one asked questions about the election's outcomes. And all but one posed questions about what they considered to be election issues. In every case, a different organisation was the odd one out. Only two pollsters sought respondents' views of the parties. Only one asked respondents what they thought about individual candidates. The total number of questions asked by any of the polls ranged from 14 to 247. The kinds of questions the polls asked varied considerably as well.

The attention given to *issues*, overall, was relatively small – less than that given to the leaders and only half as great as that devoted to ascertaining how respondents might vote. If the Australian election, as one economics commentator argues, was 'fought on genuine policy differences on business tax cuts, education spending, super tax changes, multinational tax avoidance and Labor's negative gearing tax changes' (Irvine 2017), there was little sign of it in the polls. While border security may have been an issue that strengthened the Liberals and economic insecurity an issue that drew voters to Labor, the polls showed very little interest in these issues either. The only issue in which most of the polls showed an interest was Medicare – an issue of security, to be sure, but not one that occupies a central place on most analysts' 'security' agendas. The polls showed an interest in Medicare relatively late in the piece, not because they thought respondents' views in themselves worthy of consideration, but because they sensed the issue might be decisive ('Mediscare').

A comparison of the Australian and British polls shows some striking similarities; among them, the near-collapse of questions about respondents' position on issues – the polling, Gallup argued, which justified the place of polls in a democracy because it conveyed to the parties what voters actually wanted, regardless of which party they voted for or which party formed government (Gallup and Rae 1940, v, 12–14). But a comparison also demonstrates important differences between the Australian and British polls, including differences in: the intensity of polling; the greater emphasis in Australia on establishing how respondents were likely to vote; and the greater emphasis in Britain on reporting party images, engagement with the campaign and expectations about the election's outcomes.

The polling organisations and the organisations for which they polled

In Australia, polling organisations were either commissioned by the media or paid their own way. Newspoll was commissioned by News Corp's flagship *Australian* newspaper. Ipsos, commissioned by Fairfax (and promoted by Fairfax as Fairfax Ipsos), published polls in the *Sydney Morning Herald*, the (Melbourne) *Age* and the *Australian Financial Review*. Omnipoll was commissioned by Sky News, part-owned by News Corp's 21st Century Fox. Galaxy was commissioned by News Corp's mainland metropolitan mastheads – the *Daily Telegraph* (Sydney), *Herald Sun* (Melbourne), *Courier-Mail* (Brisbane) and *Advertiser* (Adelaide). ReachTEL was commissioned variously by Channel 7, Fairfax, the Hobart *Mercury* and the *Sunday Tasmanian* – the last two owned by News Corp as well. Essential Research, close to the the union movement and the Labor Party, was self-funded though published by the political website Crikey, as was the Roy Morgan Research Centre, which polled on a continuing basis in the hope of being able to sell its findings; but it also posted some of its results online, perhaps as teasers.

The time when all the campaign polling, other than the exit polls, was commissioned by the print media had long passed. Of the questions and answers published during the 2016 campaign less than half (46.2 per cent) were sponsored by a newspaper or newspaper group. A substantial proportion (16 per cent) was paid for by a television station or TV network. But more than a third (37.8 per cent) were provided by companies that paid for their own fieldwork. During the British campaign, the proportion of the questions asked on behalf of the press and TV (ITV News) was much higher (79.7 per cent), the proportion asked independently of the media (20.3 per cent) much lower (derived from Cowley and Kavanagh 2016, 235; Goot 2017, Table 7.2).

If some of the firms were new to election polling, most were not. Of the new entrants, Ipsos used standard telephone interviewing techniques (CATI or Computer Assisted Telephone Interviews), as had its predecessor at Fairfax (Nielsen) – though Ipsos extended Nielsen's telephone reach to include mobiles – while Omnipoll polled online. Among those that had polled in 2013, some used the same techniques they had used then: Morgan deployed a mixture of face-to-face interviewing and SMS; ReachTEL, using landlines, continued to robopoll – a technique formally known as IVR or Interactive Voice Recognition. Others had changed their methods since 2013: Galaxy and Newspoll – previously conducted via CATI – used a combination of online and robopolls restricted to landlines.

Most of the polling was done by robopoll or conducted online. CATI polls, not long ago the industry standard, had become too expensive; with revenue from media advertising and newspaper sales in sharp decline, cost-cutting was imperative. The use of CATI had not entirely disappeared; Ipsos used it. But even a newspaper company inclined to CATI had to draw the line somewhere; when Fairfax commissioned polls in single seats, it couldn't afford CATI so it didn't commission Ipsos. Done well, a poll in a single seat needed a sample similar in size to a poll done nationwide. Ipsos, however, wouldn't cut corners by changing modes; nor, in 2013, had Nielsen. For Fairfax, considerations of quality in its single-seat polls were to be trumped, as they were in 2013 (Goot 2015, 124), by considerations of cost – backed, no doubt, by a quiet confidence that its reputation would be judged not by how accurate its single-seat polling turned out to be, but by the accuracy of its nationwide results.

'Despite elections being awash with polls', one advertising executive remarked after the 2013 election, 'most are national polls' (Madigan 2014, 40). In fact, most of the polls in 2016 were *not* conducted nationally (see Table 8.1); nor were they in 2013 (Goot 2015, 133). The main reason: a widespread belief, however mistaken (Goot, in press), that elections are won in the 'marginal' seats not won on the size of the national swing. Although every polling organisation produced national polls – three (Essential, Ipsos and Omnipoll) produced nothing other than national polls – barely a quarter of the 2016 polls were conducted nationally. Pollsters' mostly produced single-seat polls; 25 of the 33 polls produced by Galaxy, 25 of the 29 produced by Morgan, and 24 of the 31 from ReachTEL were single-seat polls. Two polls were state polls. One other poll was an exit poll conducted by Galaxy outside 25 polling booths.

What the polls polled

In the 55 days between the dissolution of the Parliament on 9 May and the holding of the election on 2 July, the polls that were published asked 792 substantive questions. Across 126 separate polls (Table 8.1), this meant an average of just over six (6.3) questions per poll (derived from Table 8.2). Essential, which conducted eight polls and asked 232 questions, averaged 29 questions per poll; its profile was quite different from that of any other polling firm. At the other extreme, Morgan conducted many more polls (29) but

Table 8.1: Number of polls conducted and published in Australia between the dissolution of the Parliament (9 May) and the day of the election (2 July 2016), column % in brackets.

	Essential	Galaxy	Ipsos	Morgan	Newspoll	Omnipoll	ReachTEL	Row N (%)
Mode	Online	Online + robo	CATI	Multimode	Online + robo	Online	Robo	
Sponsor [outlet]	[Crikey]	News	Fairfax	[website]	The Australian	Sky News	Fairfax/ News	
Dates	12 May – 30 June	10 May – 2 July	17 May – 29 June	14 May – 19 June	19 May – 28 June	19 May – 2 July	12 May – 30 June	10 May – 2 July
National	8	2	4	3	5	3	7	32 (25.4)
State		1		1‡				2 (1.6)
Single seats		29*		25	13*		24*	91 (72.2)
Other		1#						1# (0.8)
Column N	8	33	4	29	18	3	31	126

Notes: Excludes ReachTEL polls conducted for and released by the NSW Teachers Federation, the Lonergan Research polling conducted for and released by the Greens, and the Community Engagement poll conducted for and released by Make Poverty History and Micah Australia.
* Robopoll
‡ Aggregation of single-seat polls in South Australia
# Exit poll conducted at 25 booths

averaged only two or so (2.3) questions per poll. For the other pollsters, the corresponding figures in descending order of question intensity (the number of questions asked divided by the number of surveys) were: Ipsos, 9.5 (38 questions, four surveys); ReachTEL, 8 (247 questions, 31 surveys); Omnipoll, 4.7 (14 questions, three surveys); and Galaxy, 3.9 (128 questions, 33 surveys).

In Britain, a shorter 34-day election campaign saw 12 polling organisations produce 138 polls, using online methods or CATI but no robopolls (Sturgis et al. 2016, 22). Most were conducted across Britain; only 34 were in groups of seats, in Scotland, or across other populations. The polls generated 2,593 questions, an average of roughly 19 (18.8) questions per poll (see Table 8.3). The question intensity for four of the 12 pollsters was about as high as or higher than the highest of the Australians; for only two was it lower. In Australia, the poll with the highest intensity was self-funded; in Britain, it was not. But one of the self-funded polls in Britain, TNS, polled as intensively as the highest intensity poll in Australia, also self-funded. Even when they were not being paid, the publicity benefits meant a number of pollsters were keen to participate.

Table 8.2: Number of questions in the published Australian polls from the dissolution of the Parliament (9 May) to the day of the election (2 July 2016), % in brackets.

	Essential	Galaxy	Ipsos	Morgan	Newspoll	Omnipoll	ReachTEL	Row N (%)
Voting*	20 (8.6)	65 (50.8)	12 (31.6)	61 (91.0)	36 (54.5)		99 (40.1)	293 (37.0)
Leaders	69 (29.7)	36 (28.1)	12 (31.6)		28 (42.4)	2 (14.3)	40 (16.2)	187 (23.6)
Candidates							37 (15.0)	37 (4.7)
Parties	57 (24.6)	2 (1.6)						59 (7.4)
Issues	43 (18.5)	17 (13.3)	10 (26.3)	6 (9.0)		9 (64.3)	66 (26.7)	151 (19.1)
Campaign	27 (11.6)						1 (0.4)	28 (3.5)
Outcomes	8 (3.4)	8 (6.3)	4 (10.5)		2 (3.0)	3 (21.4)	4 (1.6)	29 (3.7)
Other	8 (3.4)							8 (1.0)
Column N	232	128	38	67	66	14	247	792

* Includes the 'leaner' asked of respondents who refused, when first asked, to say for which party they would vote. Essential N = 8; Fairfax Ipsos N = 4; Galaxy N = 43; Morgan N = 29; Newspoll N = 18; Omnipoll N = 0; ReachTEL N = 0; Total N = 133.

Table 8.3: Number of questions in the published British polls from the dissolution of the Parliament (30 March) to the day of the election (7 May 2015), % in brackets.

	Ashcroft	BMG	ComRes	ICM	Ipsos MORI	Opinium	Panelbase	Populus	Survation	TNS	YouGov	Row N (%)
Voting	54 (43.5)	5 (45.5)	69 (20.1)	15 (12.3)	14 (8.4)	18 (4.8)	35 (35.7)	37 (62.7)	111 (22.3)	66 (25.8)	104 (19.2)	528 (20.4)
Leaders	12 (9.7)	1 (9.0)	78 (22.7)	69 (56.6)	66 (39.8)	164 (43.7)	25 (25.5)	10 (16.9)	181 (36.3)	11 (4.3)	111 (20.5)	728 (28.1)
Issues	12 (9.7)	1 (9.0)	138 (40.2)	15 (12.3)	19 (11.4)	24 (6.4)	18 (18.4)	12 (20.3)	118 (23.7)	143 (55.9)	174 (32.2)	674 (26.0)
Campaigning	26 (21.0)		17 (5.0)	7 (5.7)	2 (1.2)	145 (38.7)	5 (5.1)		25 (5.0)	17 (6.6)	9 (1.7)	253 (9.8)
Parties	7 (5.6)		13 (3.8)		48 (28.9)	1 (0.3)	0 (0.0)		5 (1.2)	2 (0.8)	74 (13.7)	151 (5.8)
Outcomes	13 (10.5)	4 (36.4)	28 (8.2)	16 (13.1)	17 (10.2)	23 (6.1)	15 (15.3)		57 (11.4)	17 (6.6)	69 (12.8)	259 (10.0)
Column N	124	11	343	122	166	375	98	59	498	256	541	2,593

Source: Goot (2017: Table 1).

Voting intentions

The questions pollsters most frequently asked during the Australian campaign were those that sought to establish how respondents were going to vote; 37 per cent of all the questions were of this kind. Nonetheless, such questions were not the most commonly asked by every pollster. Questions about the vote accounted for nearly all (91 per cent) of Morgan's questions, over half (54.5 per cent) of Newspoll's and half (50.8 per cent) of Galaxy's; but for Essential, such questions figured much less prominently (8.1 per cent of its questions) (Table 8.2). Typically, pollsters asked two questions in their attempt to elicit respondents' voting intentions: one, about how they intended to vote; the other, for those who refused to answer or were 'undecided', about the party to which they were 'leaning'.

The most frequently reported figure, however, was the two-party preferred, a figure most pollsters didn't arrive at directly but calculated from the distribution of the minor party and independent votes in 2013; Essential (in its last two polls), Ipsos and ReachTEL (except for its initial polling in Tasmania) were the only pollsters that attempted to establish the respondents' two-party preferred vote directly. Essential also asked respondents whether they intended 'to vote at a polling booth on election day' or whether they would be casting their 'vote before election day' (for a fuller account, see Goot, in press).

As well as asking how they were going to vote in the House of Representatives, ReachTEL in each of the Tasmanian seats asked respondents a week before the election whether they were 'more or less likely to vote for [Jacquie[sic] Lambie/Richard Colbeck/Lisa Singh] in the Senate this time than at the 2013 election', these candidates having either disowned the party that had endorsed them in 2013 (Senator Lambie now heading the Jacqui Lambie Network) or been demoted by their party on its Senate ticket (Senator Colbeck by the Liberals; Senator Singh by Labor). These were the only questions any of the pollsters asked about voting for the Senate.

In Britain, questions about how respondents intended to vote were not the questions most frequently asked; questions about *leaders* (28.1 per cent of the questions asked) and *issues* (26 per cent) loomed larger. Questions about how respondents were *likely to vote* taken together with a number of questions not asked in Australia – about whether respondents were likely to vote, how likely they were to change their mind, their party identification, why they intended to vote for a particular party or candidate, whether they were voting tactically, how they had voted last time, and so on – accounted for a much larger proportion of all the questions asked in Britain (20.4 per cent). Comparing questions about respondents' intended (first preference) vote, the proportion of questions about voting intentions in the Australian polls was 31.6 per cent while the proportion in the British polls was not even 10 per cent, a figure lower than it might otherwise have been because of the failure, apparently, of most British polls to inquire of 'undecided' respondents about the party to which they were 'leaning' (Goot 2017, 91).

Leaders and candidates

In the Australian campaign, questions about the party leaders, overwhelmingly about the leaders of the Liberal and Labor parties, accounted for a quarter (23.6 per cent) of all the questions asked, slightly less than half the number of questions asked about how respondents would vote. But the focus on the prime minister, Malcolm Turnbull, and the leader of the Opposition, Bill Shorten, varied markedly. Newspoll and Ipsos focused almost as closely (Newspoll) or as closely (Ipsos) on the two leaders as they did on the vote. Essential was even more focused on the leaders than it was on the vote; it asked more than three times as many questions about the leaders as it did about the vote. Indeed, it asked more questions about the leaders than did any other poll. It included questions on the leaders' various attributes and on which of the leaders respondents would 'trust most to handle' a range of issues: 'regulating the banking and finance sector'; 'supporting Australia's manufacturing industries'; 'ensuring big companies pay their fair share of tax'; 'protecting the Great Barrier Reef'; 'funding hospitals'; 'addressing climate change'; 'making housing more affordable for first home buyers'; 'looking after the needs of pensioners'; 'funding public schools'; 'maintaining workers' wages and conditions'. Omnipoll, which published none of the answers to its voting intention questions, asked just two questions about the leaders. Galaxy asked many fewer questions about the leaders than it did about the vote. ReachTEL devoted less than half of the questions to leaders that it devoted to how respondents would vote. Morgan, which focused more intensely on the vote than any other pollster, ignored the leaders altogether; although in 1968 his father had introduced the regular reporting of leadership approval, Gary Morgan, his successor, didn't believe such questions now to be of much if any value (pers. comm).

Three of the pollsters raised questions about internal party rivals to the leaders. The most provocative was Galaxy's. In a national poll taken late in the campaign, Galaxy wanted to know 'If Tony Abbott was the leader of the Liberal Party' for which party would respondents vote? ReachTEL, at the beginning of the campaign, had wanted to hear from its Tasmanian respondents whether they were 'more or less likely to vote for the Coalition since Malcolm Turnbull replaced Tony Abbott as prime minister'? Omnipoll went down a quite different track: who would respondents prefer as leader of the Liberal Party (Turnbull, Scott Morrison, Julie Bishop or Tony Abbott); who would they prefer as leader of the Labor Party (Shorten, Anthony Albanese, Tanya Plibersek or Chris Bowen)?

There was also some interest in what respondents knew – not about the leaders but about other frontbenchers. Essential asked respondents to say, 'without looking it up', whether 'the current Treasurer' was Morrison, Joe Hockey or Chris Bowen. Only ReachTEL asked about MPs not on the front bench: 'How many of the 12 Tasmanian senators do you think you can name?' Whether they really could, ReachTEL didn't ask. It also asked what respondents thought of the candidates contesting seats in the House of Representatives.

In Britain, less than half of the questions about leaders were about Prime Minister David Cameron or the Leader of the Opposition Ed Miliband. Moreover, while a third (33.2 per cent) of the questions about the Australian leaders were about which of the two leaders would make the better prime minister, in Britain just 5 per cent of the questions on the leaders were of this kind. With regionally based parties of growing importance, a range of governing coalitions possible, and several party leaders participating in a televised 'leaders debate' – not only Cameron and Miliband but also Nick Clegg (Liberal Democrats), Nigel Farage (UKIP), Natalie Bennett (Green Party of England and Wales), Nicola Sturgeon (Scottish National Party) and Leanne Wood (Plaid Cymru) – party leaders from a number of parties attracted the attention, however fleeting, of more than one poll; so, too, did Alex Salmond (former leader of the SNP), though he was only an SNP candidate (Goot 2017, 95–96). While the proportion of questions devoted to party leaders in Australia (23.6 per cent) may not have been very different from the proportion devoted to party leaders in Britain (28.1 per cent), the range of leaders in the Australian polls, if not the range of questions about the leaders, was much narrower.

The parties

Across most of the polls conducted during the Australian campaign, questions about the parties – the groups they represented, the values they embodied, the ways in which they operated – figured in few of the polls. While six of the seven polls asked questions about the leaders, only two asked questions about their parties – questions other than those about which party could be 'trusted' or was 'best' on particular issues (see below) – and the poll that asked almost all these questions (Essential) did so off its own bat. Australia might have a coalition government; it might have other parties represented in the Parliament; but the polls were interested, almost exclusively, in the Liberal and Labor parties.

Essential focused on whether Liberal or Labor was best for particular groups. A battery of questions sought to report which of the two was seen as better in relation to: 'representing the interests of large corporate and financial interests'; 'handling the economy in a way that helps small business'; 'handling the economy in a way that helps the middle class'; 'handling the economy in a way that helps you and people like you the most'; 'handling the economy in a way that tries to take the interests of working families into consideration as much as it takes the interests of the large corporate and financial groups'; 'representing the interests of you and people like you'; 'standing up for the middle class in Australia'; 'being more concerned about the interests of working families in Australia than the rich and large business and financial interests'; 'representing the interests of Australian working families'. The phrase 'working families' had featured in the Your Rights at Work campaign mounted by the unions against the Howard government's *WorkChoices* legislation, a campaign in which Essential Media Communications played a central part (see Muir 2008).

Separately, Essential asked whether 'the following groups of people would be better off under a Liberal government or a Labor government' or whether it would make no difference: 'large corporations'; 'people and families on high incomes'; 'banks and other financial institutions'; 'families with children at private school'; 'small businesses'; 'farmers and other agricultural producers'; 'people and families on middle incomes'; 'average working people'; 'recent immigrants to Australia'; 'pensioners'; 'people with disabilities'; 'unemployed people'; 'single parents'; 'families with children at public school'; 'people and families on low incomes'. At the start of the campaign Essential had also asked: 'whose interests ... the [Labor/Liberal] Party mainly represent: working class; middle class; upper class; all of them; none of them'? In Adelaide and Port Adelaide, Galaxy would ask: 'Who do you think would best represent the interests of South Australia in Canberra: Labor Party; Liberal Party; Nick Xenophon Team'?

Another way of exploring party images was to focus on other things that might count towards a party's success. Presenting its respondents with 'a list of things both favourable and unfavourable that have been said about various political parties', Essential asked which of the following fitted the Labor Party and which fitted the Liberal Party: 'will promise to do anything to win votes'; 'looks after the interests of working people'; 'moderate'; 'divided'; 'understands the problems facing Australia'; 'have a vision for the future'; 'out of touch with ordinary people'; 'have good policies'; 'trust to manage a fair superannuation system'; 'clear about what they stand for'; 'has a good team of leaders'; 'too close to the big corporate and financial interests'; 'trustworthy'; 'keeps its promises'; 'extreme'.

In Australia, more than in Britain, questions about the parties sought to explore the perceived links between parties and groups. The emphasis on groups rather than issues suggests a quite different understanding of the wellsprings of electoral behaviour (see Achen and Bartels 2016). The fact that this was mostly done by Essential, a polling organisation with links to the unions, surely is not coincidental.

Issues

The attention the Australian polls gave to issues, while not high, was considerably greater than they gave to anything other than the leaders or the vote; 19.1 per cent of all the questions the polls asked were about issues. ReachTEL devoted a quarter of its questions to issues; Essential and Galaxy, rather less. Off much smaller bases, Omnipoll devoted nearly two thirds of its questions to issues, Ipsos about a quarter, and Morgan much less. Only Newspoll steered clear entirely (Table 8.2). Insofar as 'threats' figured in the polls' agendas, it was here that one was most likely to find them.

Valence issues

Most of the questions about the parties during the Australian campaign were about 'valence' issues – issues that 'involve the linking of the parties with some condition that is positively or negatively valued by the electorate' (Stokes 1966/1963, 170). Morgan twice asked a question made famous in Richard Nixon's campaign for the White House: did respondents think the country was 'heading in the right direction' or 'heading in the wrong direction'? It was the only valence issue Morgan raised and the only valence issue raised by any of the pollsters that did not require the respondent to consider, directly, the merits of one or more of the parties (or, as we have noted in relation to the Essential poll, the party leaders).

Essential asked, in two of its polls, whether respondents trusted Liberal or Labor more on 'security and the war on terrorism'; 'management of the economy'; 'controlling interest rates'; 'managing population growth'; 'treatment of asylum seekers'; 'ensuring a quality water supply'; 'ensuring a fair tax system'; 'housing affordability'; 'ensuring a quality education for children'; 'ensuring the quality of Australia's health system'; 'addressing climate change'; 'protecting the environment'; 'a fair industrial relations system'; and 'protecting Australian jobs and local industries.' Essential also asked 'which party would you trust more to secure local jobs in your area and nationally?' ReachTEL, in three of its national polls, asked 'which of the two parties [sic] [the Coalition or Labor]' respondents 'trusted most to manage': 'the economy'; 'health services'; 'education'; 'the issue of border security'. In two of its Tasmanian polls it also asked 'which of the following parties [Liberal, Labor, the Greens, Other/Independent] do you trust most to manage the economy and the core issues facing Tasmania'? The possibility that respondents might trust one party on some issues but some other party on others was a possibility for which the question did not allow.

A variant of the 'most trusted' question was a question about the 'best party'. Ipsos asked 'which of the major parties, the Labor Party or the Liberal–National Coalition . . . would be best for handling': 'health and hospitals'; 'education'; 'the economy'; 'the environment'; 'interest rates'; 'asylum seekers'. Essential asked which party, Labor or Liberal, would be best when it came to 'handling the economy overall'. And having asked respondents in Tasmania which of a number of issues would most influence their vote (see below), ReachTEL went on to ask: 'Thinking of the issue you just chose, which of the following two parties [Liberal, Labor] has outlined the best plan for this area?'

Vote drivers

Other questions were designed not to see which party was preferred on an issue but to establish whether certain issues would influence, or had influenced (some respondents having voted already), respondents' votes. These questions assumed that it was issues rather than anything else that drove the vote and that the respondents, most of them not especially interested in politics, would be able to identify which issues these were.

Early in the campaign, Galaxy asked respondents in six New South Wales seats whether 'the federal Budget handed down by Scott Morrison last week' would make them 'more likely to vote Liberal at the forthcoming federal election, less likely to vote Liberal or . . . not influence the way that you vote at the federal election?' Later Galaxy also enquired, in four South Australian seats, about the impact of 'the decision to build the next generation of navy submarines in South Australia' on respondents' likelihood of voting for the Liberals; and, in four Victorian seats, about the impact of '[Victorian premier] Daniel Andrews and the [Victorian] state government's handling of the CFA [Country Fire Authority] pay dispute' on the likelihood of respondents' voting Labor.

From the beginning of the campaign to the end, ReachTEL asked more questions about vote drivers than were asked by any other poll. In Tasmania for the *Sunday Tasmanian*, ReachTEL asked which of the following would 'influence' each respondent's 'decision most': 'education funding'; 'health funding'; 'job creation packages'; 'management of the economy'; 'the environment'; 'same sex marriage'; 'stopping the boats'. Later, for the *Mercury*, it repeated the question. In six of its seven national polls for 7News it varied this list and altered its language: 'education'; 'creating jobs'; 'health services'; 'management of the economy'; 'border protection and asylum seekers'; 'roads and infrastructure'; 'climate change and the environment'. It used the same list in the seats it polled for 7News. In the seats it polled for Fairfax, it varied the list again: 'economic management'; 'hospitals'; 'schools'; 'national security'; 'industrial relations'; 'climate change'. ReachTEL (like Galaxy) also asked respondents about the importance of particular issues in deciding how they would vote: nationally, superannuation and the NBN; in single seats, whether 'Britain voting to leave the European Union, or Brexit as it is referred to in the media, impacted your vote at all' and, if so, whether it had made it more likely respondents would vote for Labor, the Coalition, a minor party or an independent.

Omnipoll, in the field on the day of the election and the day before, also presented respondents with a list of issues and asked, in relation to each, whether it was 'very important, fairly important or not important to you on how you voted/will vote'. In descending order of support, as rated by the respondents, the issues were: 'health and Medicare'; 'education policy and spending'; 'Budget balance and economic management'; 'superannuation changes'; 'proposed negative gearing changes'; 'moves to control building unions'; 'company taxes'. Galaxy, in its exit poll, asked respondents to name, from a list, the issues that had 'influenced' their vote. (As with Omnipoll, some issues were really two issues, not one.) The Galaxy issues, again in descending order of support, were: 'health and Medicare'; 'education/TAFE'; 'the cost of living'; 'the economy/balancing the budget'; 'job creation'; 'leadership/Malcolm Turnbull/Bill Shorten'; 'climate change'; 'same sex marriage'; 'housing affordability/negative gearing'; and 'asylum seekers'.

'Health and Medicare' and 'education policy and spending' (Omnipoll)/'education' (Galaxy) topped both lists; but they were the only issues that appeared on both lists. In the Omnipoll these issues were named much more often by Labor than by Coalition respondents, the gap between the two sets of respondents exceeding 20 percentage points. 'Budget balance and economic management' and 'moves to control building unions' were named more often by Coalition than by Labor respondents – and by similar margins. Of the 11 issues in the Galaxy list, 'the cost of living' and 'climate change' were also named more often by Labor respondents (a gap of 10 percentage points or more) than by those who had voted for the Coalition, while 'the economy' and 'Turnbull/Shorten's leadership' were named more often by Coalition respondents than by those who had voted for Labor. Threats and insecurities were structured by party. However, the proportion that nominated any of these issues as important was vastly greater than the proportion whose vote was likely to have been affected by them. Did respondents name issues that they really thought had influenced their vote; or, having voted for a particular party, did they simply name the issues that they thought appropriate given their party choice?

Priorities

Morgan asked respondents not what issues would influence their vote but which of the issues would be 'most important' to them. Respondents drawn from four electorates could choose three from a list of six, all of them valence issues: 'keeping day-to-day living costs down'; 'improving health services and hospitals'; 'managing the economy'; 'improving education'; 'open and honest government'; 'reducing crime and maintaining law and order' – this last an issue regarded traditionally as a matter for state not national governments. Omnipoll, adopting another approach, asked respondents to think about 'which one of these policies is the most likely to get your vote . . . : more spending on education; a cut to the rate of company tax; reducing the government budget deficit.' Ipsos asked whether a 'higher priority' should be given to 'more money for schools or cutting tax for business.' ReachTEL wanted to know whether respondents supported 'tax cuts for companies' or 'increased spending on health and education services' most.

Perhaps what mattered were not national issues but local issues. Polling in the electorate of Leichhardt, Galaxy wanted respondents to nominate 'the most important priority for Cairns at the election'. The options, in descending order of support: 'jobs creation'; 'building new infrastructure'; 'reef protection'; 'highway upgrades'. In Herbert, it wanted to know 'the most important priority for Townsville'. In descending order of support: 'water security'; 'jobs'; 'infrastructure'; 'tax cuts'; 'roads'. Essential attempted to measure the priority of certain issues not for a region but 'for ensuring Australia grows local jobs'. In this context, it asked respondents to assess the importance of: 'local jobs and local content rules for government funded infrastructure projects'; 'better funding of TAFE programs to give people the skills to get the jobs of the future'; 'government support for local manufacturing industries like the steel industry'; 'more investment in renewable energy'; 'opening up investment for foreign companies so they bring the technology and skills to Australia'; 'tax cuts for large companies'.

Position issues

Relatively few of the questions addressed what Stokes (1966/1963, 170) called 'position issues' – issues 'that involve advocacy of government actions from a set of alternatives'. Of the 151 issue questions, less than 10 per cent were framed as position issues. And though some of the issues that the election was said to be about were raised, others weren't. One of the issues not raised was the restoration of the Australian Building and Construction Commission, the occasion for the double dissolution.

How many of these questions went to issues of threat or security is moot. Essential asked whether respondents: 'approve[d] or disapprove[d] of the budget measure . . . to introduce internships for unemployed people which pay $4 per hour for up to 25 hours per week'; approved 'the $50 billion in tax cuts for medium and large business announced in the Federal budget'; or approved 'the changes to superannuation made in the Budget, which includes capping tax concessions for those with more than $1.6 million in superannuation'. It also asked: whether the current law under which 'whistleblowers in government agencies who reveal any information about government decisions and projects may be tracked down by the Australian Federal Police and prosecuted using national security power' should stay or 'be limited to leaks of information that harms our national security'; and whether respondents 'support[ed] or oppose[d] phasing out live exports to reduce animal cruelty and protect Australian jobs'. ReachTEL wanted to know if respondents 'support[ed] or oppose[d] people who work on Sunday receiving a higher penalty rate than people working on Saturday?' Ipsos asked about legalising marriage between same-sex couples and about whether the matter 'should be decided by a parliamentary vote by MPs or a plebiscite of all Australians'. Galaxy asked whether 'the federal government should contribute a significant share in the construction of a Stadium and Entertainment Centre in Townsville's CBD'.

For issues to be framed in the form of a referendum, Gallup's ideal, the framing needed to be binary. Only a few were not. Essential wanted to know which of four actions on climate change, including 'no action', respondents would 'most support'. ReachTEL asked respondents to 'rate', on a five-point scale, 'the quality of the current Medicare system'. And in Tasmania, ReachTEL wanted to know which of the 'three tiers of government . . . could be best abolished'.

In Britain, questions about issues were more frequent (they accounted for 26 per cent of the all questions asked; 19.1 per cent in Australia), position issues especially so (19.3 per cent of all the issues questions compared to 1.6 per cent in Australia). Position issues, nonetheless, accounted for no more than 5 per cent of all the questions asked in Britain (Goot 2017, Table 7.5); just as many of the issue questions were about vote drivers, a category that accounted for 29.1 per cent of the issue questions in Australia. More of the questions (25.8 per cent) in Britain were about valence issues, as they were in Australia (37.7 per cent). And about a third were about issues of other kinds, including questions about sociotropic and pocketbook issues (Goot 2017, Table 5), issues not raised by any of the polls in Australia.

The campaign

In Australia, the number of questions about the campaign (5 per cent of all the questions asked) was small. Only two pollsters asked questions (Essential) or were instructed by the media to ask questions (ReachTEL) about the campaign.

Some questions were about respondents' interest in the campaign. Which of four statements, Essential asked, 'best describe[d] how much political news and commentary' respondents 'intended to look at during the election campaign': 'I will be looking at a lot of news and commentary as I am always interested in politics'; 'I'm not usually very interested in politics but will be looking at a lot more news and commentary during the campaign'; 'I'm not very interested in politics so won't be reading much more than usual during the election campaign'; 'I don't like politics at all and will try to avoid looking at any news and commentary during the election campaign'. Halfway through the campaign it asked: 'how much interest have you been taking in the news about the campaign and what the parties have been saying?'

Another set of questions sought to document respondents' exposure to the campaign. Had they: 'seen TV campaign ads'; 'received campaign materials in [their] letterbox'; 'watched one of the party leader debates on TV'; 'received an email about the election'; 'visited a website about election issues'; 'been surveyed on the phone'; 'had a phone call from a political party'; 'been approached in the street by party workers handing out material'; 'been door-knocked by a political party'; 'been door-knocked by another group (e.g. union, interest group)'? Asked in week four of the campaign, these questions were repeated in week seven.

Other questions asked respondents to evaluate the campaign. Was 'an 8-week election campaign', Essential asked shortly after the announcement, too long, 'too short or about right'? Halfway through the campaign ReachTEL asked respondents how they would 'rate this election so far in addressing the issues important to you?' In week seven and again in week eight, Essential asked 'Which leader and party do you think has [sic] performed best during the campaign: 'Malcolm Turnbull and the Liberal Party; Bill Shorten and the Labor Party; Richard di Natale and the Greens?' This was one of the few references in the polls, other than in the voting intention questions, to any of the parties apart from the Liberals, the Coalition and Labor or any party leader other than Turnbull and Shorten. In week six, Essential had asked: 'which party seems to be making the most spending promises' and 'which party seems to be making the most spending cuts'? But the choices each time were restricted to 'Labor, Liberal, no difference.'

In Britain, the proportion of questions devoted to the campaign was nearly three times as great (9.8 per cent). But without the Opinium polls commissioned by the *Observer* the amount of polling on the campaign in Britain would have been much reduced (Table 8.3).

Outcomes

What did respondents expect as a result of the election? All the pollsters, other than Morgan, showed an interest in this. Most of the questions focused on one outcome about government – which party, if any, would win; and on one outcome to do with a policy – the fate of Medicare. Questions about the likely winner reflected a longstanding belief among campaigners that 'win expectations' influenced the vote. Questions about Medicare picked up on a point of difference between the parties opened up in the course of the campaign by Labor's 'Mediscare' – a difference that post-election commentary, though lacking much in the way of evidence, considered nearly decisive (Goot, in press).

Government

'Regardless of who you will vote for', Ipsos asked in each of its four polls for Fairfax, 'who do you think will win the next federal election', Labor or the Coalition? At the beginning of the campaign and near the end, Newspoll asked: 'Which political party [the Liberal–National Coalition, the Labor Party] do you think will win the federal election (on Saturday)?' Towards the end of the campaign and in its final poll, Omnipoll also asked 'which political party' or 'which of the major parties' respondents thought would 'win the federal election' or 'win the July 2 election' and named two options – Labor and the Coalition.

Other polls offered a third option. In each of the last two weeks of the campaign Essential asked respondents which party [sic] – the Liberal–National Coalition or the Labor Party – they 'expect[ed]' to 'win the Federal election', or would 'neither' win, leaving a 'hung Parliament'? ReachTEL, in its last two national polls, also wanted respondents to predict the outcome: a Coalition win; a Labor win; or a hung parliament – though the meaning of a 'hung parliament' was left hanging. 'One possible outcome of the election', Omnipoll had explained to respondents earlier in the campaign, was 'a "hung parliament" where neither party has enough seats to form government in its own right.' 'The 2010 federal election', it went on to explain, 'resulted in a "hung parliament"'. It then asked: 'If the 2016 election also results in a hung parliament, which of the following do you personally think would be best for Australia: one of the major parties should form government with the Independents or the Greens as happened in 2010; there should be a new election'?

Policy

Other questions focused on likely policy outcomes. Essential wanted to know: which party, Labor or Liberal, 'would be most likely to reduce Australia's debt'; whether respondents thought a Labor government 'would keep the Coalition government's policy on asylum seekers arriving by boat' or would Labor 'change the policy'; and whether it was 'likely or unlikely' that the Liberal Party would 'attempt to privatize [sic] Medicare' if it won. Medicare was the focus of most of the policy questions. ReachTEL asked whether respondents thought Medicare was 'more or less likely to be privatized [sic] under a Liberal–National Coalition government than a Labor government' and later whether respondents 'believe[d] that Malcolm Turnbull will keep his promise and not privatise Medicare' – questions prompted by Labor's claim, in the last weeks of the campaign, that Turnbull would privatise Medicare. 'Mediscare' excited the *Courier-Mail* as well. In six Queensland seats, Galaxy asked whether respondents believed Bill Shorten's claim that 'the Coalition wants to privatise Medicare' or whether it was 'just a scare campaign'. Later it asked, nationally, whether respondents 'believe[d] Bill Shorten's claim that the Coalition intended to privatise Medicare'. It also asked whether respondents 'believe[d] Malcolm Turnbull's claim that Labor's negative gearing policy would drive down house prices'? Essential was the only poll to broach a broader question. Would 'the result of this election', it asked: 'fundamentally change Australia'; 'have a significant impact on the future of

Australia'; 'have a limited impact on the future of Australia'; 'have no impact on the future of Australia'?

In Britain, the polls had paid more attention to questions about outcomes; such questions made up 10 per cent of the questions they asked (Table 8.3). The difference is easily explained: the majority of the British questions were about things that the polls in Australia didn't touch – not which party would win, but which party or parties respondents wanted to see form government (Goot 2017, Table 7.8). In Britain, a hung parliament was widely expected; in Australia, it was not.

Conclusion

Public opinion polls in Australia and in Britain, originally focused on issues – position issues above all – have changed. Today, the press particularly like questions that focus on voting intentions and on the alternative national leaders – polls that inform their audiences, politicians and party managers included, about which party and which party leader is ahead and which of them is behind. In this way they not only report the state of opinion on the 'horse race'; they also maximise their influence on it. Nowhere was the focus greater on how the parties were faring (the two-party preferred being the key measure) or how the two main leaders were faring (the gap in the preferred prime minister measure) than in the country's elite press: the *Australian*, the *Australian Financial Review*, the *Sydney Morning Herald* and the *Age*. All but two of the 66 questions asked on behalf of the *Australian* – the paper read by all or almost all federal politicians – during the campaign were either about how the country was going to vote or about the alternative prime ministers. Two thirds of the questions asked on behalf of Fairfax were of this kind, too. In Britain, the *Guardian* focused on voting and leaders (68.9 per cent of the questions asked by ICM were of this kind); but the proportion of the questions asked by Opinium for the *Observer* and by YouGov for the *Times* and *Sunday Times* was not as great (Table 8.3 for the data; Cowley and Kavanagh 2016, 235, for the newspaper links).

The focus of Australia's elite press on the distribution of party support and the contest between the leaders is not a function of who owns the papers; both the *Australian* and the *Times* are owned by News Corp. Nor does it appear to be principally a function of costs; given that Newspoll used a combination of robopolling and polling online, it would have cost the *Australian* very little more to have had Newspoll add other questions. Rather than being a matter of comparative costs, the differences are more likely to reflect contrasting levels of competition, with Australia's newspaper market, largely a regional one, being less competitive than Britain's national market. That the *Australian* was more focused on the vote and the leaders than any other newspaper might reflect the fact that it has less competition nationally than the *Sydney Morning Herald* and the *Age* have locally, with the latter losing circulation at a faster rate than their morning competitors, the *Daily Telegraph* and the *Herald Sun* (B&T 2015). No doubt what these papers thought of interest to their readers influenced matters, too.

The ABC's VoteCompass attempted to keep track of its viewers' positions on issues, helping those who logged in locate their own positions in relation to those of the parties – inscribing a hyper-rationalist view of politics that made issue positions the beginning and end of political choice – while occasionally, and rather cack-handedly, broadcasting the results. But it is unlikely that this discouraged News Corp or Fairfax from polling on issues, whatever the crossover in audiences.

The production of pre-election polls has spread across the mediascape and beyond. The only campaign polls commissioned for television in Australia prior to the 2010 election appear to have been exit polls (Goot 2012a, 85). In 2016, for every three questions asked for the News Corp or Fairfax papers another question was asked for 7News or Sky News. Between them however, the press and television commissioned less than two thirds of all the questions asked.

The rise of polls that are self-funded is relatively new. In Australia it dates from the aftermath of the 2001 election when the *Bulletin* cut its ties with Morgan (Goot 2002, 84–88). Morgan's days of dominance are long gone. Of the two independent polls – Morgan and Essential – it was Essential that proved the much more interesting, readers benefiting from its need to keep its online panel engaged via questions that weren't product-related, the interest among of its social movement clientele in seeing certain issues pursued, and its determination to generate media publicity on its own account. Not only did Essential ask more questions than were commissioned by either News Corp (Galaxy and Newspoll) or Fairfax (Ipsos and ReachTEL); it asked almost as many questions about the parties, issues, campaign and outcomes as all the other pollsters combined. In addition, Essential stood out for the distinctiveness of some its approaches – the use of batteries of questions and the attempt to link parties with groups among them.

The availability of new technologies helps explain why seven firms conducted polls (two online, two online plus robopoll, one robopoll and one via CATI) and why 11 did so in Britain (seven online, four using CATI). The low cost of entry also helps explain why some firms, both in Australia (two) and in Britain (four plus one, Panelbase, in part), were keen to conduct polls even though, at a time when increasingly the commercial media find themselves financially stressed, no newspaper or television station was prepared to pay them. The value of the publicity helps explain why so many pollsters entered the field even if few of them made any money out of it.

Despite the similarities, the contrasts between polling in Australia and in Britain are equally noteworthy. Robopolling, now common in Australia, is almost unheard-of in Britain (Goot 2014, 24–25); where British pollsters have changed their mode of data-gathering it has been from CATI to online, not to robo. The number of polls conducted in Australia was much smaller than the number in Britain, notwithstanding Australia's much longer campaign. The balance between polls based on a group of constituencies or single seats, on the one hand, and polls conducted across the whole electorate, on the other, was quite different as well. Why the intensity of the polling – the number of questions, on average, in each of the surveys – was much lower in Australia is not clear. Perhaps the more competitive British press has got something to do with it. Perhaps the British media are more prosperous. Or perhaps the British and Australian media have different views about the questions polls need to ask, and of whom they need to ask them, if they are to interest their audience.

What is clear is that the Australian polls placed much more emphasis than the polls in Britain on estimating the vote, notwithstanding that Australian pollsters, unlike British pollsters, don't have to worry much about measuring the likelihood of their respondents' actually voting. The polls conducted in Britain placed much more emphasis on ascertaining respondents' views of the parties, of the campaign and of the election outcomes – the pollsters' response, perhaps, to the number of British parties likely to win seats; a reflection on the traditional concern in the British polls with measuring campaign involvement (see Goot 2017, 78); and a comment on the range of possible coalitions and other uncertainties surrounding the outcome. In Australia, an interest in how respondents viewed the leaders came second to an interest in how respondents were going to vote. In Britain, interest in the leaders came first.

In both campaigns the polls' focus on issues was less marked. More remarkable, especially in Australia, was how few of the issue questions were about position issues. It is true that the distinction between valence issues and position issues can be overdrawn: respondents may think one party better than another on an issue precisely because the policy of one party is radically different from the policy of the other. Nonetheless, the very limited attempt by the polling organisations to determine respondents' issue positions signifies the collapse of the Gallup model, confirming at the national level what was evident already in New South Wales, the most populous Australian state (Goot 2012b, 281). It suggests a change in the view that respondents know enough about the alternatives to have positions on most issues, a decline in the view that the parties themselves have readily distinguishable policy positions, or a shift in the view that media audiences care.

However flawed Gallup's reasoning about the ability of the polls to convey the electorate's policy preferences, the reluctance of pollsters to embrace this argument moves the justification for polling in a democracy away from its roots in American progressivism. And it does so at precisely the time when the other and more recent justification for the polls – that they constitute an independent measure of party support against which to assess the integrity of electoral outcomes – has come to be viewed, in many quarters, with increasing scepticism.

Acknowledgement

Research for this chapter was funded by the Australian Research Council's Discovery Project 150102968. For his perspicacious comments on earlier drafts and for his persistence I am grateful to Shaun Wilson.

References

Achen, Christopher H. and Bartels, Larry M. (2016). *Democracy for realists: why elections do not produce responsive government*. Princeton, NJ: Princeton University Press.

APOP (1943a). Australian Gallup polls, 'Australia speaks' – Nos 132–40. Published July 1943.

APOP (1943b). Australian Gallup polls, 'Australia speaks' – Nos 141–52. Published August–September, 1943.

B&T (2015). Newspapers: our breakdown of the latest ABCs. *B&T Magazine*, 13 November. http://www.bandt.com.au/media/newspapers-our-breakdown-of-the-latest-abcs.

Cowley, Philip and Dennis Kavanagh (2016). *The British general election of 2015*. Basingstoke, UK: Palgrave Macmillan.

Gallup, George and Saul Forbes Rae (1940). *The pulse of democracy: the public-opinion poll and how it works*. New York: Simon & Schuster.

Goot, Murray (in press). National polls, marginal seats, and campaign effects. In *Double dissolution: the 2016 federal election*, Anika Gauga, Ariadne Vromen, Peter Chen and Jennifer Curtin, eds. Canberra: ANU E-Press.

Goot, Murray (2017). What the polls polled: towards a political economy of British election polls. In *Political communication in Britain: polling, campaigning and media in the 2015 general election*. Dominic Wring, Roger Mortimore and Simon Atkinson, eds. 77–111. Cham: Palgrave Macmillan.

Goot, Murray (2015). How the pollsters called the horse-race: changing technologies, cost pressures, and the concentration on the two-party preferred. In *Abbott's gambit: the 2013 election*. Carol Johnson and John Wanna (with Hsu-Lee), eds. 123–42. Canberra: ANU E-Press.

Goot, Murray (2014). The rise of the robo: media polls in a digital age. In *Australian Scholarly Publishing's essays 2014: politics*, 18–32. North Melbourne: Australian Scholarly Publishing.

Goot, Murray (2012a). To the second decimal point: how the polls vied to predict the national vote, monitor the marginals and second-guess the Senate. In *Julia 2010: the caretaker election*. Marian Simms and John Wanna, eds. 85–110. Canberra: ANU E-Press.

Goot, Murray (2012b). The polls and voter attitudes. In *From Carr to Keneally: Labor in office in NSW, 1995–2011*. David Clune and Rodney Smith, eds. 270–81. Sydney: Allen & Unwin.

Goot, Murray (2002). Turning points: for whom the polls told. In *2001: the centenary election*. John Warhurst and Marian Simms, eds. 63–92. St Lucia: University of Queensland Press.

Irvine, Jessica (2017). High anxiety: Trump is officially scary. *Sydney Morning Herald*, 6 February.

Madigan, Lee (2014). *The hard sell: the tricks of political advertising*. Carlton: Melbourne University Press.

Muir, Kathie (2008). *Worth fighting for: inside the Our Rights at Work campaign*. Sydney: UNSW Press.

Stokes, Donald E. (1966/1963). Spatial models of party competition. In *Elections and the political order*. Angus Campbell, Philip E. Converse, Warren E. Miller and Donald E. Stokes, eds. 161–79. New York: John Wiley & Sons.

Sturgis, Patrick, Nick Baker, Mario Callegaro, Stephen Fisher, Jane Green, Will Jennings, et al. (2016). *Report of the inquiry into the 2015 British general election opinion polls*. London: Market Research Society and British Polling Council.

Part 3
Changing social institutions

9

Howard's queens in Whitlam's republic: explaining enduring support for the monarchy in Australia

Luke Mansillo

Support for retaining the constitutional monarchy in Australia was widely seen to be in an inexorable decline (Bean 1993) but in recent years, successive Australian opinion surveys have shown *increasing* levels of support for the monarchy. After the unsuccessful 1999 referendum to replace the Queen with a republican style of government, Australians have warmed to the monarchy. The Australian monarchy's survival is an especially curious socio-psychological phenomenon because the Crown is not in residence and is shared between 16 nation-states. Moreover, Australian national mythology is steeped in the promise of the 'fair go' for all in an egalitarian society (Moran 2011). Given this, Australia's reluctance to dismiss the Queen from her constitutional duties seems more 'bizarre' than British persistence with this institutional arrangement (Billig 1998, 1). A society that avows egalitarianism but retains its inegalitarian symbolism is perplexing. But this is not unique to Australia: Canada, New Zealand, Sweden, Denmark, and Norway also wed the monarchy to a polity with tendencies towards egalitarianism.

This chapter provides an explanation for the recovery in support for the monarchy. In particular, I find that the Baby Boomer generation's experiences with the sacking of the Whitlam government have left an impression on that generation's preferences. It turns out that Baby Boomers are *not* more progressive than other generations, but remain more republican than other generations.

Trends in Australian attitudes to the monarchy

Australian attitudes towards the monarchy have been far from stable for the last two decades (Mansillo 2016). Before the 1990s, there was considerable stability of the Australian public's views on the question of abolition (Bean 1993; McAllister 2011). By abolition, I refer to the removal of the institution of the Crown in Australian law. This chapter focuses on the trend in Australian opinion from 1993 onwards and disaggregates movements in public attitudes by key socio-political characteristics. I look more closely at the role of cohort socialisation and value change in shaping the electorate's attitudes over that period. The data analysed in this chapter is taken from the Australian Election Study (AES) (1993–2016).[1]

---

1   The Australian Election Study is a mail-out cross-sectional survey with repeated measures conducted in the three months after each federal election since 1987.

Figure 9.1 Attitudes on retaining the monarchy, 1993-2016, %.

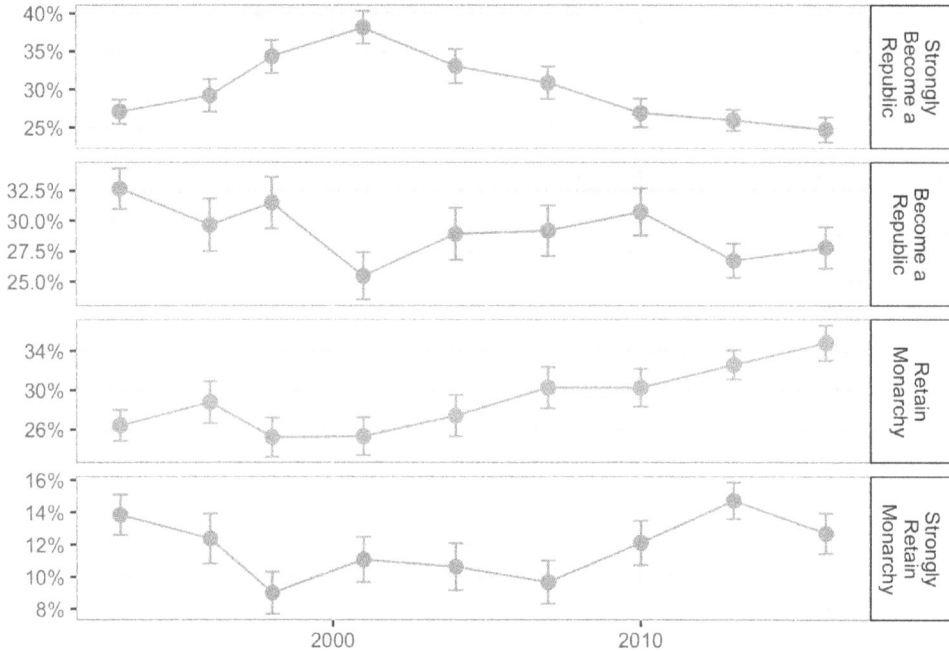

Source: Australian Election Study, 1993–2016.

To begin, this chapter focuses on the abolition question. Respondents were asked: 'Do you think that Australia should become a republic with an Australian head of state, or should the Queen be retained as head of state?'[2] Figure 9.1 shows public opinion trends between 1993 and 2016. In 1993, 60 per cent of Australians preferred that Australia would become a republic. By 1998 this rose to 66 per cent – a year prior to the 1999 Referendum. Total support for the republic then withered over the next 15 years to 52 per cent in 2016. Not only has overall support for a republic fallen but its intensity has collapsed. In 2001, 38 per cent of Australians *strongly* preferred an Australian republic, and by 2016, this had fallen to 24 per cent.

Attitudes to the monarchy and age

There is an interesting paradox between age and attitudes towards the monarchy. It is regularly assumed that young people in most advanced democracies hold generally progressive attitudes. This is thought to be a product of increasing physical and economic security and 'generational replacement' (Inglehart 1977; 1990). For example, young Australians typically hold more progressive views towards asylum seekers (Carson et al. 2016) and are more open to deeper links with Asia (McAllister and Ravenhill 1998). Young Australians also accept climate change science and support policy to curtail its effects at higher rates than older

---

2   The closed measures were: 'Strongly favour [Australia] becoming a republic'; 'Favour becoming a republic'; 'Strongly favour retaining the Queen [as the head of state]'; and 'Favour retaining the Queen'.

Figure 9.2 Attitudes about retaining the monarchy by age group, %.

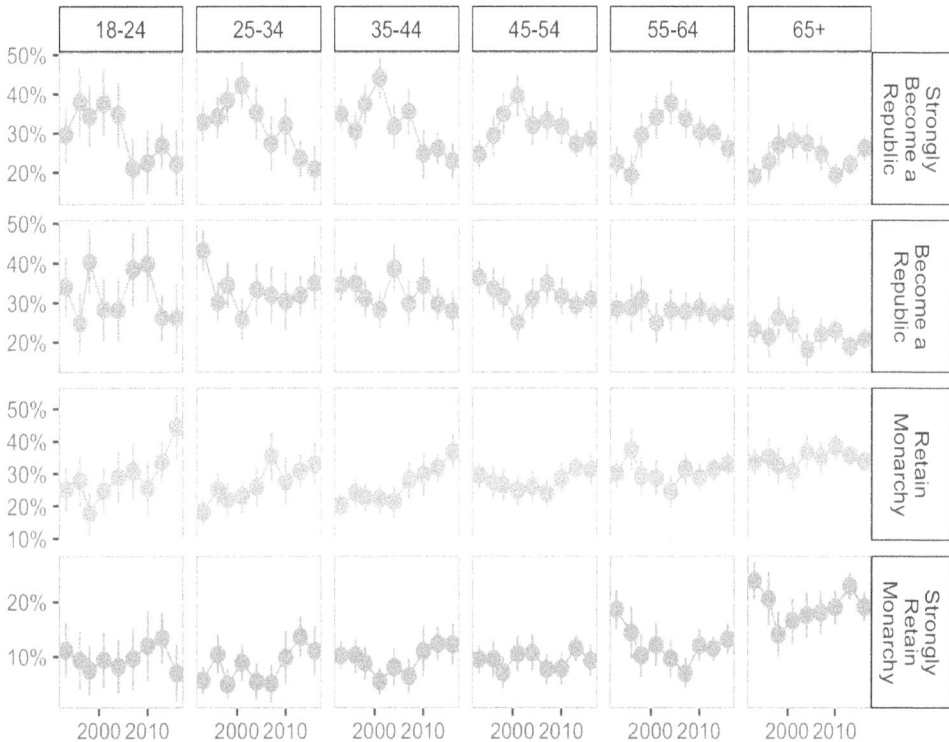

Source: AES 1993–2016.

Australians (Tranter 2011; see also Chapter 4 in this volume). They position themselves to the left of centre and typically vote for progressive parties (McAllister 2011), and historically, they have been more supportive of the abolition of the Australian monarchy (Bean 1993). But, as Figure 9.2 shows, young Australians no longer prefer a republic in such large numbers (see also Mansillo 2016).

There are distinct age, cohort and period effects in the electorate's attitudes. In 2016, young Australians aged between 18 and 24 years supported retaining the monarchy at higher rates compared to 1998. Due to data limitations these effects cannot be entirely separated through modelling. However, the attitudes of each cohort have an age profile which can be tracked over time. For instance, those aged between 18 and 24 years in 1993 had an approximate age range of 25 and 34 years old in 2001, and 35 and 44 years old in 2010 and 2013. This cohort's overall support for a republic increased from 64 per cent in 1993 to 68 per cent in 2001. Over this period support intensified, with a 10 per cent increase in those who strongly favoured a republic. But by 2016, overall support had decreased to 51 per cent favouring a republic, with 12 per cent fewer who strongly held this preference. The observed changes over the period for this cohort's attitudes demonstrate some flexibility in attitudes.

By 2013, there is clearly a nonlinear relationship with age: more of those aged between 18 and 24 years old (48 per cent) wished to retain the monarchy than those aged between

55 and 64 years old (43 per cent). However, more Australians aged 65 years or older (59 per cent) preferred to retain the monarchy than those aged between 55 and 64 years. Baby Boomers express the most pro-republican views overall. Baby Boomers' views have not been adopted by their children. This is against expectations that 'generational replacement' would produce higher levels of republicanism (Bean 1993, 202–3).

Baby Boomers have higher levels of support for an Australian republic, but why? Is this generation generally more progressive than other generations or did the experience of the Whitlam government make Baby Boomers exceptional? To assess whether Baby Boomers are more progressive than other generations, a series of social attitudes are compared by generation (see Appendix 9.1, Fig. 9.1A). Baby Boomers maintain more progressive views towards abolishing the monarchy than other generations. However, Generation Y is more progressive in their attitudes to same-sex marriage, allowing asylum seeker boats, higher immigration, Aboriginal land rights, censorship of nudity and sex in films, decriminalisation of marijuana, and greater opportunities for migrants. Baby Boomers and Generation Y have similar levels of support for allowing a readily accessible abortion, greater opportunities for women, and greater links with Asia. Australian republicanism is exceptional to Baby Boomers, who demonstrate little evidence of being more progressive than other generations. Despite historiography that stresses Baby Boomer involvement in progressive politics and social movements during the 1960s, 1970s, and 1980s, the generation is not more progressive on many social attitude indicators than younger generations.[3] The Baby Boomer generation is regularly characterised by the radical activists who broke away from Old Left activities to participate in more informal, participatory and expressive practices which formed the basis of activities ranging from the freedom rides campaign for Indigenous rights, women's liberation, gay liberation, and similar groups (Macintyre 2004, 232–36). Many sections of the contemporary feminist movement mourn 'the passing of feminism' and its rejection by many young women (Adkins 2004, 429), a historiography that idealises the 1960s and 1970s feminist movement and the Baby Boomer generation. For Australian Baby Boomers, the republic is *their* issue.

A Whitlam generation?

Political socialisation has an invaluable role in explaining an otherwise perplexing fact: unlike most issues debated in Australian politics, young people have less progressive attitudes than their parents when it comes to the monarchy. No individual is born an adult. Socialisation is a process whereby attitudes and social norms are developed through social learning (Bourdieu 1990, 135). Research suggests that the prime age for political socialisation is between the ages of 12 and 18 years (Schuman and Rodgers 2004; Torney-Purta 2004) but socialisation continues throughout life and the 'fresh encounters' with politics between the ages of 17 and 25 years also play a crucial role in forming political predispositions (Erikson 1968; Mannheim 1952; Somit and Peterson 1987). Figure 9.2 suggests that those who entered the 65 years or older cohort in 2016 – those born between 1949 and 1951 – were first-time voters in 1972.[4] The first government they could elect

---

3   Namely, the emergence of feminist, gay liberation, anti-nuclear, anti-war, civil rights, freedom of
     speech, and environmentalist social movements
4   In 1972, the voting age was 21 years old; it was lowered to 18 years in 1973.

was dismissed three years later. It is unsurprising that, at a time these Australians were becoming politically aware, the dismissal led these first-time voters to reject retaining the monarchy. This shift is reflected in the small drop in support for the monarchy compared to 2013 for those aged 65 years and over.

Major political events socialise voters and crystallise attitudes that remain decades later. The 1975 dismissal of the Whitlam government uniquely focused the public's attention on the role and powers that the Constitution affords the governor-general and provided the foundations for the later growth in public support for Australian republicanism. Many Baby Boomers were politically socialised during this crisis, which appears to have left a mark on the cohort's view of the monarchy (Mansillo 2016). While Baby Boomers have never had a particularly favourable opinion of the monarchy, their children have only really been presented with a generally favourable media image, and were socialised during the Howard era which some characterise as a conservative period (Johnson 2007; Gulmanelli 2014). Despite royal scandals in the 1990s (Benoit and Brinson 1999; Black and Smith 1999), in the twenty-first century, Buckingham Palace has maintained a good public image (Balmer 2009; 2011; Bastin 2009; Greyser et al. 2006; Wardle and West 2004). Billig (1998, 215) holds that both young and new royals provide 'a breath of fresh air' that can be seen to be 'moving with the times' as '[e]ach generation becom[es] less formal, less remote; the deferential society [becomes] more egalitarian'. In other words, younger members of the royal family appear more human and tolerable than older members. This change also goes some way to explain the age profile of support and opposition to the monarchy.

Australian republicanism is dear and salient to those who were adolescents or young adults when Whitlam was dismissed, but the issue does not interest many beyond this narrow cohort. Still, contemporary political elites in Australia are drawn overwhelmingly from cohorts who were politically socialised when the role of the monarchy was problematic. The Australian political class and media elites may be attracted to the issue with their pronounced opinions, explaining the many calls to restart the republican movement in recent years. Difficulty in a relaunched republican campaign gaining traction may arise with the young's lack of fervency on the issue. A successful campaign would craft a campaign strategy mindful that the political figures who run the campaign are generationally distinct from those whom they must persuade on the reform. It is quite likely that elite and mass opinions on the republic are dissimilar. Such situations have the potential to cause political acrimony and campaign stagnation, with elites unable to relate to, or strategise appropriately to, the mass public opinion they seek to influence and convert into votes (Dalton 1987).

The republican movement has further demographic and political challenges. The median voter has become more supportive of retaining the monarchy and this has become increasingly diffuse across constituencies of interest. The median voter theorem would imply that parties would be motivated to reduce risks of dealignment, especially from new competitors (Downs 1957). Those most keen for a republic became eligible to vote in 1981. This cohort became the median-aged voter 18 years later when the 1999 referendum was held. Since then, policy demand for a republic from the public has declined, unlike demand from political elites. At the 2016 election this cohort was aged between 53 and 59 years while the median voter was aged 47 years. This constituency is relatively stable in their voting behaviour, with little risk of defecting from their partisan voting behaviour. Those whom political elites are most interested in competing for are increasingly less likely to be republicans. Recent canvassing for a new republican campaign has come from those politically socialised when Whitlam was dismissed. Political elites who currently have power will find appeals to young people that do not have cause to problematise the monarchy frustrating. Vexation may be amplified by a link between monarchism with ethnocentric and civic nationalisms (Mansillo 2016, 224). There would be difficulty employing republican appeals to national identity if nationalists associate the nation with monarchy. Disassociation of nationalism and monarchy requires stimuli. Perhaps the 1990s royal scandals produced a unique opportunity structure that facilitated the republican campaign's inroads into public opinion. Political elites keen on abolition face a difficult strategic question: when to push for another referendum, given the risks. For any political elite who can foresee possible failure in abolishing the monarchy at a second referendum, the greatest unease would be the wait until a third referendum. Success has become less certain in recent years.

Attitudes to the monarchy divided by gender

There are reasonably large attitudinal differences between men and women, with about 15 per cent more women tending to support retaining the monarchy than men (see Figure 9.3). These differences were particularly pronounced in 1993 and from 2010 onwards in the AES data. For half a century, there have been persistent differences by gender on the question of abolition (Mansillo 2016, 218–20). Gender differences in attitudes have converged on many social issues (McAllister 2011, 112–20). However, attitudes towards retaining the monarchy are an exception.

The difference observed between the genders in Australia, however, does not appear in Britain (Billig 1998, 173). Billig (1998) found only differences in interest in royalty by gender in Britain but no difference on the question of abolition – something present in Australia. Billig describes a 'household division of labour' where royalty is a 'female' topic of conversation, and identified this 'gendered territory' in the interviews he conducted: 'Royalty was being marked out as female business. Mothers, not fathers, would be interested in royal books; girls, not boys, would stand in the playground chatting about the Royal Family' (Billig 1998, 179).

Socioeconomic status, education, and attitudes towards the monarchy

Socioeconomic status produces great differences in attitudes to retaining the monarchy. For simplicity, I use self-assessed class identification. There are stark differences in attitudes by class identities, as depicted in Figure 9.4. There is generally stronger support for a republic by those who identify with the upper and middle classes. Class social identities enable citizens to position themselves within a society's intergroup social dynamics and such identification is a cognitive shortcut to understanding societal complexities (Hogg 2000).

Middle and upper class republicanism observed in Figure 9.4 fits well with assessments made by Stuart Macintyre (2004, 258–66) about the Keating government's foray into the politics of a new national identity. He argues that Prime Minister Paul Keating – the chief advocate for a republic – had a 'preoccupation' with 'big picture Australia'. This gave an impression of obsession with 'noisy minority groups' and their postmaterialist 'pet' issues such as the republic, reconciliation with Aboriginal Australians,

Figure 9.3 Attitudes about retaining the monarchy by gender group, %.

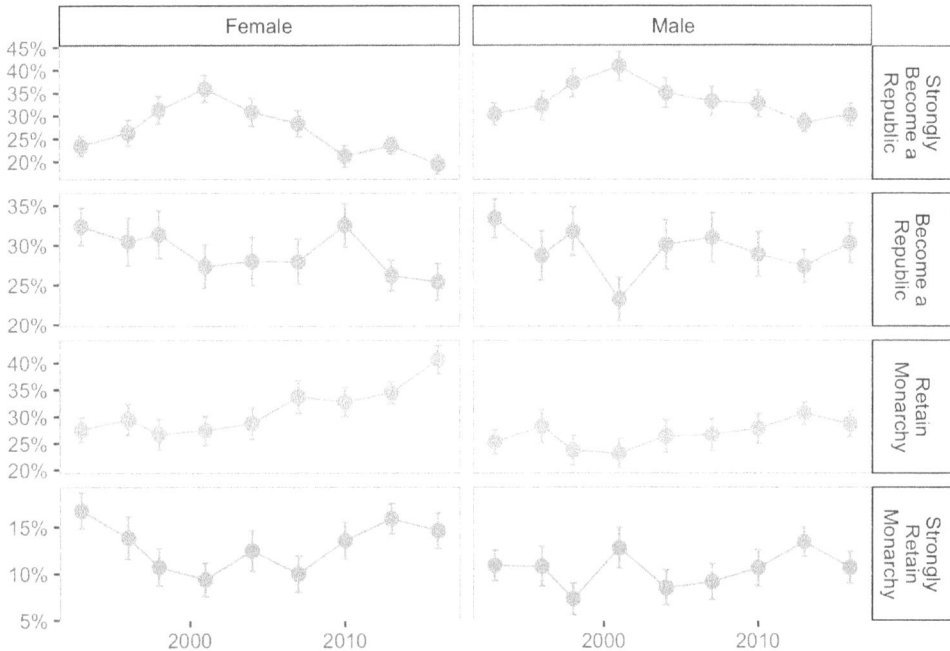

Source: AES 1993–2016.

and strengthening multicultural Australia, all as 1990s Australia languished through high unemployment. Those experiencing economic hardship and economic insecurity when confronted with insecurity of both culture and national identity cannot be expected to embrace republicanism with as much vigour as the well-to-do.

Despite enduring differences in attitudes between the upper/middle and working classes towards the monarchy, attitudes within classes have fluctuated. The AES data details more nuance than Macintyre (2004) suggests. In 1993, middle-class Australians were statistically indistinguishable from working-class Australians on whether Australia should retain the monarchy or become a republic. However, from then on, the middle class diverged from the working class, increasing their support for the republic. It should not be lost that when Keating was elected, middle- and working-class Australians had the same level of republicanism. By 1998 far more middle-class Australians were republican-leaning compared with working-class Australians. This difference persists but the degree has diminished over time. Since 1999 there has been convergence of views by class, as the referendum becomes a more distant memory. Overall, the middle and working classes have become less republican but small differences remain in their level of support for retaining the monarchy.

There is an expected similarity in the relationships of both class identification and *education* on attitudes towards retaining the monarchy (see Figure 9.5). This is unsurprising as a higher class position affords greater educational opportunities and greater education levels enable access to higher social class positions. The well-educated can improve their socioeconomic status through more lucrative jobs and those from high socioeconomic

Figure 9.4 Attitudes towards retaining the monarchy by class identification, %.

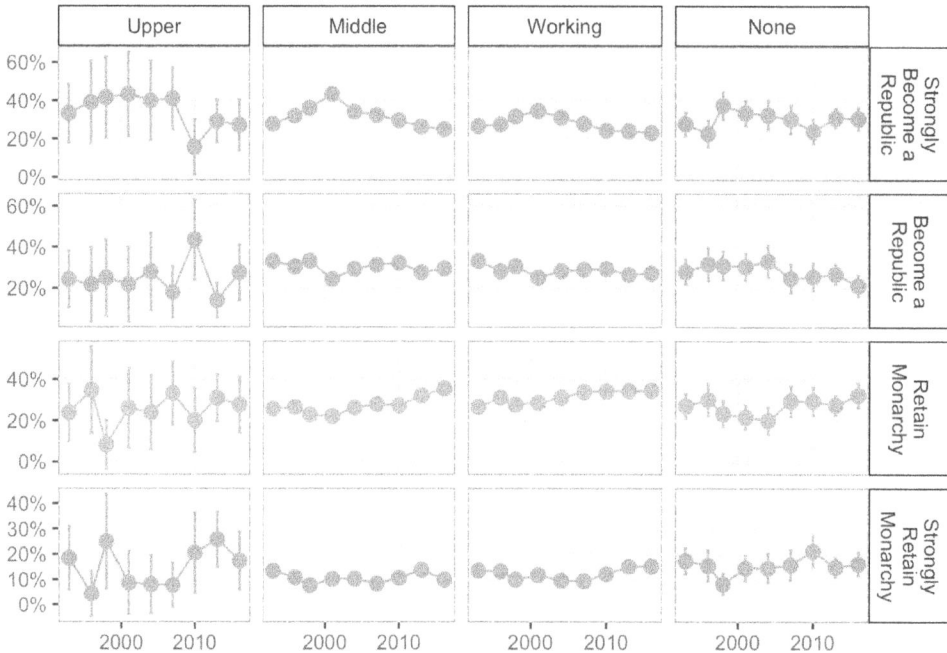

Source: AES 1993–2016.

backgrounds have relative advantages through their greater capacity to afford their children educational opportunities not available to lower socioeconomic backgrounds.

University-educated Australians have the lowest level of support for retaining the monarchy. However, more university-educated Australians supported retaining the Crown in 2016 than in 1993. In the 15 years from 2001 to 2016, university-educated Australians have also 'weakened' the strength of their republicanism, with half as many strongly preferring a republic. In 1993, Australians with a *non-university* post-school qualification were statistically indistinguishable from Australians without a post-school qualification. Both groups became more republican in the late 1990s, but both have since reduced that support. Those without a post-school qualification have a warmer opinion of the monarchy in 2016 than in 1993. Education is a good distinguishing feature of attitudes between Australians but over time there is little stability of attitudes produced by education. While the direction of support has remained relatively consistent in the period studied, the base level of each education level has fluctuated. Education as a proxy for political interest may have acted as an intermediary for media salience in the formation of attitudes.

Partisanship and attitudes towards retaining the monarchy

Political partisanship is the attachment to a political party that offers citizens a shortcut to navigate an otherwise complex political world and thereby reduces cognitive burden on citizens (Burden and Klofstad 2005). Moreover, political partisanship has long been

Figure 9.5 Attitudes towards retaining the monarchy by education levels, %.

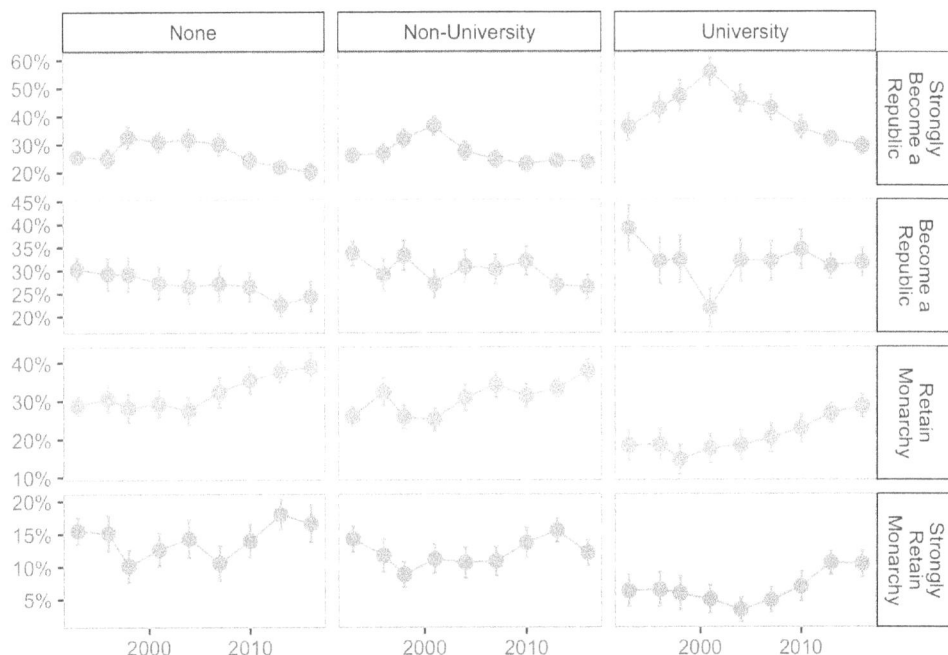

Source: AES 1993–2016.

known to be influential in determining social and political attitudes (McAllister 2011; McAllister and Kelley 1985) – including attitudes towards the monarchy (Bean 1993). Partisan identities condition voters' attitudinal positions. Parties provide cues that activate latent predispositions or biases in citizens' minds. These cues affect the degree to which individuals support attitudinal positions. Despite partisanship levels declining in post-industrialised countries, partisanship is comparatively stable in Australia and remains an essential conceptual tool to comprehend mass public opinion (Dalton and Wattenberg 2002).

Overall, Liberal–National Coalition partisans prefer to retain the monarchy (see Figure 9.6). In 1998, there was slim majority support for a republic (53 per cent) among this group, but this has since collapsed to a minority in 2013 (39 per cent). Labor partisans from 1993 to 1998 overwhelmingly supported a republic. In 1998, 21 per cent of Labor partisans preferred to retain the monarchy but this grew to 37 per cent in 2016. Attitudes were highly durable in the 1990s when issue salience made partisanship a relevant cue to inform attitudes. This effect may have weakened as the monarchy–republic issue featured less on the political agenda. Greens partisans are generally republicans: only 9 per cent in 2001 supported retaining the monarchy but this has since increased to 29 per cent by 2016. Those who identify with other minor parties since 2001 have increased in their support for retaining the monarchy.

In 2016, with 37 per cent of Labor partisans monarchists, Labor is more 'cross-pressured' on the issue than at any other time in the previous two decades. Of the 44 Australian referendums presented to the public since Federation, only eight have successfully passed

Figure 9.6 Attitudes towards retaining the monarchy by partisanship, %.

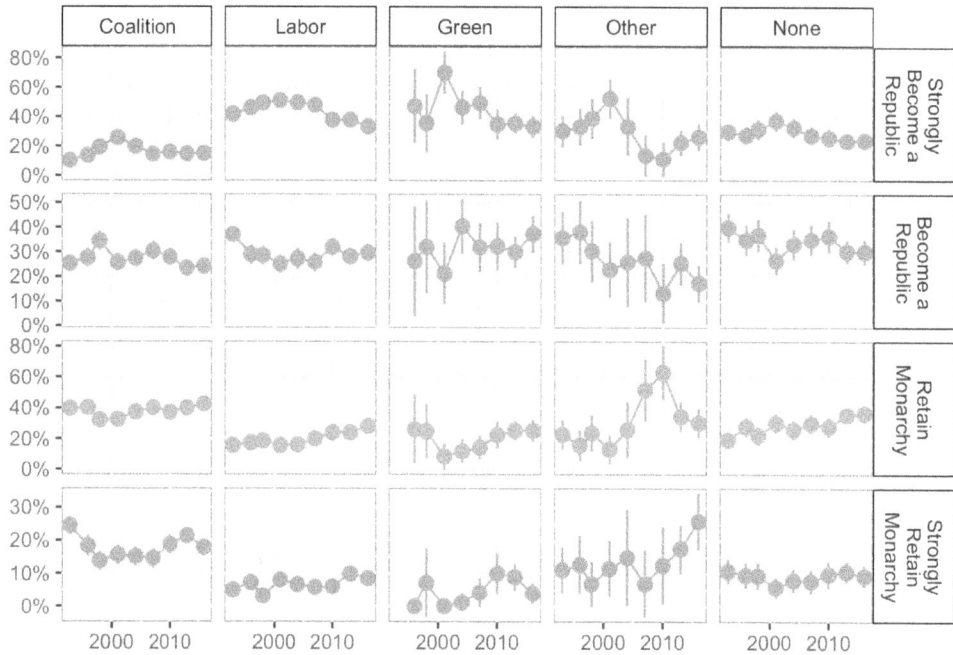

Source: AES 1993–2016.

and all have been with effective bipartisan support for the proposed reform. For republican campaigners to have a chance at success, support from *both* the Coalition and Labor would be required. Moreover, Labor partisans who are conflicted on the issue – or 'cross-pressured' in the language of Hillygus and Shields (2008) – could be persuaded at a general election to defect to another party if the Coalition tried to wedge Labor on this issue (see Carson et al. 2016; Wilson and Turnbull 2001). At the same time, the re-emergence of One Nation could pose the Coalition a potential threat to its electoral competitiveness. Monarchism taps into a strain of ethnic nationalism in the electorate which may be a source for One Nation or another far-right party to wedge the Coalition between inner-city 'small-l liberal' Liberal voters and culturally threatened (socially conservative) suburban Liberal and rural National voters. The issue may help facilitate One Nation's appeal among ethno-nationalist Australians – the same people attracted to the party in 1998 when there was an active republic campaign.

Both Labor and Coalition party strategists have little interest in campaigning for a republic when they seek each other's cross-pressured partisans to win office. In addition, partisans of other parties and the non-partisans are becoming an increasingly large component of the electorate. These crucial voters are evenly split on the issue. It remains to be seen how willing Labor and Coalition elites are to campaign on the issue given the risks of electorate realignment from the major parties.

Political interest and attitudes towards retaining the monarchy

An enduring debate in political science surrounds the public's political sophistication and its implications for how citizens behave politically in a democracy. The level of public knowledge of and general interest in politics has long been thought to be essential for any democracy. For citizens to make meaningful decisions they must understand their options when political questions are presented. Citizens must understand their political system if they intend to wield influence and control their representatives. Core to a well-functioning democracy is that voters maintain an interest in political affairs (Almond and Verba 2015). The political knowledge and interest in politics of Australians are both quite low, similar to the situation in other post-industrialised countries (McAllister 1998).

Attitudes toward retaining the monarchy should be affected by levels of political interest. People who are interested in politics tend to consider political questions and have firmer and more consistent views. People who are not interested in politics are not likely to frequently encounter political information but, when they are exposed, they are potentially easily swayed. Unlike most advanced democracies, Australia compels the least sophisticated voters to the polls. These voters do not typically turn out to vote in comparable democracies where voting is not compulsory. This makes the views of those with less political interest and little political sophistication more crucial to political outcomes for Australian democracy. Figure 9.7 disaggregates attitudes to retaining the monarchy by level of political interest. In 1993, attitudes were statistically indistinguishable between those with high and low levels of interest in politics. The monarchy became increasingly contested during the 1990s and therefore politically salient in the lead-up to the 1999 referendum. Those with the greatest levels of political interest became increasingly more republican. Those with 'some' interest in politics from 1993 to 2016 have become marginally more inclined to prefer retaining the Queen. Those uninterested in politics were far less republican. Those completely uninterested or with 'not much' interest in politics were statistically indistinguishable in 2001 from their 1993 views. As expected, even after enduring the most intense republic campaigning, these citizens' attitudes did not shift.

All in all, those interested in politics are less likely to support a republic in 2016 compared to 2001. A marked shift in support for retaining the monarchy by those with 'some' or 'not much' interest in politics occurred between 2010 and 2013 (again, see Figure 9.7). This increase corresponded to a period that captures the marriage between Prince William and Catherine Middleton, lending weight to the argument that public spectacles like royal weddings legitimise royalty and improve attitudes towards the monarchy (Mansillo 2016, 230). Those citizens who are ambivalent on the issue appear to have greatly shifted their views in that period. Perhaps the period effect of royal scandal and the referendum in the 1990s (which enabled the sudden collapse in support) has ceased to be influential.

Monarchy yields to postmaterialism?

Advanced industrial societies following the Second World War experienced unprecedented levels of security through economic growth and stable international politics (Kremer 1993; Mearsheimer 1993). After the Great Depression and world wars, social-democratic parties in advanced industrialised democracies developed welfare states to reinforce the security offered by unprecedented prosperity. Postwar birth cohorts whose

Figure 9.7 Attitudes towards retaining the monarchy by political interest, %.

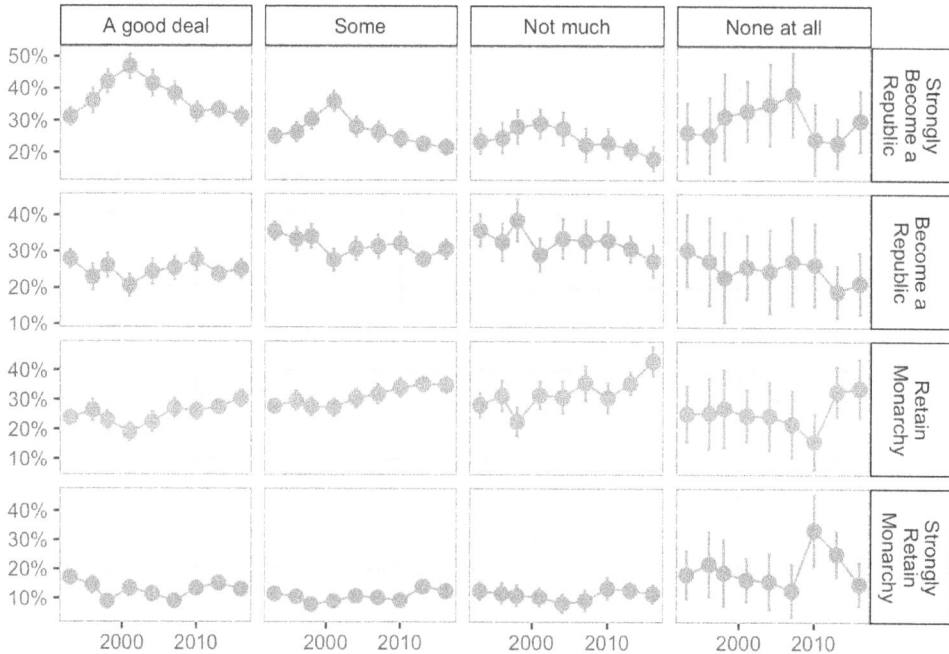

Source: AES 1993–2016.

survival was secure developed more 'postmaterialist' values, i.e. prioritising self-expression, autonomy and quality of life (Inglehart 1977; 1990). After the Second World War, values and cultural norms have shifted through generational replacement, advanced by new social movements (Inglehart 1990, 314). Accordingly, these values should be important in determining attitudes towards the monarchy.

A postmaterialism index is constructed from responses to a set of two questions on important goals for a nation. They include two materialist options: 'maintain order in the nation' and 'fight rising prices'; and two postmaterialist options: 'give people more say in the decisions of the government' and 'protect freedom of speech'.[5] Respondents who select only materialist or postmaterialist categories are classified as such. Those who select a postmaterialist option then a materialist option are mixed postmaterialists and conversely those who select a materialist option before a postmaterialist option are classified as mixed materialists.

Unsurprisingly, postmaterialists favour the replacement of the monarchy more than materialists (see Figure 9.8). There is relative stability in the levels of republicanism for

---

5   Postmaterialism is measured here by the Minkenberg and Inglehart (1989) operationalisation of the Inglehart (1977; 1990) index. Identifying and measuring postmaterialism in public opinion surveys is highly debated since there are major concerns about frequent measurement validity (Bean and Papadakis 1994; Davis and Davenport 1999). The index items have been repeated on surveys for decades to maintain consistency in surveys of record despite these measures being unable to capture the full complexity of value change that early scholars of value change theory could not have predicted. While the index has its limitations it still contains value for social researchers.

Figure 9.8 Attitudes towards retaining the monarchy grouped by the Postmaterialism Index, %.

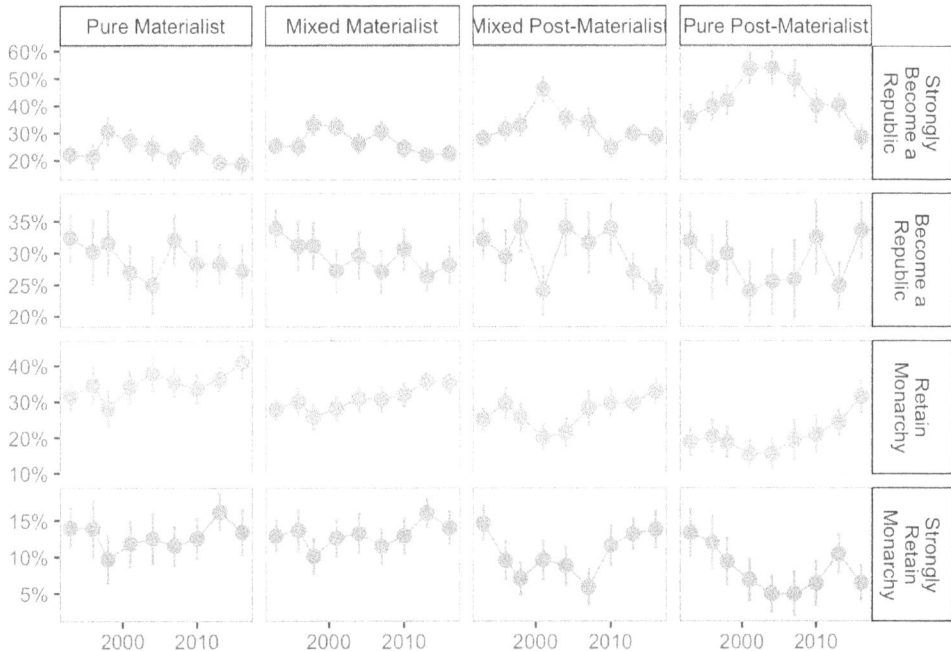

Source: AES 1993–2016.

materialists. Postmaterialists have had more fluctuation in their attitudes with support for retaining the monarchy increasing in recent years. Pure postmaterialists and mixed postmaterialists declined markedly in their support in the 1990s. There was a small drop for mixed-materialists' and pure-materialists' support for the monarchy in 1998 before then returning to trend. Mixed-materialists and mixed postmaterialists began in 1993 at the same position. By 2016 mixed-materialists had increased their overall support for retaining the monarchy somewhat, but mixed postmaterialists remain at their 1993 levels.

What determines attitudes towards the monarchy in Australia?

This chapter identifies several socio-political characteristics that structure opinion towards retaining the monarchy in Australia. To assess which factors are the most consequential and what durability they have in structuring attitudes, I employ a semiparametric generalised additive model (Wood 2011). Semiparametric regression was selected because age and income have nonlinear relationships with attitudes towards retaining the monarchy.[6] For each of the nine studies attitudes towards replacement of the monarchy are regressed over birth year, family income, gender, university education, the postmaterialism

---

6   Additivity or linearity cannot be reasonably attributed to age or income on the dependent variable. For example, the effect of a change in family income by $10,000 from $20,000 to $30,000 for an individual would be more consequential than the same increase in family income from $100,000 to $110,000.

index, Coalition partisanship, and level of political interest.[7] The parameter and curve estimates are provided in Table 9.A2 and Figures 9.A2 and 9.A3.

The effects that birth year and income have on opinions move concurrently with each other. Years where birth year has a linear relationship, family income has a nonlinear relationship and vice versa. This fluctuation in effects between years could suggest a period effect or perhaps an over-identified model. In 1993, and 2007 through to 2013, birth year has a nonlinear relationship with support for retaining the monarchy greatest among older and younger birth cohorts. The lowest support is from those born during the late 1950s and 1960s who were socialised during the 1970s. These results confirm the cohort socialisation hypothesis that Mansillo (2016, 220–24) proposes. Consistently, those oldest birth cohorts record the highest level of support for the monarchy while those socialised at the time when the Whitlam government was dismissed maintain the lowest level of support.

However, the results show that, by 2016, young Australians were more supportive of retaining the monarchy than their seniors. When the issue held more salience amid royal scandals in the 1990s and politics surrounding the referendum, younger birth cohorts also had low levels of support. Salience of the issue conditions cohort opinion. Overall, moving from the highest support to lowest support there is 0.6 change in the dependent variable on the 1 to 4 scale.

Similarly, there are modest effects for family income in the survey years of 1993 and in surveys taken between 2007 and 2013, but there is far greater support for the monarchy in lower-income households than high-income households (with an income threshold effect that improves support for a republic around $60,000). When the issue salience was high, low-income households and those in the youngest birth cohorts shifted their support away from the monarchy. Support returned as the issue declined in salience.

How have the influences on attitudes to retaining the monarchy changed over time?

Education has an enduring effect on opposition to the monarchy. Overall, on the dependent variable's 1 to 4 scale the effect of a university education produces on average a 0.2 change. The direction of the effect has been durable but its size has shifted. Education had a small effect in 2013 and when the issue was at its most salient in the late 1990s. Otherwise, when the issue has not been salient, education has had a larger effect on attitudes. Gender has typically had a significant effect, with women tending to support retaining the monarchy more than men. The effect was at its highest in 2016 at 0.3, which was *twice* the effect size of a university education for that year. Most years it has been lower. Mansillo (2016, 225) found during high and low issue salient periods, female British migrants and Australian-born women had identical attitudes on the issue; this was not the case for male British migrants, who exhibit more support for the institution than Australian-born men. Furthermore, the same study found a significant effect for education levels only for women in low salience periods; men and women in high salience periods did not demonstrate a significant effect for education levels, and age had a linear effect for men but no effect among women (Mansillo 2016, 226, 229). The finding that the effect for gender has strengthened in recent years and the evidence from Mansillo (2016)

---

7   Family income has been inflation-normalised to 2016 dollars.

suggest there is significant scope for future research to unpack and explain these gendered differences in attitudes.

Over time, there has been a collapse in the effect size of Coalition partisanship on attitudes. Between 1993 and 2001, the effect size *halved*, indicating a realignment was underway that left an enduring structural weakness in support for the monarchy. Measured on the 1 to 4 scale of the dependent variable, Coalition partisanship had an effect of 0.84 in 1993 but has remained between 0.45 and 0.51 since the referendum in 1999. Postmaterialism has a small but enduring effect that produces opposition to the monarchy. The small effect sizes were counter to expectations that social values *predominantly* inform attitudes.[8] Social values are typically thought to be central to attitude formation. Like the dependent variable, the index scaled from 1 to 4. The models find significant but ranging effect sizes. Moving from pure materialist to pure postmaterialist positions, the models find effects that range between 0.12 and 0.41 change in the dependent variable on its 1 to 4 scale.

The level of political interest has an overall stable effect in weakening support for the monarchy. The change in the dependent variable from the lowest to the highest level of political interest ranges from 0.13 to 0.46 over the period studied. The effect is about four times the size of gender for most years, or twice the effect size of a university education. This result suggests that the disengaged in politics prefer the status quo.

Overall, however, the largest effect identified is produced by birth cohorts. This is followed by large effects for political partisanship, political disinterest and postmaterialism while controls for gender, family income, and education have relatively small effects on attitudes.

Cohorts and media attention in shaping support for the Australian republican cause

These findings raise a follow-up question. If much of the variance can be explained by generational socialisation, what could explain the improvement across most generations long after their formative years? There is substantial attitudinal variance by political interest levels despite attitudes being structured around birth year cohorts. Scholars such as Kullmann (2008) argue that Australia's republican 'penchant' exists, unlike in New Zealand, because the issue has received long-term media attention. Media increases the exposure of citizens to various issues, which increases the issue's perceived importance and attitudes are considered with reference to media frames, partisanship or ideological predispositions. Media activity has the potential to prime public opinion. Media salience – the prominence given to a topic in media content – of the Australian republic issue provides stimuli that could influence the public's attitudes. I now turn to test the hypothesis that the topic's high media salience provides a stimulus that reduces support for the monarchy. This also provides an opportunity to more confidently identify the non-monotonous birth year effect curve shape.

Agenda-setting theory holds that media organisations have an ability to influence the salience of issues on the public agenda (McCombs 2005). Editors and producers use their editorial judgement to determine whether they will cover an issue and how

---

8   The finding of small effect size reinforces measurement concerns in the literature (Bean and Papadakis 1994; Davis and Davenport 1999).

much prominence they assign to it. Media consumers infer issue importance from its prominence within a news broadcast or page position and article length allocated in a newspaper. News media content is more likely to reach those who have reasonably firm opinions – people interested in politics seek out news and current affairs and those uninterested do not. News media salience may not directly prime attitudes of uninterested Australians who do not expose themselves to significant volumes of news and current affairs media. News media salience may indirectly prime attitudes of the politically uninterested by changing the topic's salience in other media types such as comedy programs with a political flavour (Xenos and Becker 2009) or through introducing information through discussions with peers (Huckfeldt and Sprague 1995). Salience of a topic in news media content could directly or indirectly have implications for attitudes.

To test whether media salience has implications for attitudes towards retaining the monarchy, the previous regression model is repeated on the pooled AES data with a measure of media salience and an interaction with political interest. Media salience of the republic issue was created using a Factiva keywords search of print media mentions of an 'Australian republic' in major Australian newspapers over a year. Details of the scale are in Appendix 9.1. The results are reported in Appendix 9.2 and Figure 9.9.

The model indicates there is a significant negative interaction effect between low political interest and high media salience for the republic (as described in Appendix 9.1). This means that high media salience for the republican issue makes citizens who are politically uninterested less inclined to support retaining the monarchy. Gender, partisanship, education, and income have similar effects to the previous results for individual years.

By pooling the sample over the 23-year period, there is more data to better assess the cohort socialisation thesis discussed earlier. Figure 9.9 captures birth year's nonlinear relationship with support for the monarchy. As described previously those who were politically socialised around the Whitlam government's 1975 dismissal are the *least* supportive of the monarchy. Those who were socialised outside this period have less reason to oppose this institution. The other nonlinear relationship, the effect of family income, finds those with the most republican attitudes have equivalent 2016 inflation-normalised family incomes between $100,000 to $180,000. Family income has a considerably smaller effect on attitudes than birth year cohorts.

Conclusion

Australian attitudes towards the monarchy's retention have changed over the past two decades. Advocates for another republic referendum face an uphill battle to convince Australians of their cause. This is especially the case because of the growing cohorts of voters with higher support for the monarchy than their parents. Social scientists writing about this subject two decades ago did not foresee a shift in public opinion contrary to expectations that 'generational replacement' would create a perpetual decline in support for the monarchy (see Bean 1993). These unexpected improvements in support for retaining the monarchy witnessed in recent years can be explained by existing social theory. Earlier assumptions that generational replacement would produce an ever-declining level of support for the monarchy is inconsistent with the observations made. These earlier thoughts on the topic can be built upon and nuanced. By acknowledging that different birth cohorts were politically socialised at different times with different experiences, changes in the electorate's attitudes to the monarchy and the republican

Figure 9.9 Support for retaining the monarchy by birth year and family income (normalised to 2016 dollars).

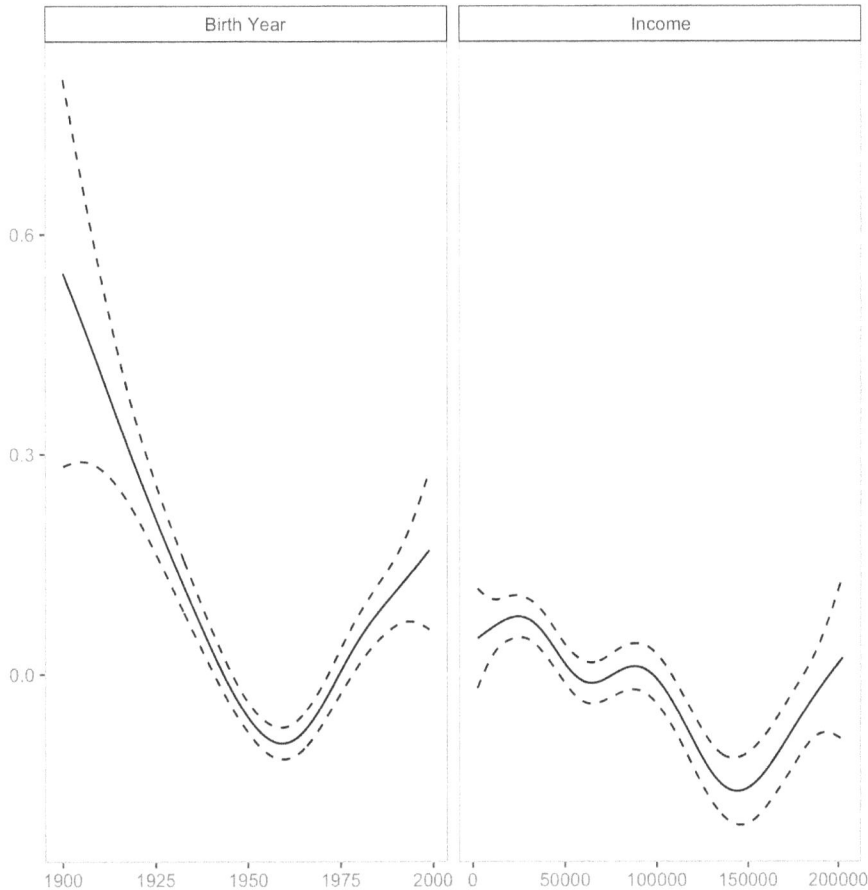

Source: AES 1993–2016.
Note: Family income is mean-centred on the dependent variable, which is from 1 to 4.

cause can be understood. On top of this, changes in media attention to the issue (that generate salience) provide a further temporal dimension to fluctuations in public opinion. Citizens that have little interest in politics are more prone to be swayed on the issue in high media salience periods. When media salience was last high, the media frame was typically negative and support for the monarchy was lower. It remains to be seen if media framing contributed to the formation of more negative public opinion towards the monarchy or if media salience itself changes public opinion, as the Kullmann (2008) comparison with New Zealand suggests.

Australian attitudes towards the monarchy have been remarkably stable but there has been a degree of malleability among Australians who are less politically interested. The structure of attitudes for socio-political characteristics such as gender, education, partisanship, and social values has remained relatively stable. There have been major movements in attitudes as a product of the interaction effect of media salience of the republic issue and low levels of political interest. Levels of political interest has remained relatively stable (McAllister 2011,

63).[9] The evidence presented here suggests media salience has been crucial to the fluctuation in attitudes observed.

There is a distinct birth cohort who are keenest on Australia becoming a republic. This has implications for the potential for another republic campaign. Those keenest are increasingly distant from the median voter and their political demands are more likely to fall on deaf ears among political party elites who compete for votes. Despite some attitudinal rigidity from Baby Boomers, there has been some warming to the monarchy over time by cohorts who have little reason to problematise this institution (Mansillo 2016). The role that improved public relations and media image (Benoit and Brinson 1999) as well as 'banal nationalism' has had in self-legitimising the institution should not be neglected (Billig 1998).

Australian Baby Boomers, despite being keener on an Australian republic, are on most issues less progressive compared to Australians from Generation Y. The republic is a Baby Boomer preoccupation and a product of their unique political socialisation. A successful coalition for change would require more than Baby Boomers. Presently there is not enough support for another referendum to be successful. Any campaign would need to convince a significant proportion of the electorate to change the Constitution. The 1999 referendum failed as those who supported a republic could not agree on the form that an Australian republic should take (McAllister 2001). The double majority requirement for a majority of voters and majority of voters within a majority of states is a very high barrier to a campaign's success. Short of royal scandals similar to those of the 1990s that undermined the monarchy, there are few social forces that could stop the royals from holding on to *their* throne.

References

Adkins, Lisa (2004). Passing on feminism from consciousness to reflexivity? *European Journal of Women's Studies* 11(4), 427–44.

Almond, Gabriel A. and Sidney Verba (2015). *The civic culture: political attitudes and democracy in five nations*. Princeton, NJ: Princeton University Press.

Australian Election Study (2016). The AES studies: 19932016. http://www.australianelectionstudy.org/voter_studies.html.

Balmer, John M. (2009). Scrutinising the British monarchy: the corporate brand that was shaken, stirred and survived. *Management Decision* 47(4), 639–75.

Balmer, John M. (2011). Corporate heritage brands and the precepts of corporate heritage brand management: insights from the British monarchy on the eve of the royal wedding of Prince William (April 2011) and Queen Elizabeth II's Diamond Jubilee (1952–2012). *Journal of Brand Management* 18(8), 517–44.

Bastin, Giselle (2009). Filming the ineffable: biopics of the British royal family. *Auto/Biography Studies* 24(1), 34–52.

Bean, Clive (1993). Public attitudes on the monarchy–republic issue. *Australian Journal of Political Science* 28(4), 190–206.

---

9   There is a question to be raised over declining data quality as response rates to the AES has halved over the period (Goot 2013). Response to a survey on politics is predicated to some degree on interest in politics. Nonresponse bias causing missing data on the variable of interest is a potential issue for the validity of such findings. If people who are uninterested in politics systematically do not answer surveys, there is a nonresponse problem for the characteristic we are drawing inferences from.

Bean, Clive and Elim Papadakis (1994). Polarized priorities or flexible alternatives? Dimensionality in Inglehart's materialism–postmaterialism scale. *International Journal of Public Opinion Research* 6(3), 264–88.

Benoit, William L. and Susan L. Brinson (1999). Queen Elizabeth's image repair discourse: insensitive royal or compassionate queen? *Public Relations Review* 25(2), 145–56.

Billig, Michael G. (1998). *Talking of the royal family*. London: Routledge.

Black, Elisabeth and Philip Smith (1999). Princess Diana's meanings for women: results of a focus group study. *Journal of Sociology* 35(3), 263–78.

Bourdieu, Pierre (1990). *In other words: essays towards a reflexive sociology*. Cambridge: Polity.

Burden, Barry C. and Casey A. Klofstad (2005). Affect and cognition in party identification. *Political Psychology* 26(6), 869–86.

Carson, Andrea, Yannick Dufresne and Aaron Martin (2016). Wedge politics: mapping voter attitudes to asylum seekers using large-scale data during the Australian 2013 federal election campaign. *Policy and Internet* 8(4), 478–98. doi: 10.1002/poi3.128.

Dalton, Russell J. (1987). Generational change in elite political beliefs: the growth of ideological polarization. *The Journal of Politics* 49(4), 976–97.

Dalton, Russell J. and Martin P. Wattenberg (2002). *Parties without partisans: political change in advanced industrial democracies*. Oxford: Oxford University Press .

Davis, Darren W. and Christian Davenport (1999). Assessing the validity of the postmaterialism index. *American Political Science Review* 93(3), 649–64.

Downs, Anthony (1957). *An economic theory of voting*. New York: Harper.

Erikson, Erik (1968). *Youth, identity and crisis*. New York: W.W. Norton.

Glass, Jennifer, Vern L. Bengston and Charlotte C. Dunham (1986). Attitude similarity in three-generation families: socialization, status inheritance, or reciprocal influence? *American Sociological Review* 51(5), 685–98.

Goot, Murray (2013). Studying the Australian voter: questions, methods, answers. *Australian Journal of Political Science* 48(3), 366–78.

Greyser, Stephen A., John M. Balmer and Mats Urde (2006). The monarchy as a corporate brand: some corporate communications dimensions. *European Journal of Marketing* 40(7–8), 902–8.

Gulmanelli, Stefano (2014). John Howard and the 'Anglospherist' reshaping of Australia. *Australian Journal of Political Science* 49(4), 581–95.

Hillygus, D. Sunshine and Todd G. Shields (2008). *The persuadable voter: wedge issues in presidential campaigns*. Princeton, NJ: Princeton University Press.

Hogg, Michael A. (2000). Subjective uncertainty reduction through self-categorization: a motivational theory of social identity processes. *European Review of Social Psychology* 11(1), 223–55.

Huckfeldt, Robert R. and John Sprague (1995). *Citizens, politics and social communication: information and influence in an election campaign*. Cambridge: Cambridge University Press.

Inglehart, Ronald (1977). *The silent revolution: changing values and political styles among Western publics*. Princeton, NJ: Princeton University Press.

Inglehart, Ronald (1990). *Culture shift in advanced industrial society*. Princeton, NJ: Princeton University Press.

Johnson, Carol (2007). John Howard's 'values' and Australian identity. *Australian Journal of Political Science* 42(2), 195–209.

Jones, Barry (2007). *A thinking reed*. London: Allen & Unwin.

Kremer, Michael (1993). Population growth and technological change: one million BC to 1990. *The Quarterly Journal of Economics* 108(3), 681–716.

Kullmann, Claudio (2008). Attitudes towards the monarchy in Australia and New Zealand compared. *Commonwealth and Comparative Politics* 46(4), 442–63.

Macintyre, Stuart (2004). *A concise history of Australia*. Second edition. Cambridge: Cambridge University Press.

Mannheim, Karl (1952). The problem of generations. In *Essays on the sociology of knowledge*. Paul Kecskemeti, ed. 276–322. London: Routledge & Kegan Paul.

Mansillo, Luke (2016). Loyal to the crown: shifting public opinion towards the monarchy in Australia. *Australian Journal of Political Science* 51(2), 213–35.

McAllister, Ian (1992). *Political behaviour: citizens, parties and elites in Australia*. Melbourne: Longman Cheshire.

McAllister, Ian (1998). Civic education and political knowledge in Australia. *Australian Journal of Political Science* 33(1), 7–23.

McAllister, Ian (2001). Elections without cues: the 1999 Australian republic referendum. *Australian Journal of Political Science* 36(2), 247–69.

McAllister, Ian (2011). The Australian voter. Sydney: UNSW Press.

McAllister, Ian and Jonathan Kelley (1985). Party identification and political socialization: a note on Australia and Britain. *European Journal of Political Research* 13(1), 111–18.

McAllister, Ian and John Ravenhill (1998). Australian attitudes towards closer engagement with Asia. *The Pacific Review* 11(1), 119–41.

McCombs, Maxwell (2005). A look at agenda-setting: past, present and future. *Journalism Studies* 6(4), 543–57.

Mearsheimer, John J. (1993). Why we will soon miss the cold war. *Atlantic Monthly* 266(2), 35–50.

Minkenberg, Michael and Ronald Inglehart (1989). Neoconservatism and value change in the USA: tendencies in the mass public of a postindustrial society. In *Contemporary political culture: politics in a postmodern age*. John Gibbons, ed. 81–109. London: Sage Publications.

Moran, Anthony (2011). Multiculturalism as nation-building in Australia: inclusive national identity and the embrace of diversity. *Ethnic and Racial Studies* 34(12), 2153–72.

Schuman, Howard and Willard Rodgers (2004). Cohorts, chronology, and collective memories. *Public Opinion Quarterly* 68(2), 217–54.

Somit, Albert and Stephen A. Peterson (1987). Political socialization's primacy principle: a biosocial critique. *International Political Science Review* 8(3): 205–13.

Torney-Purta, Judith (2004). Adolescents' political socialization in changing contexts: an international study in the spirit of Nevitt Sanford. *Political Psychology* 25(3), 465–78.

Tranter, Bruce (2011). Political divisions over climate change and environmental issues in Australia. *Environmental Politics* 20(1), 78–96.

Wardle, Claire and Emily West (2004). The press as agents of nationalism in the Queen's golden jubilee: how British newspapers celebrated a media event. *European Journal of Communication* 19(2), 195–214.

Wilson, Shaun and Nick Turnbull (2001). Wedge politics and welfare reform in Australia. *Australian Journal of Politics and History* 47(3), 384–404.

Wood, Simon N. (2011). Fast stable restricted maximum likelihood and marginal likelihood estimation of semiparametric generalized linear models. *Journal of the Royal Statistical Society: Series B (Statistical Methodology)* 73(1), 3–36.

Xenos, Michael A. and Amy Becker (2009). Moments of Zen: effects of *The Daily Show* on information seeking and political learning. *Political Communication* 26(3), 317–32.

Appendix 9.1

Table 9.A1: Survey item coding for regression models.

Measure	Coding	Notes
Response variable	1 = Strongly favour Australia becoming a republic 2 = Favour Australia becoming a republic 3 = Favour Australia retaining the Queen 4 = Strongly favour Australia retaining the Queen	
Gender	0 = Male 1 = Female	
Partisanship	0 = Not a Coalition partisan 1 = Coalition partisan	
University qualification	0 = No university qualification 1 = University qualification	
Postmaterialism	1 = Pure materialist 2 = Mixed materialist 3 = Mixed postmaterialist 4 = Pure postmaterialist	This is the coding scheme adapted in Minkenberg and Inglehart (1989).
Political disinterest	1 = A good deal [of interest in politics] 2 = Some [interest in politics] 3 = Not much [interest in politics] 4 = None [No interest] at all [in politics]	
Family income	Annual family incomes in dollars that have been standardised for inflation	Family income, specifically gross annual family income, is measured ordinally in the AES between various enumerated incomes points on a scale. This scale's measures have changed over the period the AES has collected its data to reflect the changes in the Australian economy, especially inflation and the income distribution. To standardise these ordinal measures, a ratio scale is created by taking the median of the incomes range for a category. This is then multiplied by the total change in inflation between the quarter that the election took place in and the quarter of the 2016 election occurred to standardise these measures. Inflation data was sourced from the Reserve Bank of Australia.
Birth Year	Year	
Republic media salience	0 = Least standardised media content on an Australian republic for a year 1 = Most standardised media content on an Australian republic for a year	The number of mentions of 'the republic', 'Australian republic', 'Australian president', and 'Australian Head of State' – but excluding 'the republic of' to prevent foreign states such as the Republic of the Congo from being added to the tally – in the print editions of the *Advertiser* (Adelaide), the *Age* (Melbourne), the *Australian*, the *Australian Financial Review*, the *Courier-Mail* (Brisbane), *Daily Telegraph* (Sydney), *Herald Sun* (Melbourne), *Hobart Mercury* (Tasmania), *Northern Territory News, Sun Herald* (Sydney), *Sunday*

Measure	Coding	Notes
		Age (Melbourne), the *Sydney Morning Herald*, and the *West Australian* (Perth) in a year was divided by the number of articles published in the print editions of each year. This was confined to general news and excluded articles categorised as relating to business, sport or music. The use of proportions rather than mentions was to control for the changing volume of articles written year to year and missing publications for earlier years. This was divided by the number of articles in the sample for that year and standardised to a 0 to 1 scale.

Table 9.A2: Regression coefficients (support for retaining the monarchy).

	1993	1996	1998	2001	2004	2007	2010	2013	2016	Pooled
Gender	0.110***	0.056	0.089*	0.009	0.180***	0.076	0.245***	0.129***	0.304***	0.143***
	(0.036)	(0.049)	(0.048)	(0.049)	(0.050)	(0.048)	(0.044)	(0.033)	(0.040)	(0.014)
Coalition Partisanship	0.840***	0.663***	0.549***	0.446***	0.511***	0.493***	0.453***	0.479***	0.504**	0.542***
	(0.037)	(0.050)	(0.051)	(0.051)	(0.053)	(0.050)	(0.046)	(0.036)	(0.042)	(0.015)
University Education	-0.197***	-0.309***	-0.184***	-0.210***	-0.352***	-0.183***	-0.263***	-0161***	-0.157***	-0.195***
	(0.052)	(0.062)	(0.064)	(0.063)	(0.063)	(0.059)	(0.052)	(0.036)	(0.044)	(0.018)
PostMaterialism	-0.024	-0.063*	-0.071***	-0.128***	-0.137***	-0.117***	-0.038*	-0.085***	-0.072***	-0.078***
	(0.018)	(0.025)	(0.024)	(0.025)	(0.026)	(0.025)	(0.023)	(0.017)	(0.020)	(0.007)
Political Disinterest	0.041*	0116***	0.081**	0.154***	0.026	0.082*;	0.097***	0.102***	0.046*	0.096***
	(0.024)	(0.034)	(0.033)	(0.032)	(0.034)	(0.032)	(0.029)	(0.022)	(0.025)	(0.012)
Republic Media Salience										-0.055
										(0.060)
Political Disinterest * Republic Media Salience										-.060**
										(0.029)
Constant	1.86***	1.927***	1.876***	1.916***	2.177***	2.065***	1.959***	2.148***	2.126***	2.032***
	(0.070)	(0.104)	(0.097)	(0.102)	(0.109)	(0.093)	(0.088)	(0.070)	(0.083)	(0.033)
N	2,444	1,399	1,440	1,543	1,330	1,436	1,853	3,386	2,212	17,043
Adjusted R^2	0.234	0.177	0.129	0.132	0.159	0.144	0.115	0.103	0.105	0.129

Source: AES 1993–2016.

Figure 9.A1 Political attitudes by generation, %.

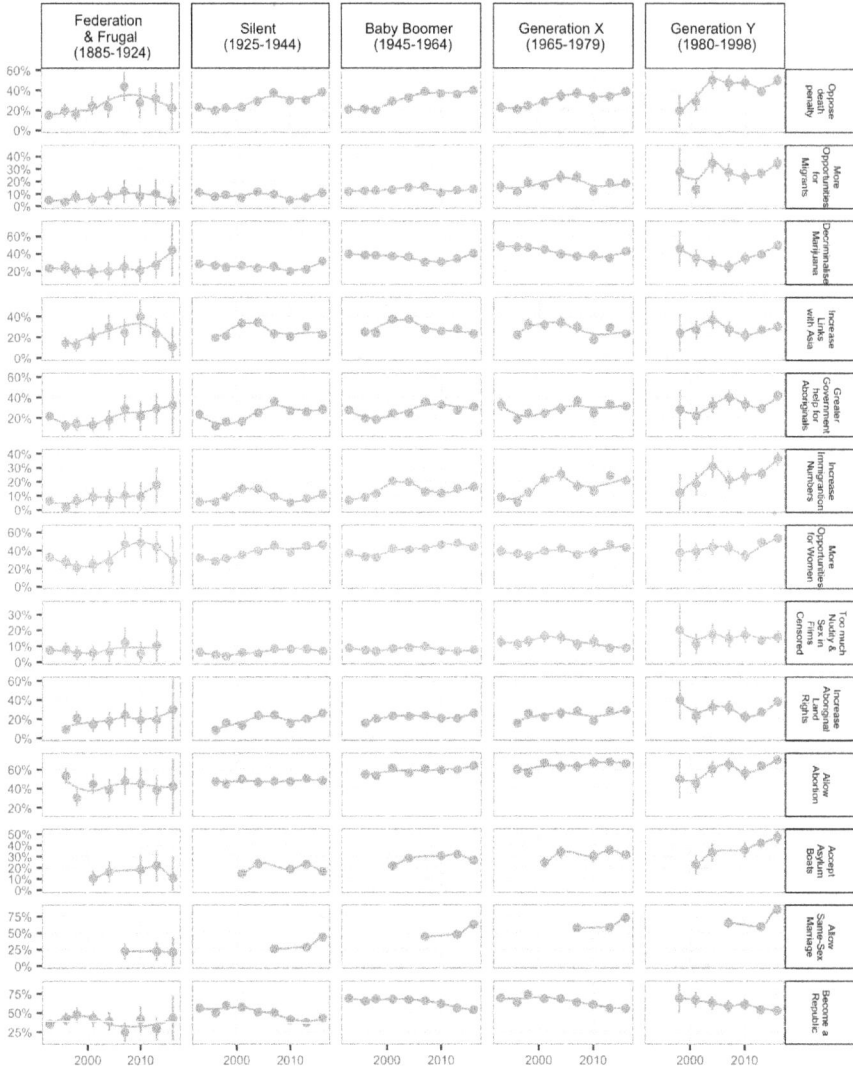

Source: AES 1993–2006.

Figure 9.A2 Birth year mean-centred effects on attitudes towards retaining the monarchy grouped by each study.

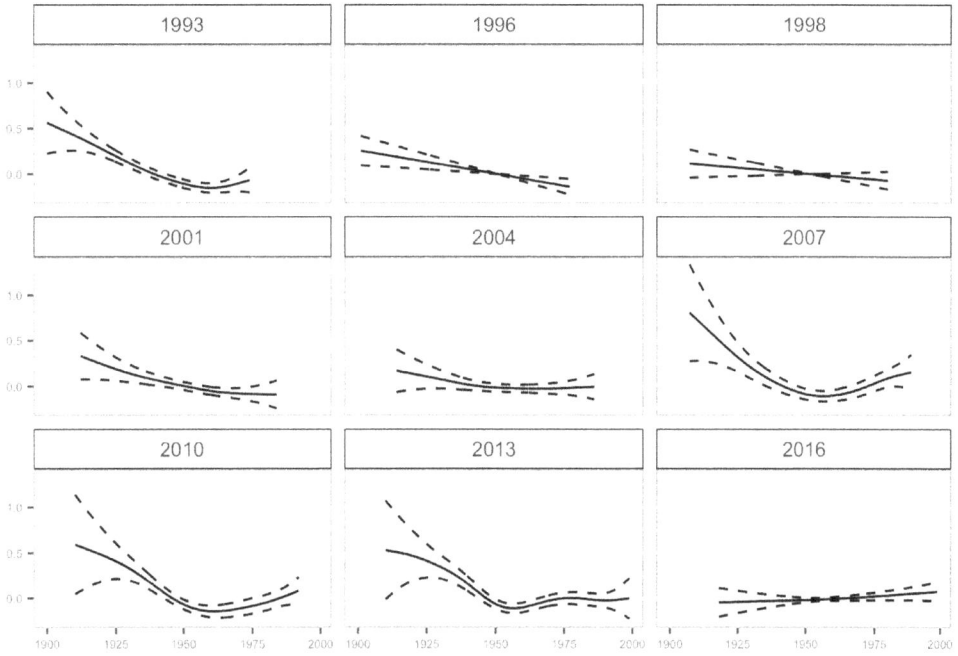

Source: AES 1993–2016.

Figure 9.A3 Family income mean-centred effects on attitudes towards retaining the monarchy grouped by each study.

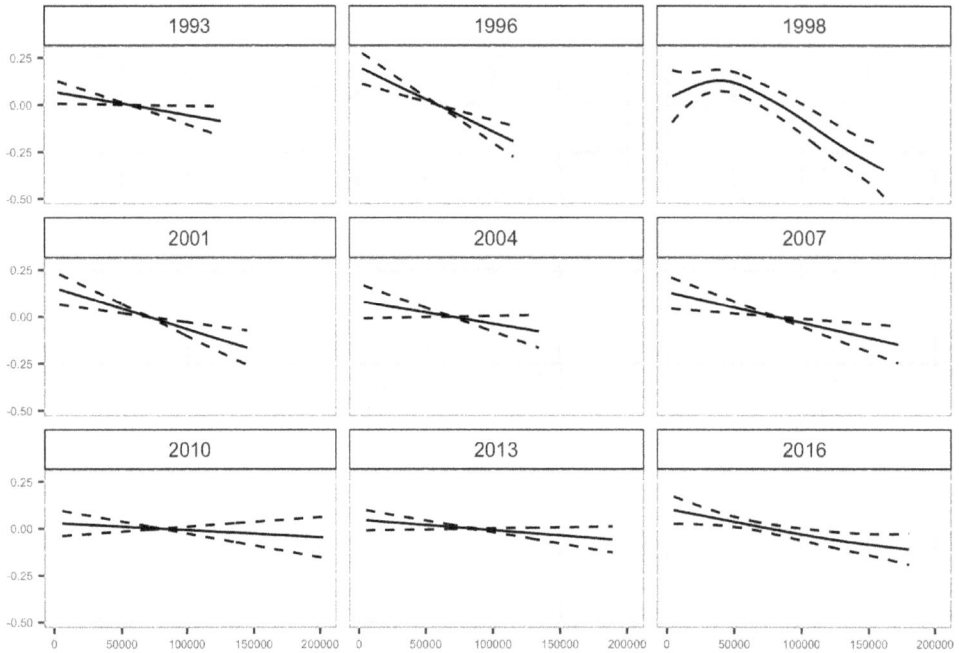

Source: AES 1993–2016.

10

Marriage and happiness: changing Australian attitudes to marriage

Ann Evans and Edith Gray

In this chapter, we begin by outlining some dramatic changes in relationship formation, and then ask whether there has been an accompanying shift in attitudes surrounding perceptions of marriage. We examine three key attitudes about marriage. First, we look at whether Australians believe that people in a marriage are happier than their unmarried peers. Second, we look at opinions about childbearing outside of marriage. Third, we investigate to what extent Australians consider marriage to be an outdated institution. We conclude with some observations about the future of marriage.

Recent changes in marriage behaviour

While marriage remains a central institution in Australian society, with most Australians still 'tying the knot', there have been many recent changes to how and when people marry. To set the scene, we start by outlining some of the major trends in marriage over the last 35 years (Table 10.1). Although the absolute number of people marrying every year has increased over time, so has the population of Australia. The crude marriage rate, which measures the number of marriages occurring in a given year per 1,000 people, has experienced a steady decline from 7.4 marriages per 1,000 people in 1980 to 4.8 marriages in 2015.

Not only have overall marriage rates fallen, but how and when people get married has also changed. Australians are increasingly marrying later and after first living together in a cohabiting relationship. In 1980, the average age for men marrying for the first time was 24 years, and the average first-time bride was 22 years of age. Of couples marrying in that year, about three out of ten lived together before tying the knot and the majority of marriages were performed by a minister of religion. Thirty-five years later, in 2015, the characteristics of couples marrying was very different. The average man marrying for the first time is 30 years old, and the average woman is 29. Living together before marriage is much more prevalent and now practised by eight out of ten couples. Most marriages are now performed by a civil celebrant rather than a minister of religion.

The declining rate of marriage has not occurred uniformly across sub-populations. There is evidence of growing socioeconomic differentials in the probability of marrying among young Australians (Heard 2011). For many young people, financial security and home ownership are still important preconditions for getting married, and as a result,

Table 10.1: Selected marriage statistics, 1980–2010, 2015.

	1980	1990	2000	2010	2015
Crude marriage rate (marriages per 1,000 estimated resident population)	7.4	6.9	5.9	5.4	4.8
Median age at first marriage					
Men	24	27	28	30	30
Women	22	24	27	28	29
% couples living together before marriage	29	45	71	79	81
% marriages performed by minister of religion (vs civil celebrant)	64	60	47	31	25
% of births born outside of marriage	12	22	29	34	35
Crude divorce rate (divorces per 1,000 estimated resident population)	2.5	2.6	2.3	2.3	2.0
Median interval between marriage and final separation	7.5	7.3	8.2	8.8	8.5

Sources: Australian Bureau of Statistics (1994, 2000a, 2000b, 2010, 2016a, 2016b).

marriage rates appear to be declining fastest among those with the lowest education and income (Heard 2011; Hewitt and Baxter 2012).

Alongside changes in entering into marriage, there has been dramatic change in the ending of marriages. The introduction of the 'no fault divorce' in the *Family Law Act 1975* led to a sharp increase in divorces in the late 1970s. Since then, however, the divorce rate has stabilised somewhat and only fluctuated slightly. As a result of these changes, Australians are increasingly less likely to find themselves married at any point in time. According to the Census, in 1981 about 8 per cent of men and 4 per cent of women aged 40–44 had never been married. By 2011, the figure had increased to 25 per cent of men and 19 per cent of women. However, people who are not married may still be living with a long-term partner in a committed de facto[1] relationship. De facto relationships are ones where the couple lives together but is not formally married, although the relationship may transition to a marriage at a later stage. In the early 1980s it was estimated that only around 5 per cent of couple relationships were de facto (ABS 1994). By 1992, this had increased to 8 per cent of all couples and by 2011 to 16 per cent (ABS 2012).

With cohabitation now a socially acceptable alternative to marriage (Evans 2015), many more children are also born out of wedlock, and the link between marriage and childbearing has weakened. The proportion of babies born outside registered marriage also rose from just over one in ten in 1980, to just over three out of ten births in 2015 (Australian Bureau of Statistics 2016a).

Changing attitudes to marriage

It is clear from the statistics presented above that it has become increasingly common for people to marry later (or not at all), and to have children outside of marriage. But how have people's attitudes to marriage changed over time?

---

1   In this chapter we refer to de facto and cohabiting couples interchangeably.

At both individual and societal levels, attitudes and behaviours about marriage can be expected to reinforce each other via various 'feedback loops' (Nazio and Blossfeld 2003; Emens, Mitchell and Axinn 2008). If we use cohabitation as an example, at the individual level a person who has more favourable attitudes towards cohabitation is more likely to cohabit themselves. Similarly, if at a societal level cohabitation becomes an increasingly accepted alternative to marriage, more people will engage in this behaviour as they will not have the fear of being stigmatised. But behaviour can in turn impact on attitudes. Someone who was previously opposed to divorce might find themselves more accepting of it once they experience it themselves. And, as the proportion of the population who have experienced divorce increases, so does the population who is exposed to this behaviour via their peers. This in turn can make divorce a more socially acceptable behaviour.

Drawing on data from the National Social Science Survey (NSSS), the International Social Survey Programme (ISSP), the Australian Survey of Social Attitudes (AuSSA), as well as the Household Income and Labour Dynamics in Australia (HILDA) survey, we examine how attitudes about marriage have changed from the late 1980s until 2012. We outline the overall change over time in attitudes but also specifically look for the influence of respondent gender, age, and relationship status on attitude change.

An influential idea in the world of family research is that there are 'his' and 'her' marriages, and that men and women receive different benefits from marriage. As Bernard (1972, 14) noted over four decades ago: 'there are two marriages in every marital union, his and hers. And his . . . is better than hers'. Although this 'differential benefits' hypothesis has since been questioned (Williams 2003; Jackson et al 2014), we look at the gender differences in how questions were answered in order to take into account possible differences in how men and women perceive marriage. We also compare attitudes towards marriage by age of respondent as studies on a wide range of social issues find that older people tend to have more conservative views than younger people (Tilley and Evans 2014). Social attitudes towards marriage are also influenced by each individual's own experience with marriage, so we therefore distinguish between respondents based on their current relationship status. Furthermore, as social attitudes commonly differ between urban and rural residents, we include an indicator of where respondents live. Finally, we also consider the impact of education on respondent attitudes to marriage – previous research suggests education levels matter to both attitudes and behaviour in this area (Treas et al. 2014; Hewitt and Baxter 2012).

Are married people seen as being happier than unmarried people?

Research conducted across time and in different countries generally finds that married people are happier than their unmarried peers (Easterlin 2003), although the exact relationship between marriage and happiness is complex (Stutzer and Frey 2006). In countries where cohabitation is more widespread there is little difference in the wellbeing of cohabiting versus married people (Vanassche, Swicegood and Matthijs 2013; Lee and Ono 2012). However, in Australia, some researchers still find evidence that married people have higher life satisfaction than their cohabiting peers (Evans and Kelley 2004). In this section we do not examine the effect of marriage on happiness per se, but rather what Australians think about marriage and happiness. If married people are generally seen as

Table 10.2: Married people are generally happier than unmarried people, %.

	1989	1994	2003	2012
Strongly agree	12	9	10	4
Agree	33	34	35	22
Neither agree nor disagree	28	34	32	37
Disagree	20	17	17	25
Strongly disagree	5	6	6	9
Can't choose	2	n/a	n/a	3
Total	100	100	100	100

Sources: National Social Science Survey (NSSS) 1989 (N=4,060; Kelley et al. 1990), International Social Survey Programme (ISSP) 1994 (N=1,662; Kelley et al. 1994); Australian Survey of Social Attitudes (AuSSA) 2003 (N=1,215; Gibson et al. 2004); Australian Survey of Social Attitudes (AuSSA) 2012 (N=1,421; Blunsdon 2016).
Note: Sample sizes shown are for the final analytical sample after missing values were excluded.

being happier than others, then this can be seen as a declaration of the superiority of marriage (Treas et al. 2014).

The following statement has been presented in surveys in 1988, 1994, 2003 and 2012 'Married people are generally happier than unmarried people'. Respondents were asked to consider this statement and could choose between the following response options: Strongly agree, Agree, Neither agree nor disagree, Disagree and Strongly disagree, or Can't choose (in 1989 and 2012). The distribution of responses is shown in Table 10.2.

Looking at the broad trends over time allows us to see whether there has been any change over the last few decades in how Australians view marriage and the extent to which it is seen as superior to being unmarried. A strong and consistent shift away from agreeing that married people are generally happier than unmarried people is evident. In 1989, 46 per cent of respondents agreed or strongly agreed with the statement. By 2012, this had fallen to just 26 per cent.

One important point to keep in mind is that, in responding to the question, it is unclear whether the implied comparison is between married people and single people or de facto couples – or both. Given the fact that the question is open to interpretation, different respondents may use different comparison groups. For example, someone who is currently cohabiting might compare married people to cohabiting people. In a general sense, in answering the question, respondents are likely to draw on their own experiences: someone who was unhappily married and is now divorced may not rate marriage as a source of happiness.

To further examine this question, we grouped together everyone who said they agreed or strongly agreed that married people are generally happier and compared the percentage of respondents who agreed across different characteristics, such as gender, age, and relationship status. The results can be seen in Table 10.3. Starting with gender, it is clear that in every year men were more likely than women to agree with the statement that married people are generally happier. This sex difference has been observed in other studies that have examined this question (Parker and Vassalo 2009; Thornton and Young-DeMarco 2001; Treas et al. 2014). This difference in how men and women responded to

Table 10.3: Percentage agreeing that married people are generally happier than unmarried people, by selected characteristics for each year, %.

	1989	1994	2003	2012
Gender				
Male	51	50	52	35
Female	40	37	39	20
Age				
<30	28	34	30	12
30–39	40	33	40	18
40–49	45	41	46	25
50–59	56	45	44	25
60–69	65	54	54	30
70+	75	68	60	42
Relationship status[a]				
Married	52	––	51	34
Cohabiting	18	––	35	13
Separated/divorced	31	––	37	17
Widowed	61	––	45	16
Single & never married	28	––	24	10
Urban/rural				
Rural	49	45	44	28
Urban	44	43	45	26
Education level				
Incomplete secondary	49	45	45	30
Completed secondary	39	41	42	22
University	42	45	47	26
Total %	46	44	45	26
Total N	3,988	1,662	1,215	1,421

Note: [a] 1994 cohabitation information was not available in this year. Sources: NSSS 1989; ISSP 1994; AuSSA 2003 & 2012.

this statement could result from differences in how men and women view marriage and the benefits they believe marriage has. Previous research has shown that men may derive more benefits from marriage and that husbands report greater marital satisfaction than wives (Bernard 1972; Fowers 1991).

A very strong relationship was also evident between agreeing with this statement and a person's age. Compared to younger people, older people were significantly more likely to feel married people were happier than unmarried people. This is consistent with what we expected: older people tend to have more traditional views about marriage and are therefore likely to believe being married is superior to not being married.

As suspected, current relationship status was an extremely important influence in responses to this statement. Married people, and widowed people, were the most likely to agree with the statement. Conversely, in every year those who were single and never married, or cohabiting, were the least likely to agree. For example, in 2002, just over half of married people agreed or strongly agreed that married people are happier than unmarried people, compared to a quarter of those who were single and never married and about a third of those who were cohabiting. Separated or divorced people also had low levels of agreement on the question, likely reflecting their own unhappy experiences. Contrary to what we expected, neither the geographic location of respondents nor their education level mattered to attitudes.

Shifts in opinion about marriage appear to have occurred across all the individual characteristics of people examined above, but it is most evident when looking at age. Apart from some small inconsistencies between 1994 and 2002, agreement with the statement fell across the board, with the biggest shift from 2003 to 2012. One possibility for this change over time could be that the composition of the respondents has changed in terms of their characteristics. We know that, for example, the percentage of people who are married has decreased over time, and that levels of education have increased. This could account for some of the differences in the views expressed. However, we find that even after taking account of these compositional differences in respondents, there was a large shift in opinion across the years.

Should people who want children get married?

While one third of babies born in Australia today are born outside of a marriage, the majority are still born in a marriage. In this section, we look at how people view the link between marriage and family formation and their level of agreement to the statement: 'People who want children ought to get married'. Again, the available response categories ranged from Strongly agree to Strongly disagree. Looking at the overall trend from 1989 to 2012, there is a clear decline in the level of agreement. In 1989, 72 per cent of respondents agreed or strongly agreed that people who want children ought to get married. By 2012, this had fallen to 47 per cent (see Table 10.4).

As before, we grouped together those who stated they agreed or strongly agreed with the statement that people who want children ought to get married, to examine the distribution of answers further. Unlike the earlier question, with regards to childbearing and marriage, men and women appear to have very similar views with little difference between the sexes. The only exception was in 2012 where men were more likely to agree with the statement (54 per cent) than their female counterparts (41 per cent). Once again, age was very strongly related to how they answered the question with older people being significantly more likely to agree compared to young people. However although this pattern is observed in all years, over time agreement has fallen across all age groups (see Table 10.5).

Again, current relationship circumstances heavily influenced responses to this statement. Married and widowed respondents were most likely to express the view that people who want children ought to get married, with single and cohabiting respondents less likely to agree. Interestingly, separated and divorced people still registered high levels of agreement with the statement, indicating that in many cases they still believe people should be married if they want to have children.

Table 10.4: People who want children ought to get married, %.

	1989	1994	2003	2012
Strongly agree	28	26	24	15
Agree	43	44	41	32
Neither agree nor disagree	10	12	15	18
Disagree	13	12	12	25
Strongly disagree	5	6	8	10
Can't choose	1	n/a	n/a	0.4
Total	100	100	100	100

Sources: NSSS 1989; ISSP 1994; AuSSA 2003 & 2012.

Whether people lived in an urban or rural area appeared to have little influence on how people answered this question. Education did differentiate, as those with lower levels of education were more likely than those with higher levels of education to support the view that people who want children ought to get married. This could partly be an effect of age as the older cohorts tend to have lower levels of education.

Is marriage an outdated institution?

Given the large changes in opinions regarding marriage that have accompanied actual, observed trends in society, it might be tempting to say that Australians now consider marriage an outdated institution. The HILDA survey asked about this in 2005, 2008 and 2011.[2] Over this short period of time there was no change in the distribution of responses, so for this section we only show the latest data from 2011. In HILDA, the response categories were presented on a 7-point scale with 1 labelled as 'Strongly disagree' and 7 labelled as 'Strongly agree'. There was a very strong tendency to strongly disagree with this assertion as seen in Figure 10.1.

Those who answered 1 or 2 on the scale were grouped together to see whether any patterns could be detected with regards to not agreeing and a person's gender, age, relationship status, urban or rural residence and highest education level.

Men were slightly more likely to agree that marriage is outdated (see Table 10.6). However, the difference in how men and women responded to this statement was minimal. Those aged 30 to 49 were most likely to agree that marriage is an outdated institution. Not surprisingly, married people were the least likely to agree, as were those who were widowed. There was no difference between urban and rural respondents. In terms of education there was some indication that those with lower levels of education were more likely to agree that marriage was outdated.

---

2   This chapter uses unit record data from the Household, Income and Labour Dynamics in Australia (HILDA) Survey. The HILDA Project was initiated and is funded by the Australian Government Department of Social Services (DSS) and is managed by the Melbourne Institute of Applied Economic and Social Research (Melbourne Institute). The findings and views reported in this paper, however, are those of the author and should not be attributed to either DSS or the Melbourne Institute.

Figure 10.1 Agreement with the statement, 'Marriage is an outdated institution', %.

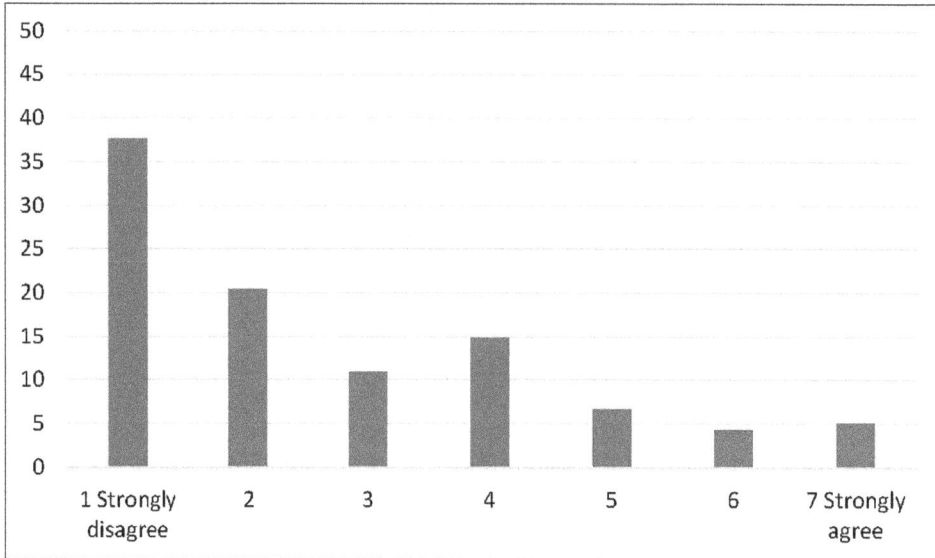

Source: Household Income and Labour Dynamics in Australia (HILDA) Survey Wave 11, 2011 (N=15,127).

We also conducted further analysis to examine the interaction between different factors on the probability of agreeing that marriage is outdated. For the most part men at all ages were more likely to agree that marriage is outdated but particularly men in their 50s. However the difference between men and women was not significant.

What is the future of marriage?

We have shown here that there have been large shifts in attitudes about marriage in Australia, but that these shifts have only occurred in the last 15 years or so. Brown and Wright (2016) also find a similar and equally significant change in attitudes between 2003 and 2012 in the United States. Given the nature of survey data it is possible that this is an artefact of the way survey questions are posed or in the types of people who respond. It is also possible that the exposure that the Australian public has had to changing family types – both in their personal lives and as well as through media – has led to a large shift in how open we are to different ways of forming relationships and raising children. Compared to 20 or 30 years ago, it is now increasingly likely for an individual to know of someone close to them who has never married, who is cohabiting or has had children outside of marriage, who has divorced and formed a new relationship, or is part of a 'blended' family. We speculate that the large shift from 2003 to 2012 could be a result of this spread of 'knowledge awareness' (Nazio and Blossfeld 2003) through old and new media.

But can we expect further shifts in attitudes to marriage and relationships? What is clear is that most respondents do *not* think that the institution of marriage is outdated. Perelli-Harris (et al. 2014) show that the nature of marriage is evolving across cultures

Table 10.5: Percentage agreeing that people who want children ought to get married, by selected characteristics for each year, %.

	1989	1994	2003	2012
Sex				
Male	73	71	68	54
Female	70	70	64	41
Age				
<30	52	44	42	33
30–39	62	53	48	30
40–49	77	67	63	41
50–59	86	79	74	43
60–69	92	87	83	53
70+	96	93	88	80
Relationship status				
Married	77	--	71	54
Cohabiting	41	--	40	21
Separated/divorced	64	--	68	45
Widowed	92	--	77	62
Single and never married	57	--	45	35
Urban/rural				
Rural	74	72	68	50
Urban	71	70	65	46
Education level				
Incomplete secondary	75	77	72	54
Completed secondary	66	64	62	43
University	66	60	57	45
Total %	71	70	66	47
Total N	3,988	1,662	1,215	1,421

Sources: NSSS 1989; ISSP 1994; AuSSA 2003 & 2012.

as individuals manage the changing role of intimate relationships in their lives. It is also likely that the change in Australian legislation to allow same-sex marriage will lead to a reimagining of marriage for both homosexual and heterosexual couples. What we do know is that most Australians still marry and that there is no evidence that marriage will disappear, despite predictions in the media. Perhaps as Cherlin (2004) posits, marriage in Australia has become 'de-institutionalised' and lost its practical importance; however, its symbolic importance seems to still be high and, in many ways, getting married is still seen as a marker of prestige. As Lauer and Yodanis (2010) note, new ways of forming relationships and childbearing are not a threat to the institution of marriage; they are just a sign that there are now more partnership options available to people.

Table 10.6: Percentage who agree that marriage is an outdated institution, by selected characteristics, %.

	2011
Sex	
Male	18
Female	15
Age	
<30	16
30–39	17
40–49	19
50–59	16
60–69	14
70+	13
Relationship status	
Married	11
Cohabiting	26
Separated/divorced	25
Widowed	12
Single and never married	20
Urban/rural	
Rural	16
Urban	16
Education level	
Incomplete secondary	18
Completed secondary	16
University	14
Total %	16
Total N	15,127

Source: HILDA Survey Wave 11 (N=15,127).

References

Australian Bureau of Statistics (1994). Marriages and divorces, Australia, 1994. Catalogue No. 3310.0. Canberra: Australian Bureau of Statistics.

Australian Bureau of Statistics (2000a). Births, Australia, 2000. Catalogue No. 3301.0. Canberra: Australian Bureau of Statistics.

Australian Bureau of Statistics (2000b). Marriages and divorces, Australia, 2000. Catalogue No. 3310.0. Canberra: Australian Bureau of Statistics.

Australian Bureau of Statistics (2010). Marriages and divorces, Australia, 2010. Catalogue No. 3310.0. Canberra: Australian Bureau of Statistics.

Australian Bureau of Statistics (2012). Marriages and divorces, Australia, 2011. Catalogue No. 3310.0. Canberra: Australian Bureau of Statistics.

Australian Bureau of Statistics (2016a). Births, Australia, 2015. Catalogue No. 3301.0. Canberra: Australian Bureau of Statistics.

Australian Bureau of Statistics (2016b). Marriages and divorces, Australia, 2015. Catalogue No. 3310.0. Canberra: Australian Bureau of Statistics.

Bernard, Jessie (1972). *The future of marriage*. New Haven, Conn.: Yale University Press.

Blundson, Betsy (2016). Australian Survey of Social Attitudes, 2012 [computer file]. Canberra: Australian Data Archive, Australian National University. doi: 10.4225/87/57e0d745ba4e8.

Brown, Susan and Matthew Wright (2016). Older adults attitudes toward cohabitation: two decades of change. *Journal of Gerontology, Series B: Psychological Sciences and Social Sciences* 71(4), 755–64.

Cherlin, Andrew J. (2004). The deinstitutionalization of American marriage. *Journal of Marriage and Family* 66(4), 846–61.

Easterlin, Richard A. (2003). Explaining happiness. *Proceedings of the National Academy of Sciences* 100(19), 11176–83.

Emens, Amie, Colter Mitchell and William G. Axinn (2008). Ideational influences on family change in the United States. In *Ideational perspectives on international family change*. Rukmalie Jayakody, Arland Thornton and William G. Axinn, eds. 119–150. London: Taylor & Francis.

Evans, Ann (2015). Entering a union in the twenty-first century: cohabitation and 'living apart together'. In *Family Formation in 21st Century Australia*. Genevieve Heard, Dharmalingam Arunachala, eds. 13–30. Dordrecht, the Netherlands: Springer.

Evans, Mariah D.R. and Jonathan Kelley (2004). Effect of family structure on life satisfaction: Australian evidence. *Social Indicators Research* 69(3), 303–49.

Fowers, Blaine J. (1991). His and her marriage: a multivariate study of gender and marital satisfaction. *Sex Roles* 24(3–4), 209–21.

Gibson, Rachel, Shaun Wilson, David Denemark, Gabrielle Meagher and Mark Western 2004). The Australian Survey of Social Attitudes, 2003 [computer file]. Canberra: Australian Data Archives, the Australian National University.

Heard, Genevieve (2011). Socioeconomic marriage differentials in Australia and New Zealand. *Population and Development Review* 37(1), 125–60.

Hewitt, Belinda and Janeen Baxter (2012). Who gets married in Australia? The characteristics associated with a transition into first marriage 2001–6. *Journal of Sociology* 48(1), 43–61.

Household Income and Labour Dynamics in Australia (HILDA) (2011). Wave 11 [computer file]. Melbourne: the Melbourne Institute, the University of Melbourne.

Hull, Kathleen, Ann Meier and Timothy Ortyl (2010). The changing landscape of love and marriage. *Contexts* 9(2), 32–37.

Jackson, Jeffrey B., Richard B. Miller, Megan Oka and Ryan G. Henry (2014). Gender differences in marital satisfaction: a meta-analysis. *Journal of Marriage and Family* 76(1), 105–29.

Kelley, Jonathan, Clive Bean and Mariah D.R. Evans (1990). National Social Science Survey: Family and Lifestyles, 1989–1990 [computer file]. Canberra: Australian data Archive, the Australian National University.

Kelley, Jonathan, Clive Bean and Mariah D.R. Evans (1994). International Social Survey Programme, Family and Changing Sex Roles II, Austral [computer file]. Canberra: Australian data Archive, the Australian National University.

Lauer, Sean and Carrie Yodanis (2010). The deinstitutionalization of marriage revisited: a new institutional approach to marriage. *Journal of Family Theory and Review* 2(1), 58–72.

Lee, Kristen Schultz and Hiroshi Ono (2012). Marriage, cohabitation, and happiness: a cross-national analysis of 27 countries. *Journal of Marriage and Family* 74(5), 953–72.

Lesthaeghe, Ron and Dirk van de Kaa (1986). Twee demografische transities? In *Mens en Maatschappij*. Ron Lesthaeghe and Dirk van de Kaa, eds. 9–24, Van Loghum-Slaterus: Deventer.

Nazio, Tiziana and Hans-Peter Blossfeld (2003). The diffusion of cohabitation among young women in West Germany, East Germany and Italy. *European Journal of Population* 19(1), 47–82.

Parker, Robyn and Suzanne Vassalo (2009). Young adults' attitudes towards marriage: family statistics and trends, *Family Relationships Quarterly* 12, 18–21.

Perelli-Harris, Brienna, Monika Mynarska, Caroline Berghammer et al (2014). Towards a new understanding of cohabitation: insights from focus group research across Europe and Australia, *Demographic Research* 31(34), 1043–78.

Qu, Lixia and Ruth Weston (2008). Attitudes towards marriage and cohabitation. *Family Relationships Quarterly* 8, 5–10.

Stutzer, Alois and Bruno S. Frey (2006). Does marriage make people happy, or do happy people get married? *The Journal of Socio-Economics* 35(2), 326–47.

Thornton, Arland and Linda Young-DeMarco (2001). Four decades of trends in attitudes toward family issues in the United States: the 1960s through the 1990s. *Journal of Marriage and Family* 63(4), 1009–37.

Tilley, James and Geoffrey Evans (2014). Ageing and generational effects on vote choice: combining cross-sectional and panel data to estimate APC effects. *Electoral Studies* 33, 19–27.

Treas, Judith, Jonathan Lui and Zoya Gubernskaya (2014). Attitudes on marriage and new relationships: cross-national evidence on the deinstitutionalization of marriage. *Demographic Research* 30, 1495–26.

Vanassche, Sofie, Gray Swicegood and Koen Matthijs (2013). Marriage and children as a key to happiness? Cross-national differences in the effects of marital status and children on well-being. *Journal of Happiness Studies* 14(2), 501–24.

Williams, Kristi (2003). Has the future of marriage arrived? A contemporary examination of gender, marriage, and psychological well-being. *Journal of Health and Social Behavior* 44(4), 470.

About the contributors

Clive Bean is professor of political science and director of undergraduate studies in the Creative Industries Faculty at Queensland University of Technology. He is also a principal investigator of the Australian Election Study. His research focuses on political and social attitudes and behaviour and he has published numerous papers in national and international journals and books.

Katrine Beauregard is a lecturer at the School of Politics and International Relations at the Australian National University. She completed her PhD in political science at the University of Calgary, Canada. Her research focuses on how political institutions can be used to include marginalised groups in the political process. Her previous work on this topic has been published in the *European Journal of Political Research* and *Politics, Groups and Identities*.

Anja Eder is university assistant in the Department of Sociology at the University of Graz, Austria. She works in the fields of international comparison and empirical methods of the social sciences. She is a member of the International Social Survey Programme (ISSP) and a founding member of the Center for Empirical Methods of the Social Sciences at the University of Graz.

Ann Evans gained her PhD in demography at the Australian National University (ANU). She is currently a senior fellow in the School of Demography and Associate Dean (Research) in the ANU College of Arts and Social Sciences. Ann's primary research interest lies in the area of family demography, and she undertakes research in the following areas: cohabitation, relationship formation and dissolution, fertility and contraception, young motherhood, and transition to adulthood.

Murray Goot is an emeritus professor in the Department of History, Politics and International Relations at Macquarie University, a fellow of the Academy of the Social Sciences in Australia and a lifetime member of the Australian Political Studies Association. His works spans public opinion, elections and referendums, media history, political parties and electoral systems. His most recent book, co-edited with Robin Archer, Joy Damousi and Sean Scalmer, is *The Conscription Conflict and the Great War* (2016).

Edith Gray is a family demographer with interests in family formation, repartnering, new family forms and ethical issues in research. Her current research focuses on inequality in first family formation. She is head of the School of Demography in the Research School of Social Sciences, Australian National University.

Markus Hadler is professor of sociology at the University of Graz, Austria, and an honorary professor in the Department of Sociology, Macquarie University. He is also Austrian representative to the International Social Survey Programme (ISSP) and editor in chief of the *International Journal of Sociology*. His research interest lies in the areas of social inequality, political sociology and environmental sociology.

Toni Makkai is a quantitative social scientist who has published extensively in key policy arenas including drugs and crime, political attitudes, crime statistics, victimisation, and aged care and regulation. She is located in the ANU Centre for Social Research, is a board director of the Centre for Social Research Pty Ltd, and is deputy president of the governing board of the Ted Noffs Foundation.

Luke Mansillo is a PhD candidate in the Department of Government and International Relations and the United States Studies Centre at the University of Sydney. He is interested in elections, political behaviour, public opinion and parties in Australia and other advanced democracies in addition to quantitative social research design practice. He has published in the *Australian Journal of Political Science* and holds a Bachelor of Arts with first-class honours in political science and Masters of Social Research from the Australian National University.

Ian McAllister is distinguished professor of political science at the Australian National University in Canberra. He has directed the Australian Election Study since 1987. His research interests are in the area of comparative political behaviour.

Shaun Ratcliff is a lecturer in political science at the University of Sydney, working out of the United States Studies Centre. His research focus is on the use of quantitative methods and survey data to understand public opinion, political behaviour and the role of parties in both the United States and Australia. In particular, he is interested in how these have changed over time. He teaches politics, political psychology and quantitative research methods, and is a member of the executive committee of the Australia Society of Quantitative Political Science. Shaun has a background working in politics and government relations, and has consulted for federal election campaigns.

Bruce Tranter is a professor of sociology at the University of Tasmania, Hobart. His research interests include the study of attitudes and behaviour relating to climate change, political and social movement leaders and national identity. His quantitative and qualitative research has been published widely in international sociological and political science journals and his recent book with Jan Pakulski is *The Decline of Political Leadership in Australia*.

Shaun Wilson is associate professor in the Department of Sociology at Macquarie University. Shaun works on projects related to political sociology, the sociology of work, and the sociology of labour movements, and he teaches courses on social policy, social inequality, and social movements. At present, he is writing on the shifting politics of the minimum wage in the Anglo-democracies as well as on attitudes to immigration and asylum seekers in Australia.

Index

www.ingramcontent.com/pod-product-compliance
Lightning Source LLC
Chambersburg PA
CBHW080132270326
41926CB00021B/4446